Welcome to

THE

EVERYTHING
— Family Guides —

THESE HANDY, PORTABLE BOOKS are designed to be the perfect traveling companions. Whether you're traveling within a tight family budget or feeling the urge to splurge, you will find all you need to create a memorable family vacation.

Use these books to plan your trips, and then take them along with you for easy reference. Does Jimmy want to go sailing? Or maybe Jane wants to go to the local hobby shop. *The Everything® Family Guides* offer many ways to entertain kids of all ages while also ensuring you get the most out of your time away from home.

Review this book cover to cover to give you great ideas before you travel, and stick it in your backpack or diaper bag to use as a quick reference guide for activities, attractions, and excursions you want to experience. Let *The Everything® Family Guides* help you travel the world, and you'll discover that vacationing with the whole family can be filled with fun and exciting adventures.

TRAVEL TIP

Quick, handy tips

RAINY DAY FUN

Plan ahead for fun without sun

≡FAST FACT

Details to make your trip more enjoyable

JUST FOR PARENTS

Appealing information for moms and dads

THE EVERYTHING®
— Family Guides —
Cruise Vacations

Dear Reader,

I have had the good fortune to see much of the world by boat. From Alaska to Fiji, Antigua to Italy, and New Zealand to the Galapagos Islands, my travels have proved again and again that no matter where I go, there is no better way to arrive than by way of the sea. Coming into a port is one of the most mesmerizing experiences available to us as people—it starts with a broad view of a place as it sits cradled in a valley or nestled on a hilltop; then we get closer to shore, with smells and sounds pulling us in like dreams come alive; and finally, when the boat's engines stop, we get a chance to place our own two feet ashore and explore every nook and cranny we can find.

Whether you choose a traditional cruise vacation, a smaller boat on one of the world's rivers or canals, or an adventurous itinerary off the beaten path, I hope this book will help you understand all your options, both wide angle and detailed.

May you have fair seas, warm sunlight, and bright stars along the way.

Kim Kavin

THE
EVERYTHING®
FAMILY GUIDE TO
CRUISE VACATIONS

A complete guide to the best cruise
lines, destinations, and excursions!

Kim Kavin

Adams Media
Avon, Massachusetts

Dedication

For my grandfather, Edward J. Galvanek,
to help plan his ninety-fifth birthday cruise.

• • •

Publishing Director: Gary M. Krebs
Associate Managing Editor: Laura M. Daly
Associate Copy Chief: Brett Palana-Shanahan
Acquisitions Editor: Gina Chaimanis
Development Editors: Karen Johnson Jacot,
Jessica LaPointe
Associate Production Editor: Casey Ebert

Director of Manufacturing: Susan Beale
Associate Director of Production:
Michelle Roy Kelly
Cover Design: Paul Beatrice, Matt LeBlanc,
Erick DaCosta
Design and Layout: Colleen Cunningham
Holly Curtis, Erin Dawson, Sorae Lee

• • •

An Everything® Series Book.
Everything® and everything.com® are registered trademarks of F+W Publications, Inc.

Published by Adams Media, an F+W Publications Company
57 Littlefield Street, Avon, MA 02322 U.S.A.
www.adamsmedia.com
ISBN: 1-59337-428-3

Printed in the United States of America.

J I H G F E D C B A

Library of Congress Cataloging-in-Publication Data
Kavin, Kim.
The everything family guide to cruise vacations : a complete guide to
the best cruise lines, destinations, and excursions / Kim Kavin.
p. cm. -- (An everything series book)
Includes bibliographical references and index.
ISBN 1-59337-428-3 (alk. paper)
1. Ocean travel. 2. Cruise ships. 3. Family recreation. I. Title. II. Series: Everything series.
G550.K38 2005
910'.2'02--dc22
2005017397

This publication is designed to provide accurate and authoritative information with regard to the subject matter covered. It is sold with the understanding that the publisher is not engaged in rendering legal, accounting, or other professional advice. If legal advice or other expert assistance is required, the services of a competent professional person should be sought.
—From a *Declaration of Principles* jointly adopted by a Committee of the American Bar Association and a Committee of Publishers and Associations

Many of the designations used by manufacturers and sellers to distinguish their products are claimed as trademarks. Where those designations appear in this book and Adams Media was aware of a trademark claim, the designations have been printed with initial capital letters.

Maps©Map Resources

This book is available at quantity discounts for bulk purchases.
For information, please call 1-800-872-5627.

Visit the entire Everything® series at www.everything.com

Contents

Acknowledgments

My literary agent, Jacky Sach, believed in me as a first-time author and worked hard to land me this book. I am grateful for her support. Gina Chaimanis and everyone at Adams Media were thoughtful in their feedback, and their flexibility enabled me to complete the book on time *and* cruise the Galapagos Islands. The marketing folks at the major cruise-ship companies did a fantastic job of providing information so this book could be completed on an extremely tight deadline.

Without the steady support of my parents, Marc and Donna Kavin, and my sister, Michelle Kavin, I would not be the journalist I am today. And without their phone numbers, I would have nobody to call when I need a break from writing.

Last on this list but first in my heart is Sean Toohey, who encouraged me to take on this project and always understood when I was still typing long past midnight. He is the partner of my dreams.

Top Ten Things to Do
Aboard Your Family's Cruise Ship

1. Whiz down the 214-foot spiral water slide on the top deck of the Carnival "Fun Ship" Conquest.

2. Eat some of the 4,200 pounds of chicken, 11,600 pounds of fish, and 21,600 pounds of beef stocked aboard the Celebrity Galaxy for a seven-night cruise.

3. Learn PowerPoint, Microsoft Excel, or Web site design in a classroom full of Dell computers aboard the *Crystal Serenity*.

4. Relax in the spa with a coconut body polish treatment while cruising through Hawaii with Norwegian Cruise Lines.

5. Dodge the paparazzi as you walk down the red carpet before a production of *The Golden Mickeys* aboard the Disney Cruise Line's *Wonder*.

6. Scale the rock-climbing wall after a morning on the ice-skating rink aboard Royal Caribbean's *Adventure of the Seas*.

7. Take in a lecture and cooking lesson from a Cordon Bleu-trained chef aboard the Radisson Seven Seas *Voyager*.

8. Test your luck (and your liver) by entering the Champagne Slot Tournament aboard Holland America's *Amsterdam*.

9. Play nine holes of miniature golf on the sports deck aboard Princess Cruises' *Caribbean Princess*.

10. Sit back, relax, and just take in the view as you cruise through paradise. You are, after all, on vacation!

Introduction

Back in 1995, about 4.5 million Americans took cruise-ship vacations. Today that number has doubled—and is still rising—with the majority of bookings coming from families. It seems that everybody and their brother (and their sister and parents and grandkids) is clamoring to climb aboard and set sail. As more and more families choose to cruise, more and more ships are launching with bigger and better facilities to meet demand all over the world.

Cruises used to be vacations that you could book at a reasonable price in the Caribbean or for a few dollars more if you wanted to see the Mediterranean. Not anymore! Those traditional cruising grounds are still there, of course, but they have expanded widely during the past decade. Ships that carry anywhere from 300 to 3,000 passengers now ply the waters of Northern Europe, the South Pacific, the African Coast, the Far East, Antarctica, and more. They charge anywhere from a couple hundred dollars for a few days aboard to nearly $200,000 for a four-month worldwide voyage in a penthouse suite. And they offer all kinds of excursions, land tours, travel insurance, and airfare options that can add to your experience along the way.

Now, when a vacation promises to "add to your experience," your first thought is likely to be, "Okay, how much is it going to add to my bill? Will it really be worth my hard-earned vacation dollars? And my family's time? Am I making the right choices when it comes to our ship, our itinerary, and our activities?"

You should be able to answer those questions definitively and book your vacation with confidence after you read *The Everything® Family Guide to Cruise Vacations*. It explains the worldwide cruise-ship marketplace, which brands of ship offer which amenities and facilities, what price ranges you can expect to pay for specific cruises with each company, and what extras you may end up wanting to add to your list. You'll learn which cruise lines cater to young children and which to teenagers, parents, and grandparents; which cruise ships travel to the places your family wants to see; and which excursions you might enjoy the most once you get there. You'll be able to book everything from a babysitter to a seat at an art auction by the time you reach the last page.

In short, this book helps you figure out exactly which cruise is right for you—and then shows you how to make your vacation vision a reality. You'll even find indexes that include contact information for all the major cruise companies, along with independent Web sites where you can go to do further research on your own, work with airlines directly, and more.

Whether you're a first-time cruiser or part of a family that wants to head off the beaten path for a change of pace, *The Everything® Family Guide to Cruise Vacations* can help. Put on your Hawaiian shirt and Bermuda shorts, kick back in your favorite La-Z-Boy recliner, and turn to the next page. Your family vacation of a lifetime is about to begin.

CHAPTER 1

Choose to Cruise!

AH, VACATION. IS THERE any sweeter word? It conjures the smell of salt air, the warmth of summer's rays, the sight of water so sparkling blue it's blinding. While it's true that you can bathe all five of your senses in such pleasures at a vacation resort on land, there is simply no better way to enjoy changing views and multiple destinations than a vacation at sea. You can select from dozens of ships based in hundreds of ports around the world. Welcome to the wide, wide world of cruising.

Why Choose a Cruise?

You worked hard to save your vacation money. If you're like most people these days, you only have a week or two to relax before you have to get back to the grind. Your goal is to make the most of your time at a price that won't break your budget and in a way that will give your family enough memories to last until well after your vacation ends.

Luckily, cruise-ship vacations are available at all different prices, in all different places, and with facilities and services designed to satisfy all kinds of families. Those qualities alone don't set cruise ships apart from land-based resort vacations, of course. What does set them apart is the fact that they move from place to place throughout your vacation—giving you and your family a chance to see and do far more than you likely would if you booked a hotel room ashore.

Another thing that sets cruise ships apart is that, in many cases, they are specifically designed to appeal to families. You can find cruise lines that offer everything from adult cigar bars to teen hangouts to children's activity areas to infant babysitting, all aboard the same ship. Excursions ashore range from historical tours to vineyard wine tastings to swimming with dolphins. Dining areas include everything from elegant sit-down halls to family-style buffets to Johnny Rockets burger joints. Even if you're traveling with a family that spans three or more generations, there are ships that have something aboard for everyone to enjoy. You will also find plenty of things for your family to enjoy together as a group.

Financially, cruise ships can make a great deal of sense, too. Cruise companies that compete for family bookings want you to be able to afford their vacations, and you can often find bargains that will cost you far less than you would pay for a resort vacation on land. In many cases, you can even work with your cruise-ship company or travel agent to combine a land vacation with your time at sea, still for a lower price than you would pay if you tried to do both kinds of vacation travel on your own.

≡FAST FACT

More cruise companies than ever are competing for bookings by families, and they're bringing in some big names to help get your attention. In the coming year, you're likely to see promotions for cruises that feature Mickey Mouse, Crayola, Fisher-Price, and more.

Safety is another factor that sets cruise ships apart from other vacations. As long as your children know that they should not enter any strangers' cabins or leave the ship without you, then they are, by definition, within a contained environment. You can introduce them to interesting new countries on guided excursions without having to worry about getting lost, and you can monitor your youngest children's time by signing them up for prearranged group activities on the boat. Some ships go so far as to require young children to wear identification bracelets to give you further peace of mind.

Even hard-to-handle teenagers can't get very far while aboard a cruise ship. Though some of these ships are quite big, they are, after all, still ships. There are only so many places a child can go, especially if a ship designates some areas off-limits to kids.

Last but not least, there's the food. The word "smorgasbord" does not do justice to the caloric cacophony offered aboard cruise ships these days, and on some of the more luxurious lines, you'll be eating recipes created by chefs from institutions as famous as Le Cordon Bleu. The dining can be so tantalizing that some people choose to cruise simply for the food. Where else can you eat all you want of whatever you want at multiple restaurants within walking distance of your bed?

If all of this sounds good to you, it's time for you to set about choosing the best cruise vacation for your family. With so many options out there, you may feel daunted at first, but this book will help you pare them down to a manageable number. The world of cruise ships quickly becomes much easier to navigate if you first figure out a few things about your family. You'll be able to use your preferences to weed out cruise companies that don't offer the kinds of services and facilities you might need, and you'll be able to concentrate on comparing prices and cabins aboard the ships that complement your vision of an ideal trip.

Start by asking yourself some basic questions:

- What is your budget?
- How old are your family members?
- Are you planning a family reunion with teenagers or older family members, or are you traveling with three or more children younger than ten?

- Is it important to you that your ship visit specific places, or will any itinerary in, say, the Caribbean be fine with you?
- Do you want to spend all your time aboard together as a family, or would you prefer that there be an extensive kids' club so the adults in your group can have some time alone?

These are just some of the questions you will need to answer as you try to find the cruise vacation that is right for you. As you read through the pages that follow, consider taking notes in the margins about cruise ships, facilities, services, or itineraries that sound like they would best suit your needs. When you're done, you'll have a good idea about which cruise companies fit your style, and you can contact them through your travel agent or directly by using the information listed in Appendix A.

For now, you'll want to start with an overview of the companies, ships, and itineraries that are designed specifically with families in mind and that tend to get high marks from families who have cruised them in the past.

Top Family Cruises

It's impossible for anyone but you to decide which cruise ship makes the most sense for your personal vacation. Your budget, your family members' personalities, and your ideas about ideal ports of call are going to be key factors in any cruise vacation you book.

Having said that, a few cruise companies are doing their darnedest to get your family vacation business, and they consistently rank highest in multiple surveys done by several sources throughout the industry. The reasons they tend to score highest include affordable pricing, good kids' activities and clubs, good onboard facilities and areas for children, and good adult amenities within the context of the family environment.

These cruise lines are not typically known for setting the uppermost standards of excellence in terms of luxury and refinement, but they are usually favored when it comes to getting the best family-vacation value for your dollar. The companies, in alphabetical order, are as follows:

- Carnival Cruise Lines
- Disney Cruise Line
- Royal Caribbean

Holland America Line (HAL) is in the process of trying to push itself more consistently onto this list, and the cruise line is expected to continue adding family-friendly features to its ships in upcoming months and years—especially for children in the three- to five-year-old age range. You would be wise to include HAL in your search for a family-friendly cruise, as long as you pay attention to the particular programs and facilities offered by any specific ship that you choose within the company's fleet. Also keep in mind that you may be among far fewer families than you would be aboard other cruise lines.

═══FAST FACT

Contact information for the top three family-friendly cruise lines:
Carnival Cruise Lines: ☎ 1-888-CARNIVAL ✉ *www.carnival.com*
Disney Cruise Line: ☎ 1-800-951-3532 ✉ *disneycruise.disney.go.com*
Royal Caribbean: ☎ 1-866-562-7625 ✉ *www.royalcaribbean.com*

Celebrity Cruises, Crystal Cruises, Princess Cruises, Norwegian Cruise Lines (NCL), and Radisson Seven Seas Cruises also sometimes get high marks for family-friendly cruising. Still, they can cost more, and their facilities and services for children can differ from ship to ship within their fleets and from itinerary to itinerary. You very well might be able to find an excellent family cruise with Celebrity, Crystal, Princess, NCL, or Radisson Seven Seas. Each does have a children's program, but you will need to do a tad bit more sleuthing on the particulars of your chosen dates, your destination, and the most suitable ship within each fleet. This little bit of extra research on your part could pay off with big dividends, though, in terms of your vacation enjoyment.

Top Ships for Teens

Teens are a special breed of cruise-ship passenger (just as they often seem to be a special breed in need of entertaining back on land). Older teens, especially, don't want to be lumped into the kiddie-pool area, but they also will not be allowed into the grown-up spaces aboard cruise ships such as casinos and wine bars, even if they are more mature than half the people already inside. Teenagers can often feel stuck in between two catered-to age groups on cruise ships, just as they occasionally do back home.

A handful of cruise ships have lounges and discos created especially for teens. In a few cases you can even find a "teen center" separate from the children's activity zone aboard. For the most part, a cruise ship with a lot of outdoor activities as well as at least one indoor teen-friendly area will work for your older children—especially when combined with excursions that they will find interesting ashore.

As is the case with the best boats for family cruises in general, Carnival Cruise Lines and Royal Caribbean are the companies that most frequently pop up in surveys ranking the best cruises for older children and teenagers. Holland America, Celebrity Cruises, and Princess Cruises also get the occasional nod, just as they do for cruises with younger children.

The popular and informative Web site CruiseMates.com did a survey of teenagers themselves to find out which particular ships their age group prefers. Royal Caribbean and Carnival dominated the list.

Here is what CruiseMates.com ended up ranking as its Top Ten, with the most popular ships for teens listed first:

- *Mariner of the Seas* (Royal Caribbean)
- *Navigator of the Seas* (Royal Caribbean)
- *Adventure of the Seas* (Royal Caribbean)
- *Voyager of the Seas* (Royal Caribbean)
- Carnival *Glory*
- Carnival *Conquest*
- Carnival *Miracle*
- Carnival *Victory*
- Carnival *Spirit*
- Celebrity *Constellation*

Each of these ships has the kinds of amenities you might expect teenagers to rate highly, from teen-friendly clubs with names like Fuel and Frankenstein's Lab to onboard activity areas including rock-climbing walls, ice-skating rinks, and miniature golf courses. These ships also tend to have more teenagers aboard than any other cruise line—more new friends for your child to hang out with—so perhaps that factors into the survey results, as well. If you plan to spend the majority of your time aboard the ship and not in port, or if you are taking a "cruise to nowhere," you may want to book one of these ships so that your teenagers will have plenty of options for keeping busy.

TRAVEL TIP

As with family-friendly cruising in general, your teenagers will also find dedicated activities for their age group aboard Disney Cruise Line, Celebrity Cruises, Crystal Cruises, Holland America Lines, Princess Cruises, and Radisson Seven Seas Cruises—but perhaps in a less-abundant, subtler way. Instead of a water slide and a basketball court, for instance, you might find a pizza party or a teens' card tournament.

No matter which cruise company you choose, if your child is a more studious type who would rather read books and learn about your cruising destinations than scream all night in a disco, you might consider putting your vacation dollars into a trip that offers an exotic itinerary instead of a rock-climbing wall. That way, the ship won't be a destination unto itself, and your teenager can join you in focusing on a bit more adventurous exploration ashore.

Cruising with Infants

If you plan to cruise with an infant—any child younger than age two—your cruise-ship options dwindle quickly. Some cruise companies reserve the right to refuse boarding to children in this age range, and even the ships that have extensive programming for children and teenagers don't always have facilities or services available for babies. This is beginning to change, but the movement toward better infant cruising options is still, well, in its infancy.

By far the best company for family-value cruising with infants right now is Disney Cruise Line. It is the only mid-range cruise company that has a nursery for children between twelve weeks and three years old, and group babysitting is available. (Cunard's *Queen Mary 2*, the largest cruise ship in the world, does have a nursery and British nannies available for infant care, but Cunard's prices are far higher.) Disney's nursery and infant care is offered along with its children's programming for your kids age three and older. If you're traveling with one kindergartner and one toddler, Disney is the only "family-priced" line where you will be able to use group services for both kids at once.

Royal Caribbean is working to make a dent in Disney's business, however. In 2004, the cruise line announced a partnership with Fisher-Price toys to develop fleetwide programming for children as young as six months old. There are play-groups and other activities that use Fisher-Price toys, as well as a Fisher-Price television channel that you can watch in your cabin.

However, unlike Disney Cruise Line, Royal Caribbean does not offer babysitting services for children younger than three years old. So even though there will be plenty of activities for you and your infant to enjoy together, you will have to bring your own nanny or babysitter aboard if you want to enjoy any nightlife on your own.

You'll read more about industrywide children's programming and babysitting services in Chapter 17, which breaks down details for every cruise line individually.

Cruising with Grandchildren

For the most part, cruising with young grandchildren is a lot like cruising with young children—kids are happiest aboard the ships that cater to them. The difference when you are a grandparent cruising with grandchildren is that your health needs may require a little bit of special attention too, and you will want to be aboard a boat that can provide those services.

You should start by making sure that your cruise ship has a children's program full of activities that will give you a break from your grandchildren during the day—while making them feel like they are part of something special at the same time. You can check on your particular ship's facilities and programming with your travel agent or your cruise company, or turn to Chapter 4 of this book for specific information about what each cruise line offers for special-needs travelers.

 TRAVEL TIP

If you are elderly and want to cruise with your grandchildren, make sure your ship has as many facilities and programs for you as it does for the apples of your eye. Half the fun of cruising with grandchildren is getting to spend time with them—which you can't do if, say, you are in a wheelchair without access to some areas aboard.

Next, you should select your itinerary carefully. Some ports of call require cruise ships to anchor in a harbor instead of pulling right up to a dock, in which case it can be difficult for older people to get on and off the ship, especially if they are in a wheelchair. If you fall into that category, or if you are traveling with an elderly grandparent who does, you should select an itinerary that ensures that you and your grandchildren can both get ashore together—if you prefer not to stay aboard while the kids go exploring on their own. Ask your travel agent or your cruise-ship company about the docking situation at every port of call on your itinerary—and, while you have them on the phone, check on handicap access aboard the ship.

Family Reunion Cruises

Some families cruise together without any small kids at all. In fact, cruise ships are a popular place for large-scale reunions of adult siblings, smaller-scale vacations in honor of a college graduation, or celebrations marking a grandparent's eightieth or ninetieth birthday. You can even hold your wedding aboard some cruise ships if you want to add a new member to your family in the middle of your get-together vacation!

If the majority, or even all, of the people who plan to cruise with you are adults and older teenagers, you might consider choosing a cruise line that does *not* cater so much to children. Obviously, the more activities and facilities that are aboard, the more kids and younger families a cruise ship is going to attract—and if you are part of a mature family, you might want to share your experience with a more mature crowd.

You might even consider booking your trip aboard a higher-end cruise line that does not encourage children to come aboard. Silversea and Seabourn are two examples—both are excellent lines, and they focus on luxury instead of lollipops. Swan Hellenic also tends to appeal to a more mature crowd, as does Cunard. Of course, you are also likely to pay higher rates aboard these more exclusive ships, but this option is available if you think you might prefer it.

🧳 TRAVEL TIP

You can book small public rooms aboard most ships for family-reunion fun. Consider setting up a relatives-only card tournament, or a Trivial Pursuit round robin, or even a test-your-knowledge contest about the ports of call on your ship's itinerary.

If you like the idea of fewer kids aboard but aren't opposed to their presence—and want to try to stay more in the mainstream in terms of pricing—consider one of the cruise lines that offer children's programming but balance it a bit more with adult interests. These include Celebrity, Crystal, Holland America, Norwegian Cruise Line, Princess Cruises, and Radisson Seven Seas.

Budget-Conscious Cruises

There are two schools of thought about how to get the most budget-conscious cruise fares. One is that you should comb last-minute Web site deals. The other is that you should book as much as a year in advance to take advantage of the cruise companies' early-bird discounts.

A good rule to remember is this: If you don't care what kind of cabin you get on which itinerary, you may save a few extra dollars by waiting for a last-minute deal. But if your goal is to be aboard a specific boat in a particular level of cabin on the itinerary of your choice, you are much more likely to get the best deal with the companies' early-booking programs. (You'll read more about how this works in Chapter 3.)

In general, if you want to try out cruising without busting your budget, you should look for short, two- to four-day itineraries in non-exotic ports of call. Simply choosing a three-day cruise, say, round-trip to New York that is all scenic cruising with no ports of calls will save you at least several hundred dollars because you will have no extra fees for excursions. If you can find a ship leaving from a city near your home—someplace like Fort Lauderdale, Florida, or San Francisco, California—you also will be able to put your limited budget to more use aboard your ship, as you will have no airfare expenses.

≡ FAST FACT

In the past, the last-minute deals have been the best, but that is beginning to change. As cruises have become more popular, many of the cruise lines are seeing more demand than they have cabins available—meaning they have no incentive to offer last-minute deals because their ships are already full.

Booking an inside cabin (without a view) is another way to stretch your vacation dollars, and in some cases, you really won't be sacrificing all that much. If, for example, you're the kind of person who likes to be out and about constantly, who only goes back to your cabin to shower and sleep, then paying for a balcony or an ocean-view suite really makes no sense for you. You might as well save your limited funds for excursions instead.

Sometimes, you can find longer itineraries that are good deals. Norwegian Cruise Line, for example, promotes its repositioning cruises as excellent bargains. Repositioning means the company needs to move its ship—for example, from the Caribbean at the end of the winter to the Mediterranean at the beginning of the summer. These cruises are bargains, if you don't mind sometimes skipping favorite ports of call or cruising during shoulder seasons (just before or after the summer rush, for example). Norwegian knows it cannot get top dollar for its cabins during a shoulder season going across the Atlantic Ocean with limited chances for you to get off the boat, so it lowers its rates to get at least some income during the trip. For you, this can sometimes mean cruising aboard for more than a week at less than $100 per day.

Budget-Busting World Tours

Okay, so you may not have money to burn, but if you do—or if you just like to take a peek into the lives of people who do—you can check out one of the worldwide cruises that some cruise companies offer. We're talking three to four months straight at sea, broken up into legs of about two weeks apiece in case you don't want to complete the whole shebang at one time.

Holland America calls its 105-day grand world voyage the "Circle of the Sun." It goes round-trip from Fort Lauderdale down through the Caribbean to South America, off the tip of Cape Horn to Antarctica, east to Cape Town, South Africa, and up the African coast before detouring east through the Indian Ocean to Cochin, India, and then cruising back west and up through the Red Sea to the Mediterranean (with ports of call in Rome, Italy, and Barcelona, Spain), before beginning the westward transatlantic voyage back to South Florida. Whew!

What? Not enough? You'd rather do the South Pacific and Asia instead of the Caribbean and South America? You're in luck. Crystal Cruises' "Empires of the Sun" 101-day voyage goes one-way from Los Angeles, California, west to the Hawaiian Islands before heading south to Bora Bora and the South Pacific, both islands in New Zealand, plus Australia before navigating north through Indonesia to Hong Kong, China, and other Asian ports including Phuket, Thailand, and Ho Chi Minh City, Vietnam. It then turns westward across the Indian Ocean to Africa, up the Red Sea to the Mediterranean Sea, around Turkey, Greece, and Croatia, and then visits western Mediterranean favorites like Venice, Italy, and Lisbon, Portugal, before finally arriving in London, England.

These cruises sure are exotic—and so are their prices. To do the whole Holland American itinerary, you'll have to fork over at least $19,599 per person for a standard cabin, or $149,299 for the nicest suite aboard. The lowest-priced cabin aboard the Crystal Cruises itinerary will run you at least $63,545, or $38,504 with the early-booking discount. If you want the Crystal penthouse, you'll have to pay $182,289 even with the early-booking rate.

Cruising Seasons: When to Go Where

Whether you're cruising the entire world or just a little part of it during a weeklong vacation, the weather will play a key role in your happiness. It can also make a difference in how much your trip costs.

In general, the best time to visit the Caribbean is the winter, starting in December. The temperatures in that part of the world are lovely during the fall, as well, but that's also hurricane season, and you could lose your entire vacation to rain if you happen to catch the wrong week. The high season in the Mediterranean is the summertime, from late May until early September (though it sometimes gets a bit chilly there in September). Alaska is also a summertime destination, for obvious reasons, and the South Pacific and Australia are good wintertime options, since their seasons are the reverse of whatever is happening in North America. The Galapagos Islands, which straddle the Equator, are a good year-round destination. Just be aware of the rainy seasons in such places. Galapagos, for instance, gets most of its showers between December and May.

≡FAST FACT

In order to maintain high ship occupancy and take advantage of peak season rates around the globe, cruise lines occasionally move their itineraries from one part of the world to another. For example, a cruise destined for the Caribbean may end up touring the Mediterranean. This is called a repositioning cruise, and it can save you a lot of money because the cruise line will offer large discounts to customers who are willing to be flexible about their itineraries. You many not see all the sights you had originally planned on, but you will get all the amenities of the cruise ship for much less.

These peak weather windows are, of course, the most sought-after times for cruise-ship bookings—which means that if you go when the weather is at its best, you are likely to pay top dollar. If you can live with a shoulder season, right before or after the peak times, you can sometimes save a little bit on your fares. And what you will give up in less-than-perfect temperatures, you will more than make up for with less-than-moblike crowds.

If you have your heart set on cruising to a destination during its peak season, you can still sometimes save a few bucks by booking your trip during a "weaker week" within the rush period. For example, weather in the Caribbean is about the same during the entire month of December, but the week before the Christmas holiday typically generates far fewer bookings than the celebration week itself. As such, you might be able to find a good deal if you're willing to disembark and be on your way back home in time to collect any loot that Santa Claus brings.

≡FAST FACT

The Lonely Planet travel-book company has an excellent and free Web site, ✑ *www.lonelyplanet.com*, where you can often find weather information about ports of call you are considering for your cruise. Check for seasonal predictions of rain, typhoons, hurricanes, and temperatures before you book your trip.

The same holds true for weeks before and after collegiate Spring Break in February, elementary-school break in March, the Fourth of July, and Thanksgiving. Ask your travel agent or your cruise ship company which weeks tend to be the slowest, and then look online for Web specials being promoted for those dates.

CHAPTER 2

Cruise Costs

HOW MUCH SHOULD YOU expect to pay for your family cruise vacation? It's a simple question, but the answer depends on various decisions you make. Will you cruise for three days or three months? Do you want the most spacious, top-level cabin with a private balcony? Do you want to stay aboard and enjoy the ship's free amenities? Or will you add as many shore excursions as possible? Your answers to all of these questions—and more—will determine the price of your cruise.

How Cruises Are Priced

Cruise ships are priced to appeal to people with different levels of income. As with land-based vacation resorts, you will find some cruise ships that are dirt cheap while others have prices so high that they induce nose bleeds. The trick is to determine your budget and then find a ship whose base price is low enough to let you add on all the extras you will want to enjoy while you are aboard.

You're not alone in booking this cruise—in fact, ships are filling up faster than they have in years. In 2004 alone, the estimated number of Americans who booked cruises was bigger than the entire population of New York City: 9 million, a solid 5 million more than a decade earlier. At any given time, you're likely to encounter serious competition for the best cabins and the best deals, especially during peak school-vacation weeks and holidays. You need to do your homework, do it well, and do it as early as possible so you can jump on every opportunity that comes along.

When looking at the costs, consider that the industry tends to use terminology ranging from lowest to highest, with the least expensive ships called value or mass-market, followed by premium and then luxury or deluxe. There are also niche and specialty companies whose itineraries might be, say, for two weeks aboard a small-capacity expedition ship from the southern tip of Chile to the wilds of Antarctica. This kind of cruise, as you might have already guessed, will cost you a heck of a lot more than three days aboard a value-priced ship in Florida and the Bahamas. Beyond these extremes, there are all kinds of cruises whose prices fall in between.

Some parent companies own a variety of cruise lines that fall into different price categories. Carnival Corporation, for instance, owns the premium Cunard and Holland America lines as well as the value-priced Carnival ships. Within the fleets of each individual line, you will usually find newer ships that cost more to cruise aboard than older ships.

TRAVEL TIP

Do not expect the advertised price of your cruise to be the final amount that you pay. Advertised prices do not include excursions, babysitting fees, beer and liquor purchased onboard, souvenirs, and other extras that can add hundreds or even thousands of dollars to your final bill.

While all the extras you choose, along with your cruise length and destination, will affect your specific vacation cost, you can get a good feel for the price ranges at various cruise lines by looking at a few sample itineraries from each. The examples you'll see on the following pages of this chapter are just that—examples from late 2005 promotions. Prices are, of course, subject to change (which usually means they go up). All of the prices included in this chapter are brochure fares, with discount options such as early-booking deals listed separately. In general, none of these prices includes airfare or land excursions—which can add a hefty sum to your total vacation cost, and which you'll find described later in Chapter 3.

Still, this general overview of the short, medium-length, and longer itineraries offered by each of the major cruise-ship companies will give you a place to start when considering the costs of the various cruise lines and which might be right for your budget and family needs.

Carnival Cruise Lines

Carnival is considered a traditional, value-oriented brand. This line of cruise ships caters to families with children, and as such Carnival keeps its prices at a level that working families should be able to afford.

There were twenty-one ships operating under the Carnival flag as of summer 2005, with another ship, the Carnival *Freedom*, expected to join the fleet in the spring of 2007. The ships range in size from the Carnival *Holiday*, which holds 1,452 passengers, to the newest ships—Carnival *Valor* and Carnival *Liberty* (and the forthcoming Carnival *Freedom*)—which hold 2,974 passengers apiece.

Carnival's itineraries run from three to sixteen days. Most cruising grounds are in close proximity to the United States mainland and are therefore places American families are likely to want (and to be able to afford) to go: the Caribbean, the Bahamas, the Mexican Riviera, Alaska, and Hawaii. The Carnival *Liberty*, which was due to launch in the summer of 2005, was expected to cruise in the Mediterranean and inaugurate a sixteen-day transatlantic route.

Carnival 3-Day Cruises

The Carnival *Fantasy*, one of the smaller ships in this line's fleet, offers three-day itineraries all year round from Port Canaveral, Florida, to Nassau in the Bahamas. You board late on a Thursday afternoon and wake up Friday morning in Nassau, where you stay until 7 A.M. on Saturday. The ship then spends all day Saturday at sea, and you arrive back in Port Canaveral at 7 A.M. Sunday.

Published prices for an interior cabin with upper-and-lower bunk beds start at $699 for this trip, though you can get a rate as low as $249 if you book early enough to qualify for Carnival's Super Saver fare. (Those dates vary, and you have to check with your travel agent for details.)

 **TRAVEL TIP**

If you cancel your Carnival cruise, you may be charged a penalty depending on how close to departure time it is. You can be charged 100 percent of your fare if you cancel within a week of your sailing date. Ask your travel agent about Carnival's Vacation Protection Plan, which can cover these fees and costs you as little as $19.

Published prices for a cabin with an ocean view on this cruise range from the Super Saver fare of $309 to the regular base rate of $789, while prices for a suite start at $569 with the Super Saver discount, rising to a base rate of $1,049 with normal booking time.

Carnival 7-Day Cruises

The Carnival *Triumph*, one of the line's bigger ships, offers seven-day itineraries during the month of September (fall foliage time) from New York City up to Halifax, Nova Scotia, and back down to New York City. Stops along the way include Boston, Massachusetts; Portland, Maine; and Sydney, Nova Scotia.

Published prices for an interior cabin with upper-and-lower bunks start at $599 with the Super Saver fare or $1,649 if you book later. Prices for a suite on this cruise start at $1,549 with the Super Saver fare or $2,599 if you forget to book early.

Shorter four- and five-day versions of this itinerary are also available and are priced accordingly. Check with your travel agent for details.

≡ FAST FACT

Carnival has promised to offer its Vacation Guarantee program through at least December of 2006 as a way to lure more first-time cruisers. The program lets unhappy customers disembark in the first non-U.S. port of call for any reason and get a refund for the unused portion of their cruise. Passengers are reimbursed for their coach airfare back to the ship's homeport.

Carnival 12-Day Cruises

Carnival's twelve-day Mediterranean itinerary began during the summer of 2005 with the inaugural cruise of the Carnival *Liberty*. The round-trip itinerary starts and ends in Rome, Italy, with ports of call in Naples, Italy; Dubrovnik, Croatia; Venice, Italy; Messina, Sicily; Barcelona, Spain; Cannes, France; and Livorno, Italy.

Published prices for an interior cabin with upper-and-lower bunks start at $1,099 with the Super Saver fare, or $1,999 if you book later. Prices for a suite on this cruise start at $2,899 with the Super Saver fare, or $3,999 if you choose not to book early.

Celebrity Cruises

Celebrity promotes itself as a premium cruise line—one that wants you as a customer if you are between thirty-five and fifty-four years old and earn at least $75,000 per year. Its ships boast styling touches such as artifacts from historic luxury liners and exterior glass elevators. Its newest Millennium-class ships have 25,000 square feet of spa facilities apiece, and if you book a suite, you will have access to twenty-four-hour butler service.

Celebrity's fares are usually in line with companies like Cunard and Holland America, which means prices are generally higher than family-value brands like Carnival and Royal Caribbean but not as expensive as deluxe brands like Seabourn and Silversea. Celebrity operates ten ships in traditional cruising grounds such as the Caribbean and Europe, but also has ports of call in places where value travelers aren't likely to go simply because of the airfare required to get there: the Arctic, Antarctica, the Panama Canal, South America, and elsewhere. Celebrity's ships carry anywhere from 1,354 to 1,950 passengers, not counting the Celebrity *Xpedition*, which launched in 2004 and takes only 100 passengers. (This is the legal limit for any cruise ship in the Galapagos Islands; 90 percent of this archipelago is protected parkland.)

You can view Celebrity's itineraries on its Web site by clicking links for cruises ranging from three to nineteen days. Prices vary greatly depending on locations, but you can get a basic idea about the line's pricing structure from the examples listed below.

Celebrity 3-Day Cruises

The Celebrity *Century*, a 1,870-passenger ship that launched in 1995, offers three-day cruises from Fort Lauderdale, Florida, to Cococay in the Bahamas. You might board on a Thursday afternoon, wake up in the Bahamas on Friday morning, and depart the Bahamas that night for arrival back in Fort Lauderdale on Saturday morning. An inside cabin on this trip starts at $200 per person. Ocean-view cabins start at $240, while suites are a minimum of $550.

Celebrity 7-Day Cruises

The Celebrity *Infinity*, a 1,950-passenger ship launched in 2001, does six-night, seven-day cruises in the Pacific Northwest. Ports of call include the cities of Vancouver and Victoria in British Columbia, Canada; Grays Harbor in Washington state; Astoria, Oregon; and San Francisco, California. An inside cabin for this trip will cost you a base rate of $700, while suites start at $1,520.

≡FAST FACT

Celebrity has a travel insurance program called the CruiseCare Guest Protection Plan. It pays the cost of your trip if you cancel for a covered reason, including illness or injury. If you cancel for another reason, you can get up to 75 percent of your trip's cost back in credit toward a future Celebrity cruise.

Celebrity 15-Day Cruises

The Celebrity *Constellation*, a 1,950-passenger ship launched in 2002, is scheduled to run fifteen-day itineraries in Scandinavia and Russia. The cruises are round-trip from Dover, England, and include ports of call in Oslo, Norway; Stockholm, Sweden; Helsinki, Finland; two days in St. Petersburg, Russia; Tallinn, Estonia; Warnemunde, Germany; and two days in Copenhagen, Denmark.

An inside cabin for this cruise starts at $2,780. An ocean-view cabin is at least $3,350, and the suites have a base price of $4,450.

Costa Cruises

Costa is a mass-market cruise company based in Italy whose ten ships offer itineraries in traditional destinations such as the Caribbean and the western Mediterranean as well as Iceland, Egypt, Greece, Turkey, the Canary Islands, Croatia, and Morocco. Some of Costa's ships are quite big, able to carry upward of 2,700 passengers, while others have a double occupancy maximum of just 820 people.

As with Carnival's Super Saver fares, Costa has an early-booking program that it calls Andiamo Advance Purchase. If you book far enough in advance, the Andiamo rates can save you as much as $700 per person. There are also friends-and-family discounts, along with senior and kid fares.

Costa promotes itineraries that run from five to seventeen nights, with the latter being aboard transatlantic trips.

Costa 6-Day Cruises

The Costa *Mediterranea*, a 1,494-passenger ship, offers a Christmas cruise in the western Caribbean beginning and ending in Fort Lauderdale, Florida. There are two ports of call: Progreso/Merida on Mexico's Yucatan Peninsula, and Freeport in the Bahamas. The rest of the cruise is spent at sea.

An inside cabin starts at $1,099 for this trip, or $599 if you book early enough to qualify for the Andiamo Advance Purchase fare. The least expensive cabin with an unobstructed ocean view starts at $1,399, or $899 with the Andiamo booking. A grand suite has a base rate of $2,499, or $1,999 as an Andiamo purchase.

 TRAVEL TIP

If you book a suite early enough to qualify for Costa's Andiamo Advance Purchase rates, you can receive 50 percent off the per person Andiamo fare for whomever will be sharing the suite with you.

Costa 13-Day Cruises

The Costa *Allegra*, an 820-passenger ship, offers thirteen-day itineraries that visit parts of the western and eastern Mediterranean along with northern Africa. The cruises are round-trip from Genoa, Italy, with ports of call in Gabes, Tunisia; Tripoli, Libya; Athens, Greece; Santorini, Greece; Mykonos, Greece; Rhodes, Greece; Alexandria, Egypt; and Catania, Sicily.

An inside cabin on this cruise starts at $2,569, unless you qualify for the Andiamo Advance Purchase fare, which is $1,799. The lowest fare for an ocean-view cabin is $3,379, and the suites have a base rate of $5,339. Andiamo rates are not published for the ocean-view cabins and suites, but you can ask your travel agent about them if you're interested.

Costa 18-Day Transatlantic Cruises

The Costa *Atlantica*, a 2,114-passenger ship, repositions from Genoa, Italy, to Fort Lauderdale, Florida, during the late fall. Along the way, you can cruise to a fair number of places during an eighteen-day itinerary. Ports of call include Barcelona, Spain; the Canary Islands; Barbados; St. Lucia; Antigua; Tortola; and San Juan, Puerto Rico.

If you book early enough for Andiamo Advance Purchase rates, you can save as much as 45 percent on the following prices: least expensive inside cabin, $1,759; least expensive unobstructed ocean-view cabin, $2,269; and most expensive suite, $3,909.

Crystal Cruises

Crystal is a high-end line that operates three relatively small ships: the 940-passenger-apiece Crystal *Symphony* and Crystal *Harmony*, and launched in 2003, its newest, the 1,080-passenger Crystal *Serenity*. The company promotes itself as having a standard of luxury in keeping with Four Seasons and Ritz-Carlton hotels, and you will find amenities aboard including Riedel wineglasses, Wedgwood china tea service, Frette table linens, and Brown Jordan Mission Teak deck furniture—all of which, of course, are reflected in the prices these ships charge.

Crystal offers itineraries in traditional locations such as the Caribbean and Mediterranean, along with more exotic cruising grounds such as Hawaii, Africa, Alaska, Australia, Northern Europe, the Panama Canal, and South America. Cruises range from two days to a whopping 101-day world cruise. You can also find more typical seven- to twelve-day itineraries, of course.

Crystal 2-Day Cruises

The company promotes a Memorial Day getaway cruise on the West Coast that is one-way southbound from Vancouver, British Columbia, to San Francisco, California. The entirety of the cruise is spent at sea with no ports of call, so your cruise experience will consist entirely of enjoying the amenities aboard the Crystal *Harmony*.

Inside cabins on this trip start at $805 per person, though you can get special fares for early booking and bring that base rate down to $430 in some cases. The least expensive ocean-view cabin with an unobstructed view starts at $1,070, or $650 with the discounts, and the penthouse on this itinerary goes for a base rate of $3,430, or $2,920 with the special fare discount.

Crystal 10-Day Cruises

The Crystal *Symphony* offers ten-day itineraries that run one-way from Fort Lauderdale, Florida, to Caldera, Costa Rica, and include a transit through the Panama Canal. Ports of call along the way are Tortola, St. Barthelemy, and Aruba.

For this itinerary, the least-expensive published rate you will pay for a cabin with "extremely limited view" is $5,070, or $2,095 with advance purchase and other discounts. A stateroom with a view starts at $5,270, or $2,860 with the savings, and the penthouse on this ship will run you at least $16,540, or $13,495 with the special fare breaks.

≡FAST FACT

Crystal offers a Cruise Protection Program that includes as much as $50,000 in reimbursed expenses if you have to cancel or interrupt your cruise for a covered reason, such as illness. If your booking costs more than $50,000, the rest of your purchase price is refunded in the form of credit toward a future cruise.

Crystal 19-Day Cruises

One of the great things about luxury lines is that they often cruise to exotic places. Such is the case with this nineteen-day itinerary, a one-way vacation from Melbourne, Australia, across the Indian Ocean to Cape Town, South Africa. Ports of call on this trip include

Adelaide and Perth in Australia, and the islands of Reunion and Mauritius.

The lowest published fare you will find for the trip is $14,455, which goes down to $7,950 with the aforementioned discounts. A deluxe stateroom with veranda on this trip will cost you at least $14,999, or $8,995 with the bonus savings, and the luxury penthouse rate starts at $53,890, or $51,515 per person with the discounts.

Cunard Line

The name Cunard is virtually synonymous with luxury, though its prices are more in line with premium ships than their top-shelf competitors. Cunard's two ships, the 1,791-passenger *Queen Elizabeth 2* and her new sister ship, the 2,620-passenger *Queen Mary 2*, are true luxury liners that command reasonable premium-brand prices. The *Queen Mary 2* is the biggest ocean liner in the world, with so much volume that it even boasts an onboard planetarium. The artwork alone was commissioned at a cost of more than $5 million.

Cunard's itineraries run from three days to a staggering 102-day worldwide cruise. There are, of course, more moderate offerings of various sizes in between.

Cunard 3-Day Cruises

The *Queen Mary 2* offers a three-day itinerary during the July Fourth holiday that runs round-trip from New York City with no ports of call. The entirety of your entertainment comes from the amenities aboard the ship.

A standard inside cabin, the lowest-rate booking available, will run you at least $799 without the early-booking savings, which can reduce that to a minimum of $719. A standard ocean-view cabin starts at $1,199, or $1,079 with early-booking discounts, and a deluxe cabin has a base price of $2,369 if you fail to book early (or $2,132 if you do). The grand duplex, the most expensive cabin aboard for this trip, costs a minimum of $12,499, or $11,249 with the early-booking discount.

Cunard 8-Day Cruises

The *Queen Mary 2* offers an eight-day Caribbean itinerary that is round-trip from New York to St. Thomas, St. Kitts, and St. Maarten.

A standard inside cabin starts at $1,689, or $1,449 with the early-booking special rate. Standard ocean-view cabins begin at $2,139, or $1,799 with the discounted fares, and deluxe balcony cabins will cost you at least $2,689, or $2,149 with the early-bird savings. The grand duplex on this cruise is $21,939, or $17,549 with a discounted ticket.

Cunard's 12-Day Round-Trip Transatlantic

Yes, you can spend twelve days cruising aboard the *Queen Mary 2*, starting and ending in New York City with a single port of call: Southampton, England, for a short twelve hours.

This cruise will cost you a minimum of $2,849 for the lowest-level cabin, or $2,439 with early-booking savings. Standard ocean-view cabins start at $4,059 for this trip, or $3,499 with the discount; and deluxe balcony cabins have a base rate of $5,489, or $4,389 with the savings. If you want the grand duplex for your hop across the pond, you'll have to fork over $48,649, or $38,919 if you book early.

Disney Cruise Line

The Disney Cruise Line has two ships in its fleet, the Disney *Magic* and the Disney *Wonder*. Each takes 1,754 passengers and offers three-, four-, and seven-night itineraries that are priced to appeal to the mass market of traveling families. The *Magic* was launched in 1998, and the *Wonder* in 1999. Both ships completed interior and exterior refurbishing in the fall of 2004—an important maintenance investment for any company whose ships are typically full of children with sticky fingers and sandy shoes.

As you might have guessed, you can pair your Disney Cruise Line vacation with land-based stays at Florida's Walt Disney World and California's Disneyland if you want to extend your trip beyond the seven-day sailings that are offered. You'll read more about that later in Chapter 3, which covers combined air, sea, and land deals.

The *Magic* was headed for the West Coast during summer 2005 to help celebrate the fiftieth anniversary of Disneyland in California, while the *Wonder* remained based on the East Coast.

Disney 3-Day Cruises

The *Wonder* offers round-trip itineraries from Port Canaveral (near Orlando) in Florida with ports of call in Nassau, Bahamas, and at Disney's private Bahamian island, called Castaway Cay.

A standard inside cabin on this cruise will cost you $399 to $899. Ocean-view staterooms go for $589 to $1,349, while the most expensive cabins aboard, called royal suites, range from $2,299 to $2,849.

 **TRAVEL TIP**

Consider purchasing Disney Cruise Line's Vacation Protection Plan as insurance in case you need to cancel your trip because of illness or injury. If you have to cancel for another reason, you can receive up to 75 percent of your trip's cost in the form of credit toward a future Disney cruise as long as you embark within one year.

Disney 7-Day Cruises

As with the three-day cruise above, this itinerary is also round-trip from Port Canaveral (Orlando) and includes a stop at Castaway Cay, Disney's private Bahamian island. Other ports of call on this trip include St. Maarten and St. Thomas, plus three full days at sea.

Standard inside staterooms will cost you $799 to $1,999 on this itinerary. Ocean-view cabins go from $999 to $2,399, and the grand-daddy of all cabins aboard, the royal suite, runs from $4,199 to $5,199.

Holland America Lines

Holland America, or HAL (as you'll find it likes to call itself), has thirteen ships cruising all over the world and a fourteenth, the

1,848-passenger *Noordam,* due for delivery in January 2006. The smallest ship in the fleet is the 793-passenger *Prinsendam,* and the new *Noordam* will have the same passenger capacity as the fleet's other largest ships, the *Westerdam,* the *Oosterdam,* and the *Zuiderdam.* HAL is considered a premium brand, with an ambience and pricing that fall in between the mass-market and ultra-luxury levels.

Cruises with HAL have itineraries that range from three days to the mother lode 108-day Grand World Voyage, and just about everything you can imagine in between. Cruising grounds include the traditional Caribbean and Mediterranean routes, plus Alaska, Asia, Australia, New Zealand, the South Pacific, Hawaii, the Panama Canal, and South America.

Holland America 3-Day Cruises

The 1,258-passenger *Ryndam* offers a one-way, three-day itinerary from San Diego, California, to Vancouver in British Columbia, Canada. There are no ports of call; the entire trip is spent cruising the Pacific Ocean.

Interior cabins will run you a minimum of $221 to $455. Outside cabins with varying levels of ocean views cost between $271 and $538. The penthouse aboard this ship is $1,667 during this itinerary.

≡FAST FACT

Holland America's trip protection plans come in two levels, standard and platinum. The platinum is a true vacation insurance plan, while the standard can get you as much as 80 percent of your cancellation fee back as long as you cancel your trip in writing at least twenty-four hours before it is scheduled to start.

Holland America 10-Day Cruises

The 1,848-passenger *Westerdam* cruises on a ten-day, round-trip itinerary from Copenhagen, Denmark, with ports of call in Tallinn, Estonia; St. Petersburg and Moscow in Russia (two days); Helsinki,

Finland; Stockholm and Visby in Sweden (two days); Berlin, Germany; and Arhus, Denmark.

For an inside stateroom, you can pay anywhere from $1,883 to $2,197. Outside cabins with varying levels of ocean views run from $2,083 to $2,423. The penthouse on this cruise will cost you just a hair over $14,000.

Holland America 30-Day Cruise

The 1,380-passenger *Amsterdam* offers a cruise that runs round-trip from San Diego, California, all the way into the South Pacific. Ports of call include six different stops in the Hawaiian Islands plus Christmas Island; Raiatea, in French Polynesia; two days in Bora Bora; Tahiti; Moorea; and the Marquesas. Fully half of the thirty-day itinerary is spent at sea in between these ports.

You can book an inside stateroom for a price of $5,133 to $6,993. An outside stateroom will cost you anywhere from $6,133 to $7,033, and the penthouse is available for a little more than $33,000 per person.

MSC Cruises

MSC calls itself "Premium Class with a True Italian Signature." What that means is that it is a premium Italian brand, with levels of service that are not up to par with the worldwide premium market but that are said to be a cut above the most basic, mass-market cruise lines. You'll see by its rates that MSC's itineraries are priced to appeal to a wide audience. The company has seven ships, most of which are based in the Mediterranean, though it does offer cruises in the Caribbean, Northern Europe, Panama Canal, and South America.

Ships in the MSC fleet range from the 576-guest *Monterey* to the 1,756-guest *Opera*. Two more ships are under contract to be added in 2006 and 2007. The *Opera* is currently the flagship and has been sailing in the Caribbean since December 2004.

Promoted itineraries range from five to seventeen nights.

MSC 4-Night Cruises

The *Opera* offers a four-night itinerary from Genoa to Venice in Italy, with ports of call in Naples, Italy, and Dubrovnik, Croatia. If you get the early-booking discounts, you will pay $600 for an inside cabin, $950 for an ocean-view cabin, or $2,050 for the highest-grade cabin with a balcony. Brochure fares, of course, will be much higher, as you'll see in the next two example fares.

MSC 7-Night Cruises

The *Opera* also offers a seven-night itinerary that runs round-trip from Fort Lauderdale, Florida, to the Eastern Caribbean with ports of call in San Juan, Puerto Rico; St. Thomas and St. Croix in the Virgin Islands; and Nassau, Bahamas. The early-booking rate for an inside cabin is $650, substantially less than the brochure fare of $1,400. An ocean-view cabin will cost you at least $1,000, or $1,750 without the early-bird special; and a top-level balcony cabin goes for $1,900, or $2,650 without the savings you'll get for booking early.

MSC's 17-Night Transatlantic

The 763-foot, 1,590-passenger *Liricia* offers a seventeen-night transatlantic crossing from Fort Lauderdale, Florida, to Genoa, Italy. Ports of call along the way include San Juan, Puerto Rico; St. Thomas; St. Lucia; Martinique; Barbados; as well as Funchal, Malaga, and Barcelona in Spain.

An inside cabin booked early enough to qualify for the discount will cost you at least $1,300, or $2,300 without the savings. An ocean-view cabin starts at $1,750, or $2,750 if you book late, and a top-level suite goes for at least $3,080, or $4,080 without the early-bird savings.

Princess Cruises

Princess Cruises has fifteen ships in its fleet, from the two 670-passenger vessels *Tahitian Princess* and *Pacific Princess* all the way up to the 3,110-passenger *Caribbean Princess*. You can cruise aboard Princess's ships in the Caribbean and Mediterranean, as well as in

Asia, Alaska, Australia, New Zealand, Mexico, the South Pacific, and South America. Even though some of this line's cruising grounds are exotic, it is definitely priced as a value brand. Itineraries range from single-night "sampler" cruises to two-month-long jaunts around Asia and the South Pacific. Of course, you can find cruises of various other lengths in between.

≡FAST FACT

The Princess Travel Care program will refund 100 percent of your cancellation fees for a qualified reason, or 75 percent in the form of future-cruise credit if you cancel for a reason that's not covered by the travel insurance plan.

Princess 7-Day Cruises

The 2,600-passenger *Golden Princess* does a seven-day itinerary round-trip from New York City with ports of call in Halifax, Nova Scotia; St. John, New Brunswick; Bar Harbor, Maine; Boston, Massachusetts; and the sailing capital of the world, Newport, Rhode Island.

You can expect to pay rates as low as $895 per person for an interior cabin, or prices between $1,165 and $1,220 for cabins with unobstructed ocean views (again, not counting the early-booking discounts). The nicest cabin on the *Golden Princess*, known as the grand suite, has a base price of $4,595.

Princess 10-Day Cruises

The 1,590-passenger *Regal Princess* advertises a ten-day cruise to Alaska that you can book round-trip from San Francisco, California. Ports of call include Sitka, Juneau, Tracy Arm, and Ketchikan in Alaska, plus the city of Victoria in British Columbia, Canada.

Published rates for the *Regal Princess*—not including early-booking discounts—during the peak season start at $1,499 for an interior cabin and climb to $1,818 for the least expensive unob-structed ocean-view cabin. If you want the nicest suite on the boat, expect to pay at least $3,899. Prices are, of course, a bit lower during the non-peak seasons.

Princess 30-Day Cruises

This is a one-way itinerary aboard the 670-passenger *Pacific Princess*. You will begin your cruise in Bangkok, Thailand, and end up in Cape Town, South Africa. More than half of your cruising time is spent at sea during this trip (seventeen full days), and ports of call include Ho Chi Minh City, Vietnam; Singapore; Kuala Lumpur, Malaysia; Colombo, Sri Lanka; Cochin and Mumbai, both in India; the Seychelles; two days in Mombasa, Kenya; Tanzania; and Durban, South Africa.

Not counting early-booking discounts, you can expect to pay at least $3,995 for an interior cabin on this trip. Ocean-view cabins without obstructions range from $4,240 to $4,370, and the owner's suite goes for at least $7,620 if you want the nicest accommodations aboard the ship.

Radisson Seven Seas

Radisson Seven Seas Cruises has seven ships in its fleet, all much smaller than the big boys at other companies that carry upward of 2,000 or 3,000 passengers in one shot. With Radisson, you can be among just 198 passengers aboard the *Explorer II* in Antarctica, or you may choose a slightly bigger crowd aboard the 700-passenger *Seven Seas Voyager* or *Seven Seas Mariner*. That's as big as this company's boats come—which of course translates into deluxe service and, in general, deluxe prices.

Radisson's ships cruise in the Caribbean, the Mediterranean, Alaska, South America, and New England, with select grand voyages to places such as Hong Kong and Australia. One Radisson boat, the 320-passenger *Paul Gauguin*, cruises year-round in French Polynesia.

You can book itineraries with Radisson that are as short a three-night run from Freeport in the Bahamas up to New York City or as long as a twenty-six-night grand voyage that sails round-trip from Los Angeles to the Marquesas, Tahiti, Bora Bora, Hawaii, and more. Yet as with the other cruise lines that offer such lengthy journeys, you can find more bite-size trips if that's more suitable for your budget.

Radisson 5-Day Cruises

The 700-passenger Seven Seas *Mariner* does round-trip itineraries from Fort Lauderdale, Florida, with ports of call in Port Canaveral (Orlando); Freeport, Bahamas; and Key West, Florida.

You may qualify for an early-booking discount if you make your reservations at least 120 days in advance. If you book later, the least expensive cabin you will be able to get is $1,195. Prices go up until you reach the nicest cabin aboard, the master suite, which has a base rate of $4,995.

Radisson 8-Day Cruises

The 700-passenger Seven Seas *Mariner,* when she's not down in Florida doing five-day itineraries, offers an eight-day, one-way trip from the city of Vancouver in British Columbia, Canada, up to Seward, Alaska, which is just outside of Anchorage. Ports of call along the Inside Passage route include Prince Rupert, Tracy Arm, Skagway, and Sitka.

TRAVEL TIP

Consider purchasing Radisson's Guest Protection Program as travel insurance for your cruise, and remember that you can be charged a minimum cancellation fee of $200 if you cancel less than 120 days before you are scheduled to set sail.

Radisson sometimes offers two-for-one discounts, but they aren't advertised for this itinerary. The good news is that early-bird savings are an option as long as you buy your tickets at least 120 days in advance.

The least expensive cabin you will be able to find for this trip is $4,595, or $2,987 with the early-booking deal. Prices go up for the master suite, which is $18,895 or—if you book early—$12,282.

Radisson 20-Day Cruises

The 700-passenger *Seven Seas Voyager* does a twenty-day, one-way itinerary from Fort Lauderdale, Florida, to Rome, Italy. Ports of call include the Canary Islands; one day each in Agadir and Casablanca in Morocco; Granada, Valencia, and Barcelona in Spain (a total of three days); Marseilles, France; Monte Carlo, Monaco; and perhaps the prettiest harbor in the world, Portofino, Italy.

You can get an early-bird discount if you book at least 120 days before your cruise, but you cannot combine it with two-for-one fares, which Radisson does advertise for this particular trip. Ask your travel agent about the cost savings depending on which program you choose.

If you book late and don't qualify for any savings, you should expect to pay a minimum of $9,990 for the least expensive cabin aboard, and $35,990 for the master suite, the most expensive aboard.

Royal Caribbean

Royal Caribbean has nineteen ships that, in total, can carry more than 44,000 passengers at any one time. The company's five biggest ships—*Voyager of the Seas, Explorer of the Seas, Adventure of the Seas, Navigator of the Seas*, and *Mariner of the Seas*—each take 3,114 guests. You fit the company's target profile if you are in your early forties, are an active traveler, and want a vacation that is affordable, fun, and refined. Royal Caribbean is a mass-market brand, one that competes heavily with Carnival Cruise Lines for family bookings.

You can find everything from three-night getaway cruises to fourteen-night transatlantic cruises from Tampa, Florida, to Barcelona, Spain. In addition to the Caribbean and Mediterranean, Royal

Caribbean's ships cruise in Alaska, New England, Hawaii, and the Pacific Northwest.

Royal Caribbean 4-Day Cruises

The 2,390-guest *Monarch of the Seas* does a round-trip three-night itinerary from Los Angeles, California, with a single port of call: Ensenada, Mexico. One day of the four-day trip is spent entirely at sea. You can book an interior cabin for as little as $349. An ocean-view cabin will cost you at least $369, while a deluxe cabin starts at $449.

Royal Caribbean 8-Day Cruises

The 3,114-guest *Adventure of the Seas* offers a round-trip Southern Caribbean cruise from San Juan, Puerto Rico. Ports of call include Aruba, Curacao, St. Maarten, and St. Thomas. Your bill for an interior cabin will start at $729. An ocean-view cabin will cost you a minimum of $929, and a deluxe suite will be at least $1,479.

≡ FAST FACT

Royal Caribbean's Vacation Protection Plan, which starts at $29, will insure 100 percent of your purchase price if you have to cancel your cruise for a covered reason. If you cancel for another reason, you may be entitled to 75 percent of your cruise fare as credit toward a future cruise.

Royal Caribbean's 15-Day Transatlantic

The 1,804-guest *Splendor of the Seas* does transatlantic crossings from Tampa, Florida, to Barcelona, Spain. Eight of the fifteen days are spent at sea, with ports of call in Key West, Florida; the Azores; and Cadiz, Malaga, and Barcelona in Spain (three days).

Interior cabins on this trip will run you a minimum of $899. Ocean-view cabins start at $999.

Seabourn Cruise Line

Seabourn promotes itself as offering ultra-luxury and, as such, does not encourage you to bring your younger children along on vacation. This company has three identical ships, the Seabourn *Pride*, Seabourn *Spirit*, and Seabourn *Legend*, and each carries just 208 passengers. If you look at their deck plans, you will find no special areas reserved for children's or teen-oriented activities. The average age of customers who book Seabourn cabins is between fifty and sixty years old.

Having said that, if your children are older and you want to expose them to a more refined cruising environment in exotic locales, Seabourn might be a good choice for you. The ships offer itineraries not only in traditional cruising grounds such as the Caribbean and Mediterranean, but in places like Africa, Asia, India, Australia, New Zealand, and the South Pacific. Prices are usually as deluxe as the service.

Seabourn 4-Day Cruises

The Seabourn *Pride* offers an itinerary of four days and three nights that runs round-trip from New York City with no ports of call. The entire trip is scenic cruising in Long Island Sound and up the Hudson River.

You will pay at least $1,425 for the lowest level cabin on this trip, unless you book early, in which case you might get the $1,140 rate. A mid-range cabin aboard this ship is a minimum of $2,595, or $2,076 with the early-booking discount. The owner's suite for this cruise will cost you $5,835, or $4,668 as an early-booking fare.

Seabourn 10-Day Cruises

The Seabourn *Legend* has a ten-day itinerary that goes one-way from Lisbon, Portugal, to Monte Carlo, Monaco, with ports of call including Portimao, Portugal; Cadiz, Seville, Malaga, and Alicante in Spain (a total of five days); Gibraltar; and the French island of Corsica.

Your cheapest cabin option runs $7,765, or $4,659 with the early-booking discount. A mid-range cabin for this itinerary will cost you at least $13,065, or $7,839 with the early-bird savings; and the owner's suite for the trip goes for $22,465, unless you book early and get it for $13,479.

≡FAST FACT

SeabournShield is the name of Seabourn's travel insurance program. It will refund as much as $50,000 of your reservation price for covered cancellations, or give you credit toward a future cruise if you cancel for other reasons.

Seabourn 35-Day Cruises

The Seabourn *Spirit* promotes a thirty-five day itinerary that goes one-way from Singapore to Istanbul, Turkey. Ports of call along the way include Penang, Malaysia; Ko Ngai, Thailand; Cochin and Bombay, India (two days); Muscat, Khasab and Salalah, Oman (three days); Dubai, United Arab Emirates (two days); Aqaba, Jordan; Sinai, Egypt; Rhodes, Crete and Mykonos in the Greek Isles (three days); and Ephesus, Turkey.

You can expect to pay at least $42,185 for the least expensive cabin on this cruise, unless you get the early-booking fare of $11,998. A mid-range cabin goes for about $42,735, or $21,368 with the early-bird reservation; and the owner's suite during this itinerary will cost you $75,635 unless you book early and get the $37,818 deal.

Silversea Cruises

Silversea is another high-end line that has a small fleet of ships dedicated to carrying a small number of passengers. The company was created in 1994 specifically to cater to elite guests in exotic ports of call that bigger ships could not squeeze themselves inside. The *Silver*

Cloud and *Silver Wind* each take 296 passengers, while the *Silver Shadow* and *Silver Whisper* each carry 382 guests.

As with some other luxury brands, Silversea doesn't promote facilities and services for small children. In fact, it does not allow children younger than one year old aboard, and it reserves the right to limit the number of children aboard who are younger than three. However, if you are planning a family reunion of older children and adults, Silversea does have a lot of other passengers like you.

Silversea 4-Day Cruises

The *Silver Whisper* offers a round-trip itinerary from the Caribbean island of Barbados with ports of call in St. Georges, Grenada; Roseau, Dominica; and Bequia and St. Vincent in the Grenadines. You actually are aboard the ship for five days, but you disembark at 5 A.M. on the last day after the ship arrives back at Barbados.

The lowest-price cabin you will find is $1,995, though you can also get an early-booking rate as low as $1,596. A mid-range cabin will run you at least $2,595, or as little as $2,076 with early-bird savings. The most expensive published rate—not for the grand suite, but for a one-bedroom royal suite (the second-most luxurious level available)—is $4,695, or $3,796 with the early-booking discounts.

Silversea 7-Day Cruises

The *Silver Wind* promotes a one-way, seven-day itinerary from Barcelona, Spain, to Rome, Italy. Ports of call along the way include Monte Carlo, Monaco; and Livorno, Porto Cervo, Amalfi, and Sorrento in Italy (a total of four days).

You can book the lowest-price cabin aboard for $4,195, or $3,356 with early-booking discounts. A mid-range cabin will cost you $5,595, or $4,476 with the early-bird rates. The most expensive published rate—not for the grand suite, but for a one-bedroom royal suite (the second-most luxurious level available)—is $9,495, or $7,596 with the early-booking fare savings.

≡FAST FACT

The Silversea GuestCare program provides travel insurance up to the full cost of your cruise for covered cancellation reasons. It is one of the few cruise company programs that also covers pre-existing medical conditions as long as you pay for the plan in full when you make your final cruise fare payment.

Silversea 14-Day Cruises

The *Silver Shadow* offers a one-way, fourteen-day itinerary from Tokyo, Japan, to Anchorage, Alaska. Ports of call on this cruise include Hakodate and Sapporo in Japan (two days); Kamchatka, Russia; and Dutch Harbor, Kodiak, and Homer in Alaska (three days).

Your least-expensive option for a cabin is at least $8,695, or $6,956 with early-booking savings. A mid-range cabin will cost you a minimum of $11,395, or $9,116 if you qualify for the early-bird discounts. The most expensive published rate—not for the grand suite, but for a one-bedroom royal suite (the second-most luxurious level available)—is $20,695, or $16,556 with the early-booking fare savings.

Swan Hellenic

Swan Hellenic is owned by Princess Cruises, but it offers a different kind of trip than you will find aboard Princess-brand boats. Swan Hellenic operates one ship, the 600-passenger *Minerva II*, and designs its itineraries as all-inclusive destination-oriented trips. Your rate includes round-trip airfare from London, England, airport transfers, shore excursions at every port, guest speakers, all tips and gratuities, and entrance fees to every prearranged place you will visit ashore. There are add-ons you can incur, such as spa treatments, extra excursions, and liquor purchases, but your fare includes far more than most other cruise lines offer for their published rates.

Most guests aboard *Minerva II* spend 70 percent of their cruise time exploring on land, so the ship has amenities like a 4,000-volume library instead of the more typical cabaret show hall. The company's pricing options encourage solo travelers who want to see the world, and itineraries are usually at least a week long. There are no facilities on board for children, so this wouldn't be the best option for youngsters. You are, in fact, required to leave babies six months or younger at home, and on some itineraries, Swan reserves the right to refuse any children younger than one year of age. Older teens, however, could very well find this kind of cruise experience thrilling if they are adventurous and interested in learning more about the world.

Swan Hellenic 8-Day Cruises

The *Minerva II* offers a one-way, eight-day itinerary from Gibraltar, Spain, to Dover, England. Ports of call along the way include Lisbon, Oporto, and Viana do Castelo in Portugal (three days); and Gijon and Bilbao in Spain (two days).

Your rate for a standard inside cabin—remember, this is all-inclusive with airfare—will be at least $3,116. A deluxe cabin with a balcony will cost you a minimum of $4,277.

Swan Hellenic 11-Day Cruises

The *Minerva II* publicizes a one-way, eleven-day itinerary from Callao, Peru, to Caldera, Costa Rica. Ports of call in between include Salaverry, Peru; Manta, Ecuador; the Panama Canal; and Puntarenas, Costa Rica. A standard inside cabin—again, all-inclusive with airfare—will run you a minimum of $3,583. Your cost for a deluxe cabin with a balcony will be at least $5,350.

≡FAST FACT

If you book a cruise with Swan Hellenic, you are required to purchase travel insurance either through that company or through another that it deems appropriate. Your insurance must include at least 2 million British pounds (about $3.85 million) in coverage for medical and travel needs.

Swan Hellenic 22-Day Cruises

The *Minerva II* offers a one-way, twenty-two-day itinerary from Manaus, Brazil, to Buenos Aires, Argentina. The cruise runs along the Amazon River out to the South Atlantic Ocean with ports of call including Parintins, Santarem, and Belem on the Amazon (four days); Fortaleza, Recife, Salvador, Rio de Janeiro, and Paranagua in Brazil (five days); and Montevideo, Uruguay.

A standard inside cabin will cost you at least $7,635 (again, including airfare and other inclusive-rate items). If you want a deluxe cabin with a balcony, expect to pay at least $11,062.

CHAPTER 3

Beyond the Basics

CHOOSING A CRUISE SHIP and itinerary is just the beginning of your vacation-planning process. After you've selected the cruise itself, it's time to start thinking about shore excursions, before- and after-cruise land vacation deals, airline tickets, travel insurance, and more. Luckily, most of the major cruise lines are ready and willing to help you get everything you want—and, in some cases, to offer you a few discounts along the way.

Cruise-Airline Packages

As you saw in Chapter 2, cruise vacations come in a wide variety of prices, styles, and durations. The one common denominator is that most companies promote their lowest possible, cruise-only rates to get your attention. Food and a nightly show are included, but not much else. You need to consider secondary expenses.

One of your biggest secondary expenses is likely to be airfare to and from your ship. If you live in Southern Florida, western California, or New York City, you are in luck—you can often drive to a nearby port and find a round-trip cruise itinerary that will bring you back to the same port, thus negating the need for airfare at all.

If you travel often for business, you may also be in luck. You may have enough points on your frequent-flier program to purchase round-trip airfare for your whole family at no additional charge. Blackout dates are of course a concern here, but destinations likely are not, since most cruise ships intentionally begin and end their itineraries in major cities near international airports.

If you don't have either of those options on your side, you will have to purchase airfare in addition to the price of your cruise, as do the majority of people who book cruise vacations. To make your planning process a bit easier, most cruise companies have programs that enable you to add airfare and round-trip transfers onto the price of your cruise.

 TRAVEL TIP

Be sure to include round-trip airport transfers in your budget if you book your own airfare instead of getting a cruise ship/airline package deal. If, after taxi fees and tips, you're only going to end up saving $5 or $10 total, you might want to avoid the hassle and let the cruise line do the work of making the arrangements for you.

The question you will of course ask yourself is this: Will it cost me less if I book the airline tickets myself? The answer is sometimes yes, sometimes no. It depends on where you live, where you need to fly, and what airfare specials are being advertised at the time you choose to book.

Your best bet is to start by asking your cruise-ship company how much it would charge you to add round-trip airfare and transfers to the price of your cruise package. In some cases, you will get more than just the price of the ticket; Carnival's Fly Aweigh Air Fare Supplements program and the Disney Cruise Line sometimes include complimentary overnight hotel accommodations if your flight can't get you to the embarkation port on time for a same-day departure. And Radisson Seven Seas sometimes offers free airfare upgrades to business or first class if you book your ticket through them.

In virtually all cases with all cruise-ship companies, your cruise/airline package rate will include round-trip transfers to your ship. That's a convenience sometimes worth paying extra for—especially if you are traveling during the winter from a snowy city and are worried about delays that might leave you precious little time to get from the airport to your ship.

TRAVEL TIP

If you plan to book your own airline tickets instead of using a cruise line's package deal, you may still want to purchase the cruise line's round-trip transfers from the airport to your ship. Carnival, for instance, suggests that you do this when flying to meet ships in Alaska and the Mediterranean that are sometimes more than an hour from the airport.

After you know exactly what your cruise line wants to charge you for exactly what kind of airline seats and transfers, you can have your travel agent do further research for separate airfares, or you can look around on your own. The Internet makes this kind of search much easier than it used to be. Most airlines have their own sites, where you can check the exact same flight numbers and flight times that your cruise ship is offering you. If you book through the particular airline's Web site, you sometimes get a discount on the published fares or an extra number of frequent-flier miles.

You also can do research through travel Web sites such as *www. expedia.com*, *www.travelocity.com*, and *www.orbitz.com*, which will search many of the airlines' sites and give you a list to choose from by price and flight time. Last, there are "meta-search" travel Web sites such as SideStep.com and Kayak.com that will search through the airlines' Web sites *and* the sites like Travelocity and Orbitz, providing you with a very good perspective on all the airfares available throughout the industry with a single click of your mouse.

 **TRAVEL TIP**

> If you choose a cruise/airline package, you should still contact the airline on your own well in advance of your trip to ensure that you will be getting everything you want—including good seat assignments, special meals, and frequent-flier credits. Do not expect your cruise line to do this for you.

The last thing you should consider is whether your credit-card program gives you points toward a redemption program or cash back for every dollar you spend. You'll obviously get a similar number of points whether you book your airline tickets yourself or through your cruise line, as long as the price of your airline tickets is similar. However, some newer credit cards, such as the Citi Premier Pass, offer rewards points not just for every dollar you spend, but also for every mile you or anyone else flies on a plane ticket booked with your credit card. If you can't make the airline ticket purchase through your cruise company a separate line on your credit card statement, it might be a smarter move for you to book your airline tickets yourself. You'll probably end up with enough extra redemption points to get yourself something like a nice gift certificate to a home-improvement store when you get back from your vacation.

Cruise-Land Packages

After airfare, another large secondary expense you might incur is the added cost of spending extra days ashore before or after your cruise. While some people choose to cruise because they want all their fun and food contained aboard a giant floating hotel, land extensions are a great idea if you're the type of person who wants to see and experience as much of your vacation destination as possible—beyond the few hours' worth of excursions you'll get when your ship docks at a given port. Some cruise lines offer land extensions in addition to regular cruise-ship itineraries (which basically means they'll book you a room at a land-based resort before or after your trip), while others have created land-sea packages with fully developed itineraries to appeal to customers who want simplified, prearranged travel on the ship as well as on land.

As when booking airline tickets, you can choose to make your own land-based travel arrangements. Again, the issues are cost and convenience—but with land extensions, you may not know the specific type of travel you want to do, as you would when booking airline tickets to and from your ship. In this case, unless you are a seasoned traveler or someone who knows a lot about the area you will be visiting, your best bet is probably to go with the prearranged cruise-ship/land-tour combination package. The amount of time you save trying to figure out all of your hotel, taxicab, and sightseeing options will probably be worth any extra cost you will incur by having the cruise line arrange everything for you.

 TRAVEL TIP

If you decide to book a land excursion through a company other than your cruise line, be sure your friends and family aboard the ship—or back home—know the company's name and telephone number. That way, if you accidentally miss your ship's departure from port, your loved ones will know how to find you.

Some land-extension packages are more suitable for very young children than others, depending mostly on the ports of call. Check with your cruise line for details about your family's age range if you have questions.

Carnival Pre- and Post-Cruise Vacations

Carnival's land-extension packages usually include hotel, room tax, and either round-trip airport transfers or a rental car with unlimited mileage. (You must be at least twenty-one years old to choose the rental car option.) You will be required to pay some additional fees, such as resort and car rental taxes. The company recommends extra time on land in major hubs such as central Florida, New York, and Rome, but it does not promote special itineraries on land within those cities.

Celebrity Sea and Stay Program

Celebrity's land-extension packages include one, two, or three nights at a resort before or after your cruise. You can get a rental car if you are at least twenty-one years old, but you will have to pay some additional fees, such as rental-car tax.

If you cancel your land-extension program eight to thirty days before your cruise, you will be charged 50 percent of the program's fee. If you cancel within seven days of your departure, you will receive no refund.

The company suggests extra time in cities such as Genoa, Italy; Amsterdam, Holland; and Seattle, Washington, but it offers no specific itinerary suggestions for you on land.

Crystal Extended Land Programs

Crystal Cruises offers three- to eight-night coordinated land vacations with itineraries much like your cruise-ship itinerary. The cost of the packages varies widely depending on the location and duration of the stay. In some cases, a certain number of people must sign up from your ship in order for the program to operate.

Examples include a five-night Australian Wine and Opals program in which you stay at the Four Seasons Hotel and visit the Sydney Opera House, the Barossa Valley vineyards, and the outback opal-mining town of Coober Pedy. Another example is the four-night Antiquities of Greece and Egypt package, in which you visit the Acropolis, the Parthenon, and more in Athens before a flight to Cairo, where you will see the Citadel, the Pyramids of Giza, the Sphinx, and some of King Tutankhamen's treasures at the Museum of Egyptian Antiquities.

Disney Land and Sea Vacation

If you are planning to cruise with young children, you will be hard-pressed *not* to book a land-extension package before or after your Disney Cruise Line vacation. The company has you embark and disembark so close to Florida's Walt Disney World that it almost seems silly to buy separate plane tickets at a future date.

Should you only have a single week for your vacation, you might consider the seven-night Land and Sea Vacation package. It includes three or four nights at Walt Disney World followed by a three- or four-night cruise, depending on whether you would rather spend the majority of your trip on land or at sea. The cruise portion of each itinerary includes ports of call at Nassau and Castaway Cay in the Bahamas; if you choose the longer cruise-ship option, you will spend your extra day entirely at sea.

The Land and Sea packages are priced according to the level of accommodations you want. If you are willing to stay in a standard inside stateroom aboard the ship, you will be given a room at a moderate hotel ashore, such as Disney's Caribbean Beach Resort. If you want a mid-level cabin on the ship, you will be put in a deluxe hotel ashore, such as Disney's Polynesian Resort. If you choose a top-priced suite aboard the ship, you will stay at the flagship Disney Grand Floridian Resort and Spa while you are on land.

Prices for the lowest-level Land and Sea packages range from at least $799 to $2,399; the mid-level option ranges will cost you a minimum of $1,249 to $3,499; and the top-shelf pricing will cost you at least $2,699 to $5,199.

MSC Cruises' Hotel Packages

MSC Cruises offers hotel packages for one or two nights before or after your cruise, with hotels available in dozens of gateway cities. Packages include hotel taxes, and rates start at $90 per person, per night. The company does not suggest specific itineraries in your city of choice.

Norwegian Cruise Line Pre- and Post-Cruise Packages

NCL offers hotel packages that include hotel taxes, bellman gratuities, and a one-way transfer from your ship's pier to the hotel in a variety of cities worldwide.

Some more extended packages are available depending on your ship and your cruising itinerary. For example, if you cruise aboard the *Norwegian Sun* to Vancouver in British Columbia, Canada, you can book a three-night land extension that includes a trip to the world-famous Butchart Gardens as well as a trip to Chinatown. If you are cruising in South America, you can choose an extended stay in Buenos Aires, Argentina, that includes a tango show, a walking tour at Iguazu Falls, and a tour of the capital city itself.

Rates are sometimes as low as a few hundred dollars for the extended land packages, depending on your port of call.

 TRAVEL TIP

If you think you might want to book a land extension before or after your cruise, consider staying at a hotel that offers inexpensive laundry service. You won't be running into the same people you saw every day on the ship, so you can recycle your outfits and have less to lug in your suitcase.

Princess CruiseTours

Princess CruiseTours come in myriad lengths, destinations, and prices. They are arranged as one organized itinerary whether you choose to do the land or the sea portion of your trip first, and the price of your entire vacation is rolled into one fee.

In Alaska alone, Princess offers sixteen different CruiseTours that include Denali National Park and Mount McKinley, plus another four options if you would rather spend your time on the Copper River (where the king salmon are delicious), the Kenai Peninsula, or caribou country near the Arctic Circle.

The minimum trip length is ten nights, seven of them at sea, with a minimum price for your land and cruise combined of $1,399. The longest Alaska CruiseTour is fifteen nights, including seven nights at sea, with a base rate of $2,649 per person. CruiseTours are also available before or after your cruise in Asia, Canada, New England, South America, Europe, Australia, and the South Pacific.

Radisson Seven Seas Land Programs

Radisson offers both pre- and post-cruise hotel stays without any attached scheduling, as well as land-extension programs with itineraries similar to what you will find aboard its cruise ships. In Europe alone, you can choose among more than a dozen land-extension programs that run from two to five nights, with prices that vary accordingly.

Some examples include a two-night stay at Italy's Lake Como, including a private, guided boat tour, and a four-night extension in Moscow, Russia, that includes a city tour and lunch at Cafe Pushkin, a tour of the Kremlin and Red Square, and an evening performance of the Moscow Circus.

Royal Caribbean Cruisetours

Royal Caribbean's Cruisetours come with tour guides you can follow if you choose to stay with your group, but you also have the option of exploring on your own. In some cases, you can choose whether to do your land extension before or after the sea portion of your vacation, but sometimes you are only offered one option.

Royal Caribbean offers nineteen Cruisetours in Alaska, four in the Canadian Rockies, and four in Europe. Prices vary according to your destination and your trip's length. In Europe, examples include a three-night package in the Spanish cities of Madrid and Barcelona, which you will travel between by high-speed train. You'll see the Royal Palace, the 1992 Olympic Ring and Stadium, and artist Antoni

Gaudi's La Sagrada Famila. Cruisetours in Canada include trips to the resort town of Whistler, a mecca for skiers.

Silversea Silver Sights Program

Silversea calls its land extensions the Silver Sights Program. It offers two dozen options in the Mediterranean alone that range in length from three to eight days, though you usually cannot choose whether to do the land or sea portion of your vacation first. Other Silver Sights Program options exist in Northern Europe, the Far East, the South Pacific, South America, the Amazon, Canada and New England, Africa and the Indian Ocean, the Caribbean, Mexico, Alaska, and the Pacific Northwest. Prices vary according to the number of days you choose on land and your destination.

Examples include a three-night stay at the Fairmount Royal Pavilion on the Caribbean island of Barbados with a tour of Bridgetown and the Sunbury Plantation House. In Africa, you can choose a four-night program that includes a stay at the Londolozi Game Private Reserve and drives with an experienced tracker to see lions, elephants, rhinoceroses, leopards, and buffalo.

≡ FAST FACT

Londolozi is a Zulu word meaning "protector of all living things." What better for an African game reserve that sits on nearly 35,000 acres of land?

Swan Hellenic Pre- and Post-Cruise Tours

Swan Hellenic's land-extension programs range from five to seven days and include itineraries much like the ones aboard your cruise ship. Prices vary according to the length of your program and the port where you extend your trip—with options literally all over the world. You can often choose whether to do the land or sea portion of your vacation first, and sometimes one option is less expensive than the other.

Examples include a five-day stay at the Amazon Eco Park Lodge in South America, with a rustic wooden bungalow, a guided forest walk, and a small boat trip through creeks and inlets. Prices are inclusive, just as with Swan Hellenic's cruises; this particular land extension will cost you at least $2,400 for a twin-bed room.

Another example is a six-day land extension in the Middle East, including visits in Damascus, Syria, to one of the few remaining Aramaic-speaking villages, to the Valley of the Tombs museum, and to Umayyad Mosque, one of the greatest ever designed. Your inclusive rate for this land extension will be at least $1,768.

Excursions Ashore

Like airfare and land extensions, another large secondary expense you may incur is excursions during your cruise. Of course, you never have to leave your ship if you simply prefer to stay aboard and enjoy the amenities there, but if you want to explore some of the ports where your ship will call, the odds are good that it is going to cost you extra.

It's hard to generalize about how much each excursion will cost, as they range from less than $50 on some cruise lines to several hundred dollars apiece for higher-end opportunities aboard other cruise lines. Your best bet is to ask your cruise ship staff for literature and pricing on the excursions available during your cruise, or go to your cruise line's Web site for a detailed list based on your sailing dates.

Some cruise lines, such as Swan Hellenic, include a good number of excursions in the price of your vacation, but for the most part you should expect to pay extra to do anything and everything you would like to on land. Even when some excursions are included in your overall rate, others will be offered to you that might be too hard to resist.

 **TRAVEL TIP**

The most important thing to remember about shore excursions is that they fill up fast. If your cruise ship lets you book excursions in advance of actually getting aboard, take it—by phone, by Internet, by carrier pigeon if necessary. And if you find yourself squeezed out, get on the waiting list. People do change their minds at the last minute.

Some cruise lines, such as Holland America and Crystal Cruises, will even let you customize your excursions instead of always staying with groups from your ship. Crystal has a Land Programs Department that will do everything from extending the excursions already available (such as adding a private helicopter ride to a group hike) to creating a private excursion just for you (such as a one-on-one, behind-the-scenes tour of the Vatican).

Incidentals

T-shirts, wood carvings, framed feathers with pictures of parrots painted on them—souvenirs are likely to be perhaps your largest incidentals expense during your cruise. If you tend to buy things on the spur of the moment, consider setting your souvenir spending limit in advance, and bring cash or travelers' checks along for not a penny more than you wish to spend. If you are less impulsive and prefer to carry plastic, many of the shops at cruise-ship ports do take credit cards.

Other incidental expenses include everything from sundries (which you can get onboard as well as on land) to souvenir photos and fountain soda. If you are traveling with children who are gluttons for carbonated beverages, consider purchasing an all-they-can-drink soda package before your ship sets sail. Cruise lines that cater to kids, like Carnival and Disney, usually have these available, and sometimes even include a souvenir plastic cup.

Cruise Insurance

You read in Chapter 2 about various cruise-ship travel insurance programs. Most of the cruise companies offer them with varying degrees of protection and for various prices. Should you buy a travel insurance plan? The truth is, it usually doesn't hurt to get one. Especially aboard the value-oriented cruise ships that cater to kids, prices for the travel insurance plans are kept low enough to be affordable for most families. Medical cancellations are almost always covered, and with children, it's a safe bet that somebody just may get sick as your sailing date approaches.

Also consider buying travel insurance through your travel agent if you live in a northern latitude and are planning to cruise during the snowy winter season—but be sure that weather delays are included as a covered cancellation reason. If your cruise company's policy does not cover blizzards that might close your local airport until well after your ship sets sail down south, consider booking a separate insurance policy through your travel agent that will give you peace of mind should flurries start to fall.

Discounts

So, the cruise companies got your attention with those tiered fares you read about in the previous chapter, did they? You've got it right—you can often enjoy exactly the same cruise as the family in the cabin next door for a fraction of the cost, whether your vacation is worth $1,000 or $10,000. You just need to learn a few tricks.

Cruise-ship cabins are sort of like airplane seats when it comes to pricing. The lowest, greatest, most super-duper-saver fare is advertised to get you to pick up the phone and ask about booking a trip, but usually only a limited number of cabins are available at that special rate. After those are gone, you're going to be lumped in with everybody else trying to get aboard unless you book extremely early or take advantage of some special pricing promotions that some of the cruise lines offer. Here's a look at a few of your best options if you want to save money on your cruise.

Book Early

If you have your heart set on a specific cruise during specific dates, and you can't or don't want to be flexible about your destination or the months when you will go, your best bet for saving serious dollars is to book early. And by early, the cruise companies mean *very* early—sometimes as much as a year in advance.

Princess, for instance, offers special rates on its cabins until about a month before each ship sets sail. However, these discounts become available as soon as an itinerary is announced, sometimes a year before your embarkation date, and as people book cabins and the ship gets fuller, fewer and fewer discounts are offered. If you are one of the last people to book a cabin, you are probably going to pay the highest price—and you may not get the kind of cabin you want. In this system, you're not in a race to meet an early-booking deadline with Princess itself as much as you are in a race to book before other passengers who want to take the same cruise.

Another early-booking system is the kind used by Swan Hellenic. In this case, you can save as much as 45 percent off published rates if you are willing to book your trip eight months to a year in advance—by a date the company specifies in its brochure. However, the 45-percent discount applies only to certain cruising itineraries. Other itineraries are subject to smaller discounts, some as low as 20 percent. No matter what the discounted rate, only a certain number of cabins are reserved at the lower fares. Once those are gone, you will likely have to pay full price. In this type of system, then, you're in a race to meet the company's early-booking deadline *and* to do so before other passengers who want to take the same cruise.

Silversea's program is similar to Swan Hellenic's in that you can save as much as 35 percent off published fares. You must book and make your deposit by a certain date, and you must do so before all the cabins set aside for the special fares are gone. However, Silversea offers an additional 5-percent discount—which you can combine with the early-booking incentive—if you make your final payment by a date the company specifies. Again, the trick is to book as early as possible and, in this case, to pay at or around the same time. Crystal Cruises is the same way: If you pay in full six months or more before your sailing date, you save an extra 3.5 percent off your fare.

TRAVEL TIP

Most cruise companies offer some form of early-booking discounts, but their systems and deadlines are all different. Your safest bet is to book as early as possible. If you can book a full year before your sailing date, you will likely receive the best bargains no matter which cruise line you choose.

Radisson Seven Seas offers yet another kind of early-booking program. On some of its ships, if you book travel 120 days before departure, you will receive the discounted rate. However, that rate is often not as substantial a savings as Radisson's special two-for-one cruise deals, which are—you guessed it—a full 50 percent off. Be sure to ask if the two-for-one program is available for your itinerary (or for a similar one that you might choose instead) before you rush to meet the 120-day deadline in this case. Actually, that's good advice no matter which cruise line you choose. Always call early and ask whether you qualify for any other special savings programs.

Book Back-to-Back Itineraries

If your hope is to cruise for longer than just a few days, you can sometimes save serious dollars by booking a pair of shorter, back-to-back itineraries instead of booking one big ol' mother lode trip.

Radisson Seven Seas is one of the cruise lines that promotes this concept heavily. For instance, the *Seven Seas Voyager* offers an eight-day, seven-night itinerary from Athens, Greece, to Monte Carlo, Monaco—a trip that ends at 7 A.M. on a Sunday. Just a half-day later, at

6:00 P.M. on that same Sunday, the *Voyager* sets sail again on a sixteen-day, fifteen-night itinerary from Monte Carlo to northwestern Africa and then on to its ending port of Fort Lauderdale, Florida. Radisson wants to keep its boats full, so it offers a combination of the two itineraries at a price that is quite attractive.

If you booked the lowest-price *Voyager* stateroom for just the Monte Carlo to Fort Lauderdale itinerary, you'd pay at least $9,190 per person without any early-booking discounts. However, if you plan ahead, book early, and combine the trips, you end up with a twenty-three-day, twenty-two-night cruise from Athens, Greece, to Fort Lauderdale, Florida, in the same level of stateroom for a total fare of $8,341. That's right—as long as you book early, you can do both itineraries back to back for less than you'd otherwise pay to do just one without any discounts. That's a heck of a deal.

Talk to your travel agent or cruise line about similar opportunities that involve itineraries scheduled immediately before or after yours aboard the same ship. You'll be surprised how eager the companies can be to entice you to stay aboard just a little longer.

Senior Rates

If you're a "seasoned" citizen, or if you're bringing grandpa or grandma along on your family cruise vacation, you'll be happy to learn that senior citizen discounts are indeed available aboard some cruise ships. Norwegian Cruise Line, for instance, offers discounts for anyone fifty-five years or older on some itineraries. Royal Caribbean also has senior discounts for anyone who is fifty-five years or older, though as with NCL's boats, the Royal Caribbean rates are only good aboard several ships at specific times of the year. Costa Cruise Lines gives anyone who is sixty years or older as much as $200 off their ticket on any of the company's ships or itineraries. The discount is in addition to any savings you get if you purchase the ticket with an early-booking discount (called the Andiamo Rate aboard Costa's ships).

Other companies often have senior rates, as well. Ask your cruise line of choice or your travel agent for details.

Kids' Rates

At the other end of the age spectrum, there are a couple of different ways to save money when booking a trip with your children. For starters, some cruise lines offer kids' discounts on a seasonal basis. Crystal Cruises promoted a Kids Sail Free program during the summer of 2005 aboard its ships in Alaska. The discount was good for any child age twelve or younger who shared a stateroom with two adults, and the special deal may be repeated in other parts of the world during 2006.

Other cruise lines offer permanent kids' fares all year round. Costa Cruise Line has a program called the Friends and Family Fare, in which you can save as much as $200 per stateroom off the early-booking rates as long as you book at least two staterooms at the same time. You can also choose the Costa Loves Kids program, in which children seventeen and younger who share a cabin with you may cruise for just $199 per child.

≡ FAST FACT

If you are planning to share your cabin with your kids, ask whether your cruise ship offers special rates for third and fourth passengers. Even aboard cruise lines that don't offer special kids' fares, the third and fourth passenger rates are sometimes identical to the kids' rates aboard other cruise lines.

The latter of the Costa kids' incentives is actually a program that you can find aboard other cruise lines under a different name, usually something as generic as "third and fourth guest." If you are willing to share your cabin with your children, you can often get them deeply discounted fares. With Carnival, for example, a four-day Bahamas and Caribbean cruise costs at least $799 per person with the early-booking discount, but the third and fourth guest in a single cabin are eligible for fares as low as $199 with the early-booking discount.

Look for these kinds of savings without the name "kid" in the brochure for whatever cruise line you choose, and you're likely to find a good deal.

Web Site Specials

When the cruise-ship companies have trouble filling up their boats, they keep the discounts coming—sometimes right up until the day of embarkation. Last-minute deals were more prevalent in the past than they are today, mostly because demand for cabins has increased in recent years and the companies have no reason to lower their prices when every cabin is full. Still, if you're not set on a specific ship or a specific itinerary, you can save a ton by booking a last-minute deal on a cruise company's Web site.

Sometimes, the discounts even apply to cruises far enough in the future to allow you some planning time. For instance, in the middle of March 2005, Carnival was promoting an eight-day itinerary aboard the Carnival *Legend* in the southern Caribbean that went round-trip from Fort Lauderdale, Florida with ports of call in St. Maarten, Barbados, and Martinique. The brochure fare for an ocean-view cabin was $2,099, or $829 with the Super Saver early-booking discount. The special Web fare for the same exact cabin was $749—for dates as far in the future as December 2005 *and* December 2006. The upshot: You could have booked a cabin online for nearly $100 less than the Super Saver early-booking rate and still had at least nine months before you had to cruise.

Other Web discounts are good all year round, such as the Value Collection Sailing program that Crystal Cruises offers. Some of its ships have a limited number of cabins reserved at rates as much as 63 percent off the regular brochure fares—often aboard ships cruising during slower vacation times, such as the week before Christmas, the week before Spring Break, or the weeks before popular travel seasons officially begin in some destinations. These more-than-half-off rates remain published on the Crystal Cruises Web site until all the set-aside cabins are booked, so you can instantly find out whether you are still able to enjoy the savings on the itinerary of your choice. (You could also call, but that takes longer, and these cabins go quickly!)

Payment Options

All cruise lines accept major credit cards such as American Express, Visa, and MasterCard. Some cruise lines also accept Discover; read the terms and conditions (all the print that's smaller than a mosquito's nose) in the back of your particular ship's brochure for specifics about your personal trip.

You can pay for your entire cruise fare immediately after you book, which can often net you a substantial discount on your trip. Of course, this amount does not include shore excursions, liquor purchased aboard, and any other expenses you will incur after you embark on your cruise. Those may be tallied and given to you at the end of your trip, when you can again pay with any of the major credit cards that are accepted.

 TRAVEL TIP

Some cruise lines may accept checks as payment, but your reservation will not be finalized until the check has cleared, and a returned check may result in cancellation of your booking or additional fees. You may also use a secured debit card (one with a Visa or MasterCard logo), but the best way to pay for your cruise is with one of the major credit cards.

If you choose not to pay in full, you will likely be required to make a deposit in order to secure your reservation. In some cases, you will be given precious little time before booking and paying your deposit. Princess, for example, requires that deposits be made within three days of bookings. Be prepared to pay at least 10 percent of your cruise-only fare as a down payment.

The remainder of your fare will usually be due to the cruise company no later than sixty days before your departure date. In some cases, such as for holiday-week cruises, you may have to pay the balance due no later than three months before you are scheduled to sail. If you book a cruise within one to three months of the embarkation date, you may have no choice but to pay in full at the same time that you make your reservation.

CHAPTER 4

Choosing the Ship That's Right for You

SOMETIMES, YOU WILL USE your ship as nothing more than a home base from which to explore ports of call. In other cases, your ship will be a destination unto itself—bigger and more packed with activities than some of the towns where it will dock. And in both cases, whether you want to be aboard a mammoth vessel or within a cozier setting, you can have either top-shelf luxury or more afford-able amenities. There are big ships and small ships, luxurious ships and value brands, in multiple combinations.

Ship Tours

Even if you have never before set foot aboard a boat of any kind, you can get a feel for how different ships are designed by comparing deck plans within your cruise ship brochures. Cruise companies generally create one of two kinds of deck plans to show you their ship designs: a lines plan, which shows each slice of a ship as a separate deck, or a full-scale illustration, which gives you a kind of X-ray vision peek through the side of a ship. In both cases, you can find a lot of valu-able information on the page that will help you choose the right ship for your vacation.

In a traditional lines plan you will see each deck separately, from a bird's-eye view. These kinds of deck plans are the best for choos-ing a cabin aboard, for two reasons. First, the cruise ship companies usually color-code each block of cabins by price range, which means you can find out whether that "great value" cabin you found is really in a so-so spot—say, right beneath the teen disco on the deck above it. Second, with these kinds of deck plans, you often can see the exact number of each cabin within the color-coded price-range blocks. This lets you request a particular cabin in the specific part of the ship where you want to be—for instance, closest to the elevators or the self-service washing machines.

TRAVEL TIP

> While you're looking at the deck plans, you should also see the ship's specifications—including how many passengers and crew are aboard. Some ships offer one crew member for every two passengers, while others have a far less pampering ratio of crew to passengers. If you demand superior service, select a ship with more crew.

On a full-scale illustration, you often won't be able to see the sleeping quarters, but you will be able to get a much better feel for where each of the ship's facilities are in relation to one another. You will see the entire ship from the side at one time, instead of having to try to mentally piece together how each deck stacks up atop the next. With this overall full-scale illustration view you can see, for instance, exactly where the children's playroom is in relation to the main pool. This means you will know how far your kids will have to walk through the ship to find you if you're catching a few rays while they enjoy activity time. These illustrated views also do a much better job of conveying the overall size of a ship, as people are usually represented to scale, in relative size.

There are a few things you should try to determine no matter which kind of deck plan you have. Depending on how much time you intend to spend in certain areas aboard, the following information will be useful in selecting an appropriate ship and cabins for your family's particular needs:

- Where you want your cabin to be in relation to your children's cabin
- Where you want an elderly grandparent's cabin to be in relation to facilities such as elevators, dining areas, and card rooms
- Where you want your family's cabins to be in relation to noisier parts of the ship, such as the main atrium or dance clubs
- Whether you want your balcony to sit right beneath or directly downwind of the ship's main smokestack

When you look at a ship's deck plans and begin to consider how you actually want to spend your time aboard, you may decide it would be worth it to pay a bit more and get exactly the cabin you want instead of settling for the least expensive one you can get. In many cases, even the cabins that are within the same lower price ranges offer different levels of privacy simply because of their location in a corridor.

Ocean Liners

By definition, an ocean liner is simply a large, oceangoing ship that carries passengers regularly. In terms of cruising, however, the term "ocean liner" often refers to the biggest, best-outfitted, most beautiful ships at sea. Ocean liner becomes almost interchangeable with luxury liner, a term that used to refer only to super-ships like the ill-fated *Titanic* that were built to carry the world's wealthiest people on transoceanic voyages in the utmost of style. When you ask about cruising aboard ocean liners today, you are likely to receive information about flagships—vessels that, in many ways, are destinations unto themselves. Some of these flagships are true ocean liners, while others are not.

There is perhaps no better place to begin learning about flagships than with the mother of them all, the biggest cruise ship/ocean liner/luxury liner in the world: the *Queen Mary 2*.

Cunard launched the *Queen Mary 2* in January 2004 to worldwide fanfare. The $800 million vessel is a staggering 1,132 feet long and 135 feet wide—about the width of a thirteen-story building toppled onto its side. She carries 2,620 passengers and 1,253 crew members, a relatively small number of total people given the ship's size. The idea behind her construction was to create spacious elegance, not to pack people aboard like sardines.

The *Queen Mary 2*'s top deck (she has fourteen of them) is reserved almost exclusively for sun-worshippers. Facilities on other decks include a library and separate bookstore, a beauty salon, gym with separate weight room, spa with indoor therapy pool, children's play area, royal theater with stage, college-at-sea area with stage-size movie screen, a Main Street-like array of shops and boutiques, a video arcade, casino, multiple bars and restaurants, and, oh yes, the only planetarium at sea.

Nearly 80 percent of the cabins aboard the *Queen Mary 2* have ocean views, and all but a handful also have balconies. The penthouse on this ship is a full 758 square feet and includes a living and dining room—and it isn't even the nicest accommodations aboard. That distinction goes to the Balmoral and Sandringham Duplex, a staggering 2,249-square-foot home at sea with two marble bathtubs and a private outdoor balcony that's bigger than most you would find aboard any other cruise ship. The upstairs, indoor balcony overlooks the living room below, and of course, a wall of windows facing the sea.

Mid-Range Vessels

Though gigantic in the grand scope of all man-made objects in the universe, most cruise ships in the family-value price category are considered mid-range, or average in size. You may find it hard to believe, but ships that carry a thousand or two thousand people at a time are the norm nowadays. You may also find it hard to believe that some ships carry so many people when others of similar length carry far fewer people—sometimes several *hundred* fewer. That's something to pay attention to if you are considering two ships of the same length but are particularly sensitive to crowds.

Size aside, each cruise company tries to give its ships facilities that distinguish one fleet from another. Interior designs and ambience are also different from fleet to fleet (and often, from ship to ship within each fleet). Here's a look at a few examples in the mid-range category.

≡FAST FACT

If you don't like crowds, be sure to compare a ship's length to the number of people it carries. For instance, Carnival's 727-foot *Holiday* carries about 1,450 passengers, while Crystal's slightly larger, 781-foot *Symphony* holds just 940. The latter will be less jammed with people.

Carnival *Holiday* and *Celebration*

Each of these two 727-foot ships in the Carnival fleet carries between 1,452 and 1,486 passengers along with 660 crew members on a total of eight decks. Four decks on each ship are devoted entirely to cabins, while top-dollar suites comprise the whole of the forward area on the top deck.

The remainder of the top deck and the three decks below it are reserved as public areas. Facilities include a gymnasium and spa, a casino, main lounge with stage and dance floor, separate dance club, shopping area, and several restaurants and lounges.

There are only three types of cabin categories aboard these ships: interior stateroom (no view of the ocean), ocean-view stateroom (with a window or two portholes), and suites, which have balconies. *Holiday* and *Celebration* each have standard staterooms that measure 185 square feet, which Carnival says is an average of 50 percent larger than standard staterooms aboard other cruise ships.

Celebrity *Infinity*

The *Infinity* is one of Celebrity's newer ships, launched in March 2001. She is 965 feet long and 105 feet wide, able to carry 1,950 passengers as well as 999 crew members—putting her on the borderline between mid-range and ocean liner-size ships.

As a relatively recent launch, the *Infinity* was built with modern passenger tastes in mind. She has a total of 1,059 staterooms, 853 of which (or about 80 percent) have ocean views. There are four different kinds of suites aboard, the smallest ranging from 254 to 362 square feet. The finest rooms aboard this ship are the two penthouse suites, each 1,690 square feet with a marble mosaic foyer floor, grand piano, private exercise equipment, marble master bath, whirlpool tub, private veranda with pool, and more.

Also in keeping with modern tastes, the *Infinity* devotes a full 25,000 square feet to its AquaSpa and fitness center. That area is in addition to other public spaces such as a theater, champagne bar, teen club, cinema conference center, library, separate music library, Internet café, casino, and multiple restaurants and bars.

Crystal *Symphony*

At 781 feet long, the *Symphony* is the smallest of Crystal Cruises' three ships. She entered service in March 1995 and cost $250 million to build. *Symphony* takes 940 passengers and carries 545 crew members. She has eight guest decks, and nearly 60 percent of her cabins are veranda staterooms.

Her lowest-level cabins, called deluxe staterooms, are 202 square feet with picture windows that offer limited views. There are nearly as many of these aboard as there are deluxe staterooms with verandas, which are 246 square feet apiece. The *Symphony* also carries two Crystal Penthouses with verandas, each about 982 square feet with a living room, dining area, Jacuzzi bathtub, and more.

Public spaces aboard the *Symphony* include a children's center, separate teen center, library, shopping arcade, casino, showroom with hydraulic stage, computer center, Hollywood-style theater, several swimming pools, golf driving range and putting green, fitness center and spa with beauty salon, and multiple restaurants and bars.

Holland America *Amsterdam*

Just one foot shorter than Crystal's *Symphony* is Holland America's *Amsterdam*, at 780 feet long. She hit the water for the first time in October 2000. She carries 647 crew members to tend to her 1,380 passengers, who sleep in 690 staterooms that range from inside cabins to penthouse veranda suites. By far, the greatest number of cabins are outside staterooms at 197 square feet apiece, but also available are 135 inside cabins that are just a hair smaller, at 182 square feet. Holland America's recent Signature of Excellence initiative included outfitting all staterooms (aboard every ship, not just those on the *Amsterdam*) with Premium Plush Euro-Top mattresses, Egyptian cotton linens, extra-fluffy towels, terry bathrobes, massaging shower heads, lighted magnifying makeup mirrors, and new hair dryers. There are two penthouse veranda suites aboard, each 1,159 square feet in size. Penthouse guests also have access to a private lounge.

The *Amsterdam* has ten passenger decks with public spaces, including an Internet café, live-show theater, separate cinema theater, library, casino, spa and fitness center, duty-free shops, a card room, children's activity area, and multiple lounges and restaurants.

FAST FACT

If you've cruised with Holland America before but found the cabins less than sparkling, consider giving the company another look. Its fleetwide Signature of Excellence initiative included a serious sprucing up of everything from mattresses to bathrobes.

Princess Cruises' *Caribbean Princess*

The *Caribbean Princess* is a 950-footer that carries a whopping 3,110 guests on her nineteen decks. She has nearly 900 staterooms with balconies, reportedly giving her more than any other cruise ship that sails year-round in the Caribbean. Not that you are likely to spend much time in your stateroom, given all the facilities she has aboard.

You can choose to spend your time at one of the *Caribbean Princess*'s five swimming pools, on her top-deck nineteen-hole miniature golf course, or in her spa or exercise areas, the Internet café or the Grand Casino, the arcade, the fine arts gallery, or in one of her countless restaurants and bars. There's even a deck area devoted to showing movies under the stars, as well as a nightclub called Skywalker's that you get to by crossing a top-deck walkway bridge five stories above the water.

Ocean-view cabins with double beds range from 158 to 182 square feet in total space, while the *Caribbean Princess*'s grand suite with balcony is a 1,277-square-foot area with a separate sitting room, panoramic-view balcony, and corner bathtub with whirlpool jets.

Royal Caribbean *Brilliance of the Seas*

Another mid-range to ocean-liner-size ship is Royal Caribbean's *Brilliance of the Seas*. Launched in 2002, she is 962 feet long and carries 2,501 guests as well as 848 crew members. Of her 1,055 staterooms, 817 (or just more than three-quarters) are ocean view, and nearly one-third of those have balconies. Some of the ocean-view cabins are configured for families, with sleeping arrangements for six people in beds and pullout sofas.

Brilliance of the Seas has thirteen decks, and much of the public space is devoted to Royal Caribbean's signature activities, such as a rock-climbing wall. This ship also has a fitness center and spa, separate beauty salon, three swimming pools, a half basketball court, nine-hole miniature golf course, golf simulator, jogging track, shopping area, art gallery, library, teen center, casino, cinema, theater, and an Internet center, in addition to various restaurants and bars.

CHOOSING THE SHIP THAT'S RIGHT FOR YOU

Smaller, More Personalized Ships

If you aren't fond of crowds, or if you prefer to focus on your destination for entertainment instead of your ship, you might consider booking your vacation with a cruise line that carries far fewer people aboard at once. Smaller ships force you to give up some public spaces—you'll have, say, a theater but not an additional movie cinema—but rarely do they force you to give up anything in the way of accommodations. These ships are considered more of a premium experience, and as such have high standards when it comes to cabin sizes and outfitting.

Radisson Seven Seas *Navigator*

The *Navigator* is one of Radisson Seven Seas' smaller ships, at 560 feet long and 81 feet wide. She carries 490 guests in addition to her 340 crew members, and she has twelve decks with cabins spread out among seven of them. Only two of her decks are entirely dedicated to guest cabins; the other accommodations are forward on the ship's other decks, with public spaces amidships (in the middle) and aft (toward the back) on the same decks.

All of the *Navigator*'s cabins have ocean views, and 90 percent of them also have balconies. The smallest is 301 square feet, and the largest, the master suite, is 1,173 square feet with a living and dining room and, in some cases, a full wrap-around balcony. Public spaces aboard the *Navigator* include a two-deck theater, a casino, spa and fitness center, separate beauty salon, swimming pool, boutiques, and various restaurants and bars.

Silversea *Silver Whisper*

The *Silver Whisper* is an identical sister ship to Silversea's *Silver Shadow*. Built in 2001, she is 610 feet long with seven passenger decks (ten decks in total) and accommodates 382 guests and 295 crew members. All of the cabins have ocean views, and all but the smallest, called vista suites, have balconies. The vista suites are 287 square feet, while the grand suites—the largest aboard—are up to

1,435 square feet with two verandas, marble bathrooms, Jacuzzi tubs, and more.

Public spaces aboard the *Silver Whisper* include a spa, beauty lounge, and fitness center, a golf cage, swimming pool, computer center and library, card room, two-deck theater with stage, casino, boutiques, and several restaurants and bars.

Special Accommodations

Special accommodations aboard cruise ships include staterooms, but they also run the gamut from wheelchair-accessible doorways to special dietary preparations to assistive devices for people who are hearing or sight impaired. Different cruise lines offer different types of help—and there sometimes are differences from ship to ship within each fleet. Your best bet is to call your cruise company of choice or your travel agent to ensure that your specific needs will be accommodated on the particular ship you choose, both in your stateroom and beyond.

You can—and should—expect a lot from your cruise ship in terms of special needs assistance. Royal Caribbean is a good example of what's out there as a benchmark for services.

 **RAINY DAY FUN**

If you're traveling with elderly grandparents or others who require special assistance, you can often have a terrifically fun afternoon aboard a ship in a movie theater that accommodates wheelchairs. Some ships even have special hearing devices for moviegoers who need them.

For people with visual impairments, Royal Caribbean offers Braille and large-print versions of menus, elevator buttons, signage, and daily newsletters, and the cruise line also provides for service animals and early-excursion boarding. For the hearing impaired,

Royal Caribbean offers sign language interpreters (upon request, sixty days before your sailing date), TTY/TDD, Alertmaster, cabin strobe alarm, amplified telephones, closed-caption televisions, and more. For the mobility impaired, Royal Caribbean has corridors designed to accommodate 180-degree wheelchair turns, automatic doors on most decks, accessible staterooms, specialized vans for transfers, scooters, hydraulic lifts for a pool and Jacuzzi aboard, accessible tenders, accessible blackjack tables in the casino, and more.

Other cruise lines of course offer many of these services, as well. The point is that you should expect to receive top-notch service for special needs, just like everything else.

Don't let any cruise company tell you differently.

Wheelchair Accessibility

Wheelchair accessibility has come a long way in recent years. It used to be a struggle aboard some cruise ships simply to turn a wheelchair around in a corridor. Today, cruise companies know that they need to provide accessibility in every possible way, especially as the American population ages and continues to want to cruise. Consider these four key areas when comparing wheelchair accessibility aboard any cruise ships:

- Staterooms
- Public areas
- Excursion boats
- Shore tours

Most cruise ships have a half-dozen to a dozen cabins set aside for passengers who use wheelchairs. To get a room like this, as well as ensure additional services, you should notify your cruise company in writing about your family member's needs. Do this as soon as you book your trip; in fact, you can get the appropriate contact person's name and address at the time of your booking.

Specially outfitted rooms may have wide doorways, wider areas in the living space to provide a wheelchair-turning radius, ramps to reach balconies and bathrooms, lowered closet bars, lowered light switches, roll-in showers, and bathroom fixtures as would be appropriate. In some cases, penthouses are among the wheelchair-accessible rooms (in addition to lower-priced cabins).

But who wants to sit in a stateroom all day? After you've nabbed one of these special rooms, your next step should be to inquire about wheelchair accessibility in the public areas aboard your ship. Be specific. You are likely to get a generic response if you ask, "Do you have wheelchair accessibility aboard?" You certainly will get farther if you inquire, "What specific public areas are accessible to wheelchairs aboard my ship? And how close to them are the wheelchair-accessible public restrooms?" Have a copy of the ship's deck plans with you, and highlight the areas as the cruise-ship representative names them. You can follow up with questions like, "I see you didn't mention the Captain's Observatory. Is that area off-limits to passengers who use wheelchairs?"

TRAVEL TIP

If you are traveling with a family member who uses a wheelchair, bring a collapsible model. Most airport-to-ship transfer vans can accommodate them easily if you call your cruise line in advance. If you have a collapsible model with rugged wheels, even better—it will come in handy during shore excursions.

Excursion boats are another specific area you need to ask about. Some ships have one or two specially outfitted excursion boats that will accommodate people who use wheelchairs in getting from the ship and into the port of call (and vice versa, of course). Other ships do not, or might restrict the kind of wheelchair allowed (collapsible only, for instance).

Once you've got your family member out of the stateroom, through the public areas, and into the excursion boat, you will want to get him ashore to see the sights. If your cruise ship does not have wheelchair-accessible excursion boats, your family member will be limited to shore visits at ports where the ship is allowed to tie up at an actual dock, versus dropping an anchor out in the harbor. Your travel agent or cruise-ship company should be able to talk to you in detail about every port on your itinerary—whether the ship docks, whether there are stairs to navigate to get off the dock, whether the streets in town are paved, cobblestone, or dirt, and the like.

Some itineraries and ships are obviously better for people with special needs than others. Your best bet is to ask questions well in advance of booking a trip. Do not, under any circumstance, wait until you get aboard. If you do, you and your loved one are likely to be greatly disappointed.

CHAPTER 5

Preparing for Your Cruise

NOW THAT YOU KNOW what kind of ship you might like—and whether your budget matches your desires—it's time to think about where you want to cruise and how to book your trip. Working on your own through the Internet can be a lot of fun if you're a do-it-yourself type, or you may prefer to leave all the details to a travel agent. Regardless of the route you take, you'll still need to arrange for any vaccinations or special assistance you might require. It's time to start planning.

Planning Your Itinerary

If you're new to cruising and haven't traveled much in the past, the choice of itineraries that will take you all around the planet can be overwhelming. Your first goal should be to narrow down the region where you think you might enjoy cruising—the Caribbean, Alaska, the Panama Canal, Europe, Australia, Antarctica, or any other idea you have of the perfect vacation. Start by looking through cruise ship brochures or by clicking through the itineraries on the cruise ships' Web sites. Read through some of the available excursion information to try to get a feel for what you would actually be doing in each place. Determine whether ships that meet your criteria actually cruise in the same areas. Check out the chapters of this book that are devoted to each region for even more destination-specific suggestions.

After a little time, you will start to gravitate toward a few areas of the world that appeal to you most and that the ships you like most call home base. Now it's time to start sifting through the specifics.

Let's say that your family is like the majority of cruisers from the United States. You decide to go to the Caribbean, preferably by flying round-trip into Florida and cruising from there. Right away, you spot several itineraries aboard ships that fit your taste and budget:

- A seven-day eastern Caribbean cruise aboard the Carnival *Glory,* with ports of call in Nassau, Bahamas, and the islands of St. Thomas and St. Maarten. The ship cruises round-trip from Orlando, and cabins range in price from $619 to $1,249.
- A seven-night western Caribbean cruise aboard the Disney *Magic,* with ports of call in Key West, Florida, Grand Cayman Island, Cozumel, Mexico, and Disney's private island in the Bahamas, Castaway Cay. This ship also cruises round-trip from Orlando, and cabins range in price from $799 to $5,199.
- A seven-night western Caribbean cruise aboard Royal Caribbean's *Explorer of the Seas,* with ports of call in Belize, Costa Maya, and Cozumel, Mexico, and Grand Cayman Island. The ship cruises round-trip from Miami, and cabins range in price from $649 to $1,649.

Should you automatically book the Carnival trip, since it's the least expensive? Not necessarily. For starters, you need to carefully consider the pricing details. Look again at the length of that cruise: It is seven days, not seven nights like the other two. You lose a whole day at sea, which in this case also means you stop at three ports of call instead of four. You need to decide what's more important to you: saving the $30 over the Royal Caribbean least-expensive rate or enjoying an extra day on vacation. You also need to determine how much of an airfare difference you will pay by flying into Orlando instead of Miami. If the most expensive cruise is accompanied by the least expensive airfare, or vice versa, all three cruises might end up being just a few dollars apart in total cost.

Next, you should consider the ports of call. If St. Thomas is an island that you've always wanted to see, the Carnival itinerary would knock the Disney and Royal Caribbean cruises right out of contention. If you're into snorkeling and scuba diving, on the other hand, the fact that Belize is on the Royal Caribbean itinerary might be enough to pull you to that trip.

If the prices all seem reasonable to you and none of the destinations is more important to you than any others, you should consider the ships and the kinds of programming that will be available for you and your children. As you'll see in Chapter 18, Disney is the only one among these three companies that has a nursery for infants, while Royal Caribbean's ship is consistently rated highly by teens. Then again, the Carnival *Glory* is that fleet's newest super-liner with state-of-the-art amenities, including a 214-foot water slide. You won't find that anywhere else.

TRAVEL TIP

Remember to factor in the cost of excursions as you comparison shop. One cruise may seem much less expensive than another, but you may end up paying far more in the long run to do the things you want to do ashore. Try to envision your entire day-by-day experience, and total each cruise's real cost so you can compare them accurately.

After sifting through all these details—plus the extra costs of excursions, gratuities, specialty restaurants, and all the other things you'll learn about as you continue reading this book—if you still don't have a clear-cut winner, your best bet is to go with the best deal. The ship, the itinerary, and the cost are the three most important factors for you to consider no matter where you choose to cruise. If the ships you're considering and their itineraries are equal in your mind, save yourself a few bucks—or take the least-expensive cruise and treat yourself to an upgraded cabin with a balcony.

Using a Travel Agent

You probably should use a travel agent if this will be your first cruise or if you don't travel too often. Yes, you could very easily book a lovely vacation at sea after reading this book and sifting through a bunch of Web sites to find bargains, but the odds are good that as a novice traveler, you'll forget about something important. Or you might spend half your cruise worrying that you've forgotten about something important. Just saving yourself that anxiety is worth the small additional fee you'll end up paying if you book through an agency.

Travel agents—at least the good ones—are part psychologist, part information bank, and part bloodhound. They have to be able to figure out your preferences and needs, know which cruise ships are the most likely to appeal to you, and be able to track down the best fares that those ships offer. If you find an agent giving you the hard sell on *one* cruise company instead of trying to determine *which* cruise company would be best for you, walk away and begin working with another agent. The agent's entire goal should be to give you options that match your tastes at the lowest possible prices.

Some travel agencies specialize in cruises, which gives them the advantage of having a huge base of knowledge built from the experiences of previous passengers. After any cruise, a good travel agent will call you for feedback on everything from your cabin location to unanticipated shipboard expenses to the level of organization during embarkation day. If you work with a travel agent who specializes in cruises, he or she should be able to identify not only which ships might be best for you, but which cabins are the best value, and even which seats are the best ones in the main dining room.

Last, a travel agent is a good person for you to have in your corner in case something goes wrong during your vacation. Especially if you're new to cruising, hiccups in your itinerary or problems with your airline arrangements can throw you for a big loop. Having someone on your side who knows the ropes of the industry is always helpful when such situations arise.

≡FAST FACT

The American Society of Travel Agents (ASTA) has a Web site that lets you enter your zip code and find a reputable travel agent in or near your hometown. You'll also find links to ASTA's new online consumer site that includes articles about destinations and more. Check online at ✑ *www.astanet.com.*

The Internet: Be Your Own Travel Agent

If you've cruised before or you simply prefer taking matters into your own hands, the Internet is a powerful resource. Every major cruise company has its own site that lists itineraries, prices, deck plans, excursions, and more. In many cases, you can book your trip, excursions, and travel insurance right over the Internet with the click of a mouse. Plus, there are general-interest sites dedicated to cruising where you can look for independent reviews from previous cruise-ship passengers as well as hot deals on ships all over the world. (See Appendix A for a complete list of resources.)

The biggest challenge to being your own travel agent is making sure that you remember all the small details. When booking your own cruise, at a minimum, be certain to ensure the following:

- The price you are paying is for the level of cabin you want
- Your specific cabin is in a desirable location on the ship instead of, say, right above the disco
- Your airline reservations and transfers will get you to the cruise ship terminal at least a few hours before your sailing time
- Your airport transfers are prebooked for both the beginning and the end of your cruise
- Your excursion, spa, and specialty restaurant reservations are made in advance (if possible) so you don't get shut out later

- You have hotel reservations in the city where your ship is based if you have to fly into town the day before you sail
- You have transfers arranged from your hotel to your ship
- Your travel insurance covers all of your arrangements and not just the cruise portion of your vacation

If you have any doubts about any details while acting as your own travel agent, call the cruise line before booking your vacation. Do not assume anything, and read every word of your brochure's fine print. You'll thank yourself later on when things run smoothly.

When to Book

As discussed in Chapter 3, there are two schools of thought about making cruise-ship reservations. The first is that you should book early to get the best savings, and the other is that you should wait until the very last minute to save a few more bucks than even the earliest-booking passengers. Which is correct? Both—depending on the kind of cruise you want to take.

Booking Early

Booking early is always your best option if you have your heart set on a specific ship and a particular itinerary. You will be guaranteed to get the early-booking discount—which can be substantial, sometimes more than half-off the brochure rate—on exactly the cabin you want, sometimes virtually anywhere on the ship if you do your research six months to a year in advance.

The downside to booking early is that you may not end up paying the least expensive rate available for your class of cabin. Should there be too many cabins open as your sailing date approaches, your cruise line may offer even deeper discounts to generate a slew of last-minute bookings. Usually, though, it is not wise for you to take this chance. If you know exactly what you want, book it early and be happy that you got your cruise at a satisfactory (if not the very best) price.

Booking Late

Booking late is not as good an idea as it used to be, as demand for cruise-ship vacations has increased to the point that many companies don't have to offer last-minute deals anymore. Most ships are full well in advance of the sailing date, so the cruise lines have no need to slash prices and generate more business.

Still, there are bargains to be had if you are willing to wait until zero hour and aren't particularly concerned about where your ship will cruise or where your cabin will be. If you simply want to go to the tropics and you don't mind being in a cabin without so much as a porthole, you'll almost always be able to find a last-minute deal that will save you even more than the lowest advance-purchase rate.

 TRAVEL TIP

If it's been a few years since your last cruise, don't count on having the same smorgasbord of cabin selections for last-minute bookings. Some companies have stopped offering last-minute deals altogether as demand for cruise vacations has skyrocketed.

On the other hand, if you're looking for a balcony suite on an itinerary that goes from Egypt to Kenya with a pass through the Red Sea, you may spend an entire lifetime waiting for your last-minute dream deal to materialize. Consider your odds before taking this chance, and when in doubt, choose to book early instead.

Preboarding Details

After you book your vacation, your cruise company or your travel agent will send you a packet of ship's documents. This information gives you an idea about what to expect during your trip and what the cruise ship company needs to know about you before you come aboard. Expect a lot of paper. Some ship's document packages are about sixty pages long. Royal Caribbean's fits that description. It includes sections on the following:

- Your cruise summary, with map of route
- Your cruise itinerary listed day by day, with arrival and departure times at each port
- Your preboarding to-do checklist
- Your required citizenship information
- Your arrival information
- Your hotel, airport transfer, and rental car vouchers
- Your luggage tags and instructions for using them
- Your shipboard charge account application
- Your cruise tickets and contract (with plenty of fine print)
- Your customs and immigration form
- A list of frequently asked questions with answers
- Souvenirs, flowers, and more that will be available for you to purchase on board
- A tuxedo rental form
- Travel insurance options (also with plenty of fine print)

These ship's documents are written and arranged to make them easy to understand, so don't worry that the paperwork will be overwhelming. The idea is that after you complete the forms, they will make your cruise experience easier. For instance, if you fill everything out before leaving home for your cruise, your odds of having a smooth embarkation process will improve dramatically. And the preboarding checklist will be especially helpful as you pack because it will help you remember exactly what documents you need to bring with you the day your ship sails.

Who Are You?

This is not an existential question meant to leave you waxing poetic about Plato's caves or Keanu Reeves' predicament in *The Matrix*. Though you may not "find yourself," so to speak, on your cruise vacation of a lifetime, your cruise company will expect to see some identification before you'll be allowed to step on board. If your ship is not traveling outside of U.S. waters, a driver's license with picture will suffice.

For international itineraries—including the Bahamas and the Caribbean—you will need a passport for every member of your family, including children. To purchase a passport, you must go to one of the 6,000 facilities in the United States that are allowed to dispense them. You will need two photos of yourself, proof of U.S. citizenship, and a valid form of identification such as a driver's license with photograph.

≡ FAST FACT

The current fee, including surcharges, for getting a U.S. passport is $97 if you are age sixteen or older, or $82 if you are younger than age sixteen. You can usually pay by check, major credit card, cashier's check, or money order. For more information on getting a passport, check out the U.S. State Department's Web site at *http://travel.state.gov*.

Children younger than fourteen years old must fill out a special form and make their application in person, with two photos of themselves in hand. Each of your kids will need to present a birth certificate in addition to all other possible identifying documents, such as baptismal certificate, a hospital birth certificate, an early school record, a family bible record, or a doctor's record of postnatal care. The additional documents are not so much necessary as they are helpful; the more documents you bring with you, the easier it will be for you to answer any questions. But a birth certificate will usually suffice to get the kids aboard. At least one of these documents must also verify your child's relationship to you (usually, the birth certificate takes care of that). You and your spouse, or you alone if you are a single parent, will also be asked to sign forms consenting to your child getting a passport.

Obtaining Vaccinations for Exotic Ports-of-Call

One of the worst things that can befall you during your cruise vacation is a sudden illness. You need to do everything possible to make sure you will remain healthy during the duration of your trip, especially in parts of the world where diseases like malaria are common. Some illnesses, like Mexico's dreaded Montezuma's revenge, can only be prevented by abstaining from local foods and water. Many other diseases, though, can be warded off with vaccinations.

The best source of information on recommended vaccinations is the Web site sponsored by the Centers for Disease Control (CDC), a division of the U.S. Department of Health and Human Services. It provides a wealth of information about vaccinations in general—as well as a "Destinations" link that enables you to click on your cruise destination and see all the recommended vaccinations for that area. For more information, check out the CDC's Web site at *www.cdc.gov*.

For instance, if you are cruising from Cape Town, South Africa, up the eastern coast of Africa to Kenya for a few days of watching lions and giraffes, you will want to educate yourself about malaria, yellow fever, typhoid, hepatitis, and more. Just going to the Caribbean? Check out the Web site anyway. It recommends vaccinations for that part of the world as well, including rabies, hepatitis, typhoid, and yellow fever. Once you know which vaccinations you will need, you should be able to get them from your family's regular physician.

Notifying Your Cruise Line about Dietary Requirements

All the vaccinations in the world won't help you if you starve to death because you can't eat any of the food you are served aboard your ship. This is unlikely, given the smorgasbords that today's cruise ships put out on display each day, but if you have special dietary restrictions, you should notify your cruise company immediately after you book your trip.

It is best to notify the company in writing and, if possible, to get written confirmation that your request has been received and processed. In most cases, the cruise line will need thirty to sixty days to ensure you get what you need, be it meals that are kosher, low-cholesterol, low-carb, sugar-free, or the like.

When you check in on your embarkation day, double-check that your request is in the cruise ship's computer system (you can simply ask). And be sure to personally notify your waiter in the main dining room before your first meal, as well.

Notifying Your Cruise Line about Medical Needs

As with special dietary requests, most cruise lines require thirty to sixty days' advance notice to accommodate you if you have special medical needs. Again, submitting your information in writing and getting a written confirmation in return is the smart way to go, as well as double-checking when you embark for your cruise.

If you or someone in your family uses a wheelchair or is prone to seizures, make sure she carries her medical papers with her at all times during your vacation. That way, should something happen when no other family members are around, the cruise ship's medical staff will know exactly what needs to be done to help.

CHAPTER 6

Packing Up and Heading Out

YOU'VE CHOSEN YOUR CRUISE company, your cruise ship, your itinerary, your airline tickets, your shore excursions, your travel insurance, and your land-extension tours, and have handled every other little detail that will make your family vacation perfect. Now it's time to make sure you've got everything you'll want and need while you're aboard. Plus, you've got to get your house and your personal life ready to run on autopilot while you're off having the adventure of a lifetime. It's time to pack up and head out!

Things to Buy

One of the worst things you can do before heading off on a family vacation is go on a spending spree. For starters, doing so will really dent your budget (say bye-bye souvenirs and shore excursions), and quite frankly, you probably won't need half the things you purchase on impulse while getting ready to pack. Think about it. When you're standing in the shoe aisle, dreaming about walking down the beach under the stars, is it likely that you'll be able to resist that set of six pairs of flip-flops in a rainbow of colors? Not if you're a typical human being. You need to make a shopping plan, and stick with it.

The most important items you need to buy before your cruise are things you absolutely, positively will need but may not be able to find easily during your trip:

- Prescription refills
- Disposable contact lenses
- Prescription sunglasses
- Special shampoos and skin lotions if you suffer from allergies
- Specialty snacks such as sugar-free candy if you are diabetic
- Seasickness remedies

You get the idea. It's true that you may be able to acquire some or all of these things after your ship sets sail, but you'll waste countless hours tracking them down, and they will definitely cost more than you typically pay at home. And, if you're in a part of the world whose national governance system doesn't have an equivalent to the U.S. Food and Drug Administration, you might not want to fill prescriptions or have your eyes checked there anyway.

The next things you should consider buying before your trip are items you don't really need to survive but that you'd really like to have with you on vacation—at a price that's not jacked up to the moon to take advantage of desperate tourists. A few ideas include the following:

- Hot new bestseller books
- Film
- Camera batteries
- Extra memory cards for your digital camera
- A small, empty duffel bag that you can use to carry souvenirs home
- A sun hat
- A lightweight rain slicker
- Sunglasses
- A fleece
- Suntan lotion
- Bug spray

These things will probably be available to you at some point during your cruise, but again, you'll end up paying a lot more for them than you will if you buy them in advance. Plus, you'll be able to get exactly the brands and styles you want if you shop at home, as opposed to waiting for the cruise and being stuck with whatever the sundries shop has when you get there.

If you've never cruised before and are concerned about seasickness, you might want to pack more than one kind of remedy. Some work better than others for different people, so it's impossible to tell which will be ideal for you until you're green and hanging over the rail. A good over-the-counter pill is Bonine, which you can take *after* you start feeling sick (as opposed to Dramamine, which works best if you keep it in your system continuously, starting at least a few hours *before* boarding your ship). Other inexpensive options include wristbands and a simple slice of ginger to chew on—with that last one being the favorite of sailors for centuries.

JUST FOR PARENTS

If you're watching your weight, you might consider buying a box of your favorite low-fat, low-cal, low-carb, low-whatever bars before your cruise. That way, you can choose to substitute them for one meal a day instead of feeling overwhelming pressure to join the buffet line, where it will be hard to pass by all your favorite foods.

Of course, you should also consider buying some new clothes. (Hey, this is a vacation, right?) If you're headed somewhere sunny, a new bathing suit might be in order. If you're going on a hiking cruise, check out a new pair of boots—with an extra set of heavy-duty laces. Formal nights may require you to buy and bring a new evening dress, while active touring on shore might leave you wishing you had more T-shirts and socks.

Just remember that you are likely to add to your wardrobe as the cruise goes on—say, by purchasing souvenir T-shirts or colorful sarongs to tie around your bathing suit—and that you will probably get by just fine even if you buy fewer outfits at home than you actually intend to wear during your trip.

No matter where you are planning to cruise, a good pair of walking shoes is a must. You will be on your feet more than usual simply making your way around the ship, and your feet will thank you in the long run for the extra-soft new cushioning.

What to Pack

What you need to pack depends entirely on where you are going. If you're headed for the tropics, bathing suits are in order. If you're cruising to Alaska, a warm fleece and wool socks should be in your bag. If your cruise will take you to Asia, an English/Japanese phrase book might be a good bet, while if you're cruising to Africa, you'll need wraparound sunglasses that will keep the dirt out of your eyes on safaris.

One smart move is to check with your cruise line about whether your ship will have formal evenings aboard and, if so, how many. No need to pack three evening gowns and two tuxedos if you can go to dinner in your khakis just the same. If you do fly with a fancy dress or suit, you often can carry it on in a garment bag and ask the flight attendant to hang it in a closet toward the front of your plane. This will save you the wrinkles you would have had to endure with your evening wear checked in a big suitcase.

There are a few things you'll need no matter where you intend to cruise. A rain slicker is always a good idea, along with a baseball cap or visor to protect your face from the sun. Extra socks and underwear never hurt, especially if you plan to do a lot of shore excursions (which might mean taking one shower in the morning and another in the afternoon). And if you are fair-skinned and heading to the Caribbean, bring along extra T-shirts for snorkeling (or a skin from the local scuba store) as well as a long-sleeved, loose-fitting, cotton T-shirt for sleeping in should you get a painful sunburn that induces the chills.

If you plan to scuba dive, you might consider bringing your personal gear with you. Cruise lines contract with local dive shops at your ports of call, and you never know what kind of gear those shops will have, or in what sizes. Of course, you do not need to bring tanks or weights. Just your buoyancy compensator, regulator, mask, fins, wetsuit, and dive watch or computer. Be sure to pack them in a nondescript oversized duffel bag or suitcase, instead of in a bag with scuba logos on it. You never want to advertise to strangers in the airport that you are toting around a few thousand dollars' worth of gear.

 TRAVEL TIP

If you plan to bring your best set of golf clubs along on your cruise, carry them in a plain duffel or other standard bag without any golf-related logos on it. You do not want to make it obvious to strangers that you have expensive clubs with you.

No matter what you pack, expect your main suitcase to be searched out of your presence. You may get to your ship and find a written notice inside your suitcase from the U.S. Department of Homeland Security stating that airline personnel have gone through your bag. This is standard policy since the terrorist attacks of September 11, 2001. You are no longer allowed to lock your luggage, as it would interfere with the checkers' ability to do their jobs. However, most cruise lines do suggest that you lock your luggage during airport-to-ship transfers (and at any other time when your bag is in your presence).

Some things you will want to keep in your carry-on bag, and other things you are better off checking in your main suitcase. The key is to bring everything you will need—but not a single item more—and to arrange everything in a way that will make it easiest for you to travel.

In Your Carry-on Bag

Your carry-on bag is the place for things that are essential to you, such as medications, passport, wallet, and any expensive cameras or electronic gear. Never pack your medications in your main suitcase and check them into the bowels of your airplane. Delays can and will happen, and you don't want to be separated from your blood pressure pills when they do.

It's also smart to pack a change of clothes in your carry-on, in case your luggage is lost or delayed en route to your ship. Consider your options in the event of such a calamity: You can either sit and pout in your cabin in your traveling jeans, or you can pull a bathing suit out of your carry-on bag and wait for your luggage to arrive while you sip a piña colada at the pool. Throw a toothbrush and some deodorant in your carry-on, too, just in case your checked bag doesn't show up at the ship until the following day.

≡FAST FACT

Scanners that X-ray checked luggage will damage most camera film. Airlines recommend that you pack your film in your carry-on luggage instead. As long as the film is below 400 speed, the carry-on X-ray machines will not harm it.

No matter what the temperature is where you live, or what the temperature is where you're going, it's a safe bet that it your plane will be air conditioned. If you plan to wear your favorite sandals so you will be ready to hit the beach the minute your plane lands, you might want to pack a pair of socks in your carry-on bag. That way, if your feet get cold during the flight, you can slip the socks on and off without a single person noticing that they don't match the rest of your outfit.

Serious travelers also pack a bottle of water in their carry-on bags. *Really* serious travelers even stop to fill it up at an airport water fountain before boarding the plane. You never know how busy the flight attendants are going to be, and keeping yourself hydrated is something that should not wait. If you don't drink enough water during your flight, you will be more tired than usual when the plane lands. That's no way to start a vacation.

The same idea applies to snacks. Since September 11, 2001, many airlines have cut back on meal service in an effort to recoup some of the money they lost when Americans became afraid to fly, and many now offer fewer snacks than they used to. If you haven't flown in a while, don't expect a serious lunch or dinner. Pack yourself a couple of granola bars or some fresh fruit in case your plane is delayed and there is nothing but mini-pretzels aboard.

Last, if you are traveling with children, remember to pack a deck of cards, some coloring books, and other quiet games that will keep them entertained on your plane without disturbing the other passengers around you. You are bound to have other vacation-bound families aboard with you, especially if you book your airfare through a family-friendly cruise company like Carnival, Disney, or Royal Caribbean. Making sure your kids have enough to keep them occupied will save everyone from headaches on the way to the ship.

In Your Main Suitcase

While most cruise ships do not have weight restrictions for baggage, all airlines do. This is the most important consideration for packing your main suitcase. Find out your particular airline's weight limits, and make sure you meet them. If your bag is too heavy, you will be asked to take items out of it right there at the check-in counter in front of all the other passengers—and then you'll have to figure out what to do with all of your stuff before your plane takes off.

A smart move is to buy a matched set of luggage and pack all of your things in the smaller of the two biggest bags. Then, pack that smaller bag inside the biggest bag. When you get to your ship, you'll have a separate, empty bag in which to store your dirty laundry, plus plenty of space for all the souvenirs you collect throughout your vacation. Just make sure your biggest bag isn't too mammoth—you will, after all, have to stow it somewhere in your cabin.

Most of your toiletries will end up in your main suitcase, simply because that's where they will fit. If you don't own a waterproof shaving kit-style bag, buy a box of large, double-ply freezer bags. You can fit travel-size shampoo, conditioner (or combo shampoo and conditioner—even better!), hairspray, hand lotion, toothpaste, hair gel, and more inside of one large zip-close bag. Should any bottles or tubes fall open or explode from changes in air pressure, the goop will be contained inside the zip-close bag instead of leaking all over your clothes.

You would also be smart to consider your shore excursions and whether you will need any special clothing for them. For instance, if your ship is heading to Rome, Italy, you might have only a half-day excursion to visit St. Peter's Basilica at Vatican City. How disappointed you would be if you arrived during your tiny window of time in a tank top and learned that you have to have your shoulders covered by at least a T-shirt as a show of respect before entering the church. (It's true—you do.) Ask your cruise company before you pack about any such restrictions at your chosen excursion sites, and make a habit of double-checking with your cruise line's excursion coordinator before you leave your ship every day, as well.

 **TRAVEL TIP**

If you don't own an inexpensive, willing-to-let-it-break travel alarm clock, you can use your cell phone. Even if you don't get phone service where your ship is headed, your cell phone's clock will continue to function. You can use it as your alarm on days when you don't want to trust the ship's wake-up service.

Another smart idea is to pack clothes that are of matching colors so that you can use them as mix-and-match outfits. Trying to pack an individual outfit for every day of a fourteen-day vacation requires an awful lot of space. On the other hand, if you pack four pairs of black pants and four pairs of khakis along with a dozen tops that match them both, you will get by just fine even if you can't make a trip to the ship's washing machine. Also look for wrinkle-free or wrinkle-resistant fabrics; they'll save you the weight of a travel iron.

Make an Inventory of Your Belongings

Making a list of everything as you pack it will help you in several ways. For starters, when you get to your ship and realize that your favorite blue bathing suit has gone missing, you can consult your list and figure out whether you forgot it or if it took a walk during a baggage screening at the airport (in which case you should notify the airline immediately and demand compensation).

Having an inventory of your belongings will be even more helpful when it comes time to leave your ship at the end of your cruise. You will be surprised at how far back some of your things will find their way into the corners of tiny little drawers where you won't see them. As you get ready to return to your home, you can check off every item on your list as you re-pack it, and you will be sure not to leave anything behind.

Leave It at Home!

Knowing what not to pack is as important as deciding what to bring with you. If you omit certain things from your luggage, you'll have an easier time lugging it to the airport and fewer headaches after you get to your ship. For starters, avoid packing anything that adds unnecessary weight. A hair dryer, for instance, is usually included as standard equipment in your cruise-ship cabin. Even if you have a small, travel-size model, why add the half-pound to your bag? Your shoulder certainly doesn't need the extra weight tugging down on it as you wait to check in for your flight.

Beach towels are another commonly packed item that is best left at home. They take up scads of space in your main suitcase, and you won't need them because your ship will provide them for you. Another space-hogger is extra clothing. Really think seriously about how many T-shirts you will need for the duration of your cruise, and then pack two or three fewer than that number. You will buy new ones along the way as souvenirs, so you might as well make use of those right away.

 TRAVEL TIP

Do not assume that your cruise-ship cabin will have a safe in which you can store your valuables and passport. If you intend to bring fancy jewelry or expensive electronic games aboard, double-check ahead of time with your cruise line about the availability of a personal safe.

If you are cruising overseas with your passport, make two photocopies of it. Keep one in a place separate from your passport (such as in your cabin's personal safe while you're carrying your passport around), and leave the other photocopy at home. That way, if you lose your actual passport in a foreign country, you will have documentation with you there as well as back in the United States to help straighten out any immigration problems.

Last, consider leaving valuable jewelry and electronics behind. Yes, it is nice to wear your best diamonds during formal evenings, and it's always fun to have a Gameboy or personal DVD player at your disposal, but such things attract pickpockets the way dog bones attract beagles. If you can live with leaving the valuables at home, you will have greater peace of mind throughout the duration of your cruise.

Preparing to Leave Your Home for 4, 7, 14, or 28 Days

Heading out of town on a whim for an overnight trip can be a lot of fun. Heading out of town for a few weeks during a cruise from Africa to Japan is an entirely different story. One of the best ways to ensure that you will be miserable and worrisome during your cruise is to leave your house in disorder. Before you head out to meet your ship, consider doing a few things that will make your life easier while you're gone and when you get back.

For starters, put a light or two on a timer on each level of your home. Set the timers to go on and off at intervals, say, one on at 6:00 P.M. and off at 7:30, and another on at 7:00 P.M. and off at 11:30 P.M. That way, it will look like someone is home and moving around the house until a reasonable bedtime.

If you have an answering machine that is not part of a telephone company voice mail system, adjust it so that the beep does not get horribly long as messages pile up in your voice mailbox. If your answering machine does not offer you the option of keeping the beep short no matter how many messages you get, turn your answering machine off for the duration of your vacation. Better that strangers think you're out for the afternoon and have no machine than realize you're out of town altogether because they can hear the length of your machine's beep.

Pay your bills. If you're going to be gone for a few weeks in a row, the odds are good you are going to have a mortgage payment or credit card payment due before you return. Even if you just paid your last month's bills, look ahead on your calendar to what you expect to come due. In some cases, you will be better off paying a bill three weeks in advance, before your cruise, rather than missing a due date and paying late fees or finance charges after you return.

🧳 TRAVEL TIP

If you are taking a cruise that is several weeks long, ask your pharmacist about getting a vacation waiver for your next prescription refill. If your insurance company allows it, you will be able to get a double prescription before you leave so that you don't have to worry about running out of pills on the day you get back.

Have the post office hold your mail, or arrange for a neighbor to collect it while you're gone. A pile of mail spilling out of a mailbox or collecting on a front porch is a dead giveaway to thieves that you're out of town for a long stretch.

To save a little money, set your heat thermostats lower than usual, or your air-conditioning thermostats higher. It's okay if your house is a bit too hot in summer or too cold in winter—nobody's inside.

The last thing you should do before you leave is make sure you have some easy-to-microwave meals in your freezer and a favorite pair of sweatpants or pajamas clean and ready for when you get back. You are likely to be tired and hungry for the comforts of home at the end of your cruise, and you'll be happy to find your favorite things waiting for you upon your return.

Don't Miss the Boat!

Whether you are flying or driving to meet your ship, you should plan to arrive *at the cruise ship terminal* at least a few hours before your scheduled sailing time. Do not expect to fly into Miami International Airport at 5:00 P.M. and then make it to your ship in time for a 6:00 P.M. departure. You may not even have your bags by then, especially if your plane has been delayed.

And the ship, as you might have guessed, is not going to wait. Royal Caribbean, for instance, considers you a no-show if you are not checked in at least an hour before the ship's sailing time. Even if you're on the way from the airport at that late time, your booking will be canceled and financial penalties will apply.

The smart move—especially if you arrange your flights separately from your cruise—is to plan your arrival in your departure city at least four hours before your ship is scheduled to set sail. That gives you an hour for airline delays, an hour to collect baggage, and two hours to get to the ship, get through the metal detectors, check in, receive your shipboard ID card, and step aboard. Most cruise lines insist that you be aboard a half-hour or an hour before sailing time. Many frequent cruise guests fly into their city of embarkation a day before the ship sets sail. That alleviates any concerns about making it to the terminal on time, especially if winter weather is a factor.

If you can arrive at the ship terminal even earlier, all the better. Most ships begin boarding passengers at least four hours before the scheduled sailing time. If you arrive even earlier than that, it's okay. You can wait in the lounge until your boarding section or number is announced.

In most cases, you will have to stand in line anyway to get through metal detectors before stepping aboard. If it's a bigger ship, just try to imagine the amount of time needed to check some 3,000 people. Clearing the metal detectors is just like going through them at an airport. If you're not carrying anything you shouldn't be, you won't have any problems.

Embarkation Procedures

The main portions of your embarkation procedures—beyond waiting in lines and having your first souvenir photo taken—will be clearing the metal detectors, checking in, receiving your shipboard ID card (which sometimes is also your cabin key), and handing your luggage over to cruise personnel.

Check-in and collection of shipboard ID cards, as well as ID bracelets for your children aboard some cruise lines, will go much faster if you have all your paperwork filled out and in hand when you get to the check-in desk. Consider carrying everything in one folder, including all of your family's passports, so that you can hand it over to the check-in employees as quickly and efficiently as possible. You'll get through the line faster, and you'll probably make fast friends with all the people waiting behind you!

Perhaps the most unsettling part about embarkation is the luggage procedure. When you arrive at the cruise ship terminal, you will be asked to leave your luggage with a baggage handler who will throw it into a gigantic bin along with the luggage of the other hundreds of people waiting to get aboard your ship. This can seem odd, confusing, and downright scary, but take comfort in the fact that it has been standard procedure for years. As long as you have filled out your luggage tags, everything will be fine. The ships simply don't want thousands of people banging their way through corridors with heavy luggage, so they organize everything for you and deliver your bags right to your cabin.

If You Miss the Boat . . .

You have several options if you arrive late and miss your cruise ship's departure. If you bought travel insurance, breathe a sigh of relief. Nine times out of ten, you will be covered for your delays and at least some of any additional money you have to spend to meet your ship at its next port of call. You'll even be covered in most cases if your luggage gets lost along the way.

If you did not buy travel insurance, your first move should be to call your cruise company. Some lines, such as Carnival, have dedicated travel hotlines to help you negotiate delays, flight cancellations, and other travel emergencies. Your goal will be to meet your ship at its next port of call and continue your cruise from there. Don't expect any refunds for the unused portion of your trip; just be thankful the whole thing isn't a complete bust. If you have no travel insurance, the additional airline flights you will need to take will be at your own expense, of course, as will any airport-to-ship transfers, overnight hotel stays, and the like.

 TRAVEL TIP

Most people who miss their ship become panicky and sometimes abusive toward cruise line personnel. Your best bet—if you want their help—is to stay calm and be polite. Remember that it's not their fault you were late, and that you need them on your side to get your vacation back in order.

You may be entitled to a refund, or a refund in the form of credits toward a future voyage, if you prepaid for travel insurance. Still, if you were supposed to head off on a transatlantic itinerary, you're obviously out of luck the minute the ship hits the ocean waters without you on it. Barring the rental of a personal helicopter to fly you out to sea, you'll have to chalk the experience up to bad luck and plan to get an earlier start next time.

CHAPTER 7

Classic Caribbean

CRYSTAL-BLUE WATERS, SWAYING PALM fronds, and stretches of white sand—these picture-postcard images are the first to come to mind when you think about taking a cruise-ship vacation. There is plenty to see and do in the western Caribbean, but the eastern Caribbean has long been a favorite cruising ground for boats and ships of all sizes. Its islands are plentiful and stretch from north to south along an easy-to-follow course. If your goal is to see ports of call on as many tropical islands as possible, the eastern Caribbean is a good bet for you—though don't make a final decision until you read about the western Caribbean, too, in Chapter 8.

The Caribbean: An Overview

Most of the islands in the Caribbean stretch southward in an arc from the eastern tip of Puerto Rico to the northern coast of Venezuela. The Atlantic Ocean is to the east and north of these islands, and the Caribbean Sea laps up against their southern and western shores. The best time to visit is during the dry season from December through May. The time to avoid is June through November, when hurricanes have been known to wipe out entire villages and tear apart even the sturdiest of concrete docks.

≡FAST FACT

Barbados and Trinidad and Tobago—because of their far eastern and southern locations—are usually spared the wrath of hurricane season.

Some of the islands are more developed than others, with a range that includes everything from Britney Spears–blaring Hard Rock Cafés to shacks run by women called "Ma" who dish out healthy helpings of curried goat. In the eastern Caribbean, you can enjoy everything from fantastic French shopping on St. Maarten to an awe-inspiring view of the towering Pitons on St. Lucia. In the western Caribbean (discussed in Chapter 8), the itineraries swing from the Dominican Republic's southern port city of Santo Domingo to the nature-lovers' paradise of snorkeling at Grand Cayman's Stingray City Sandbar.

No matter which part of the Caribbean you visit or which way your tastes lean, you'll find plenty to do ashore. All the cruise lines offer excursions for the entire family, some included in the price of the trip and others as additional expenses.

TRAVEL TIP

Be sure to check your cruise line's pricing policy—excursions that aren't part of an all-inclusive package can add hundreds, even thousands, of dollars to your total vacation bill.

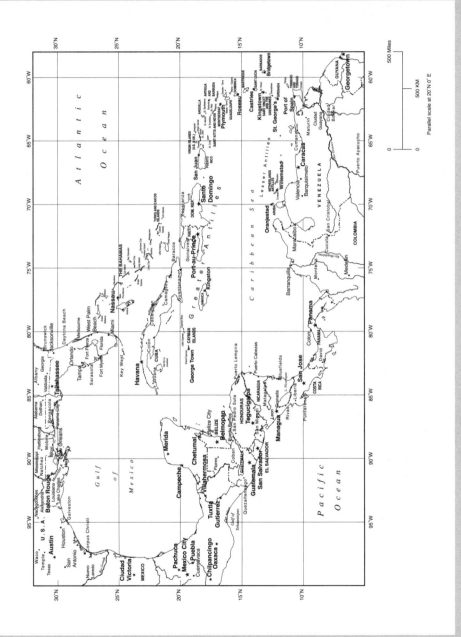

Best Caribbean Excursions

You'll be able to take off on swimming and snorkeling excursions at pretty much every Caribbean port. The waters are warm, and colorful parrotfish can be found along beaches on virtually all of the islands, so try to schedule swimming and snorkeling for days when there isn't something better for you and the kids to do ashore or on the boat.

At most ports, you will have many more excursions available than time to do them. Cruise companies try to offer an assortment for the whole family, from day trips the whole family can enjoy together to afternoons of strenuous exercise or alcoholic adventures (think mountain biking and beer tastings) from which young children are prohibited. Try to book early if you have your heart set on a particular excursion, but be open and flexible in case your mood changes from active to sleepy as the appointed date in port arrives. The last place you want to find yourself is on a five-mile hike after an all-nighter in the ship's disco.

If you need a little help making excursion choices, consider the popular activities described in the following sections.

Stingray City Sandbar on Grand Cayman

If you are in the western Caribbean, you can visit these wide-winged creatures in the wild. Fear not: They are used to tourists, so much so that they sometimes try to take food from the pockets of your swimming trunks. There are dozens of them. They swarm like bees through the crystal-blue waters and get right up next to the hairs on the nape of your neck.

Because the stingrays swim so close to you and linger, this is a great spot to practice underwater photography—terrific keepsake shots can be gotten even with a disposable camera. Talk about a memory that will never fade!

 **TRAVEL TIP**

Be careful at Grand Cayman's Stingray City Sandbar if your kids (or you) aren't the adventurous type. The stingrays *will* brush up against your bodies while you snorkel. They won't hurt you, but they might peck at your pockets in search of food.

Charlotte Amalie Shopping on St. Thomas

The merchants who have turned St. Thomas's old rum and sugar-cane warehouses into charming little shops display everything from T-shirts to fine pottery. Jewelry shopping in particular is outstanding, with everything from Bvlgari bracelets to artsy, handmade wedding bands. This is the place to get your money's worth of souvenirs, since you can bring home as much as $1,200 worth of merchandise duty-free (that's far more than you can carry from most other Caribbean destinations). You will, of course, find souvenirs at all of the destinations on your itinerary, but your selection is likely to be the biggest in Charlotte Amalie (the busiest port in the U.S. Virgin Islands). The smart move is to stock up while you're in town so you can enjoy other, more nature-oriented excursions later on less-developed islands. If you wait to shop until reaching some of the other ports, you can certainly find some lovely things. However, you will have to wander much smaller tourism districts, such as the ones on nearby St. John, which have high-end items but far fewer of them. And—even worse—you'll be so busy trying to shop that you'll miss seeing the beauty that enchanted you into coming to the islands in the first place.

Butterfly Farm in Philipsburg, St. Maarten

This is a great place to take a break from the hot sun and salty water and do a little walking on dry land. Hundreds of species of butterflies from around the world are here, on display in cages that in many cases include their native vegetation and flowers. There are also educational opportunities here for the kids. Eager young scientists have been known to take their newfound knowledge back to the ship and spend the night rolling themselves into a cocoon of blankets.

If your young ones have to give book reports as part of their schoolwork back home, this excursion is tailor-made for a science or nature presentation. The children's eyes will be so close to the butterflies, they'll be seeing them in their dreams for weeks to come.

Dunn's River Falls, Jamaica

From Ocho Rios, where many cruise-ship lines stop, you can take a ride up to these 600-foot waterfalls in the western Caribbean. The mountain waters you'll wade through will be far chillier than the warm Caribbean Sea, but the photos of your family climbing along the rocks are sure to be longtime keepsakes.

This is an especially good excursion for families who want to enjoy day trips together, since your guide is likely to ask you to hold hands and form a chain while walking up the falls. Your kids will never be happier to squeeze your palm and smile widely.

 ## JUST FOR PARENTS

If you want to go ashore in Jamaica, do a standard cruise-ship excursion. The commercial dock in Ocho Rios is gated, and your tour bus will pick you up inside the parking lot. Outside the gate, on the street, the locals sometimes line up in large groups to beg for cab fares. This can be intimidating, especially if you're traveling with small children. Stick with the organized group transportation—or leave the kids behind.

Dunn's River Falls is always one of the most popular excursions on Jamaica, so be sure to book early no matter which cruise line you choose. Seats on the buses fill up fast, and they're the safest, most convenient method of transportation to the site.

Antigua Historical Tour

This is a wonderful opportunity to include a day of culture and history into your beach-heavy vacation plan. The tour includes the picturesque Nelson's Dockyard, named after Admiral Lord Nelson, who led the Leeward Islands Squadron for the British starting in 1784. The dockyard's restored buildings are charming to wander among, and you might even catch a glimpse inside some of the private yachts tied up along the dock. The scene at Nelson's Dockyard is much as it likely was several centuries ago, only with fewer sails and more engines cruising into the slips after a day on the water. It's a boater's haven and a tourist's delight—though one with few gift shops. The ones that are based in the heart of the dockyard's property can be on the expensive side, especially during high season in the winter, but locals do set up tables full of more reasonably tagged T-shirts and shell necklaces just inside the gate to the complex.

≡FAST FACT

If your cruise to Antigua is planned for the first week in December, take the Antigua Historical Tour. Its route winds through the harbors that host the Caribbean's largest annual gathering of luxury charter yachts, which also happens during this week. The private boats are an incredible sight to see, with some costing as much as $840,000 for a single week's cruise. You won't be able to walk the docks or step aboard, but the astounding view from the marina entrance alone is worth the trip.

The tour also includes English and Falmouth harbors, which have a handful of colorfully painted open-air restaurants nearby. This is a great place to indulge in some authentic Caribbean cooking with the warm breeze coming off the water and across your table.

Dolphin Swim Adventure, Tortola

At the Dolphin Discovery Facility in this part of the British Virgin Islands, you can spend twenty to thirty minutes swimming with dolphins under the careful watch of a trainer who will help you interact with the animals in an appropriate way. Unlike Grand Cayman's Stingray City, this is a controlled environment, but it offers the same type of up-close-and-personal memories you won't find anywhere else. Be sure to bring your underwater camera—you'll never get this close to a dolphin again (unless you come back, of course).

And if you're bringing the kids, be sure they know how important it is to follow the instructor's directions. You don't want them scaring the dolphins and regretting the experience back on the ship.

Eastern Caribbean

Cruises to the eastern Caribbean islands typically start and end in the Florida cities of Miami, Fort Lauderdale, Jacksonville, and Port Canaveral, which is near Orlando. Cunard offers cruises to this part of the Caribbean beginning and ending in New York, and some Celebrity cruises to the eastern Caribbean begin and end in Cape Liberty Cruise Port, New Jersey. The latter are, of course, much longer in terms of days aboard, but all the time spent cruising south means you typically don't get to see very much more of the Caribbean than people who book the shorter cruises. On the other hand, if you just want some additional time aboard to enjoy your ship's amenities, the longer itineraries might be right for you.

 TRAVEL TIP

If you choose a Caribbean cruise that starts and ends in the New York area, keep in mind that you will likely spend two full days on open ocean while cruising to the islands, and another two full days at sea on your return. That's nearly half your time during a nine- or ten-day itinerary, so you should choose a ship with enough amenities and programs to keep everyone entertained along the way.

Many of the eastern Caribbean islands have long and interesting histories because they were the first place European sailors made landfall after crossing the Atlantic Ocean. We're talking the real deal here: pirates and explorers and soldiers like the ones Russell Crowe leads in *Master and Commander: The Far Side of the World.* The rich histories are good news during a 7-day or 10-day cruise, as you can often take cultural and historical tours to break up your time on the beach. Even the smallest, homiest museums are often worth a look, since the locals who run them will happily chat with you about their personal family history as well as their island's past. They can keep your mind occupied for hours if your goal is to really get to know the place.

Then again, the body needs to have its fun on vacation, too, and the waters and beaches on these islands are often as clean and warm as the ones in your most paradisiacal fantasies. Leave plenty of time in your itinerary for simply lolling about with snorkel gear in the sun, looking along the reefs for colorful angelfish and damselfish. Heck, if you combine the snorkeling with a fish identification book that you can get at your local bookstore before your trip, your family will have more to do during a day at the beach than hours in which to do it.

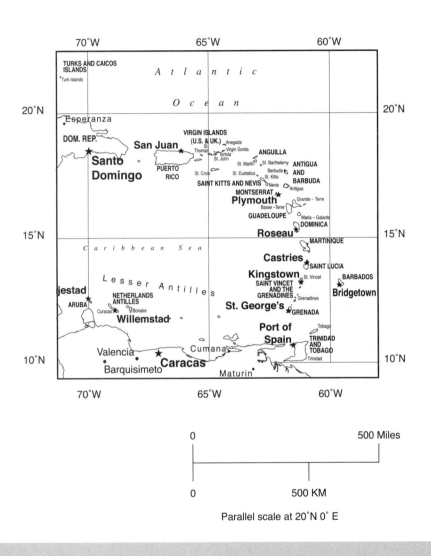

70°W 65°W 60°W

TURKS AND CAICOS
ISLANDS
Turk Islands

A t l a n t i c

O c e a n

20°N 20°N

Esperanza

DOM. REP.

San Juan

VIRGIN ISLANDS
(U.S. & UK.)
St. Anegada
Thomas Virgin Gorda
Tortola
St. John

ANGUILLA

St. Martin

St. Barthelemy

ANTIGUA
AND
BARBUDA

Santo
Domingo

PUERTO
RICO

St. Croix

St. Eustatius

Barbuda

St. Kitts

SAINT KITTS AND NEVIS Nevis

Antigua

MONTSERRAT

Plymouth

Grande -- Terre

Basse -- Terre

GUADELOUPE

Maria -- Galante

DOMINICA

15°N Roseau 15°N

C a r i b b e a n S e a

MARTINIQUE

Castries

SAINT LUCIA

L e s s e r A n t i l l e s

Kingstown St. Vincent

SAINT VINCENT
AND THE
GRENADINES

BARBADOS

Bridgetown

jestad

NETHERLANDS
ANTILLES

ARUBA

Bonaire

Curacao

Grenadines

St. George's

GRENADA

Willemstad

Tobago

Port of
Spain

TRINIDAD
AND
TOBAGO

Valencia

Cumana

Trinidad

10°N 10°N

Barquisimeto

Caracas

Maturin

70°W 65°W 60°W

0   500 Miles

0   500 KM

Parallel scale at 20°N 0° E

Anguilla

There are thirty-three beaches on Anguilla, which seems within spitting distance of the much more cosmopolitan St. Maarten but is a world away in terms of culture. Only the smaller cruise ships such as the Windjammer fleet dock here, in the village of Sandy Ground. The low flow of tourist traffic, compared with some other Caribbean islands, is refreshing, and the island is less built up because of it. The attraction of Anguilla is that it is still very much a natural beauty.

 JUST FOR PARENTS

> While shopping in port on Anguilla, look for compact discs by the favorite local artist: Bankie Banx. His guitar playing and singing voice are a cross between Bob Marley and Bob Dylan. With autobiographical tunes like "Busted in Barbados," the CDs make truly authentic island souvenirs. If you have time, catch Banx playing at his bar, The Dune Preserve. It looks like a giant tree house, and part of its ceiling is made from an upside-down boat hull.

Anguilla is definitely worth the day excursion if you are a beach lover. You'll have plenty of space for your towel ashore, and because there are so many beaches around the island, you can usually find lots of good places to pick up souvenir shells. For those who consider shelling a sport, these beaches are frequently less picked-over than the ones on more popular islands. Bring an extra zip-close bag to carry your loot back to the ship.

Antigua

The Antigua Cruise Ship Dock can accommodate as many as four cruise ships a day in St. John's, the island's capital and largest city. The town has predictably sprung up to cater to the masses. You'll find plenty of shopping here in the tourist area, as well as restaurants the whole family can enjoy in the hotel district. If your tastes run more to the traditional, stroll amid the offerings at the farmer's market on the southern edge of town each Friday and Saturday morning. It's a nice way to enjoy an off-the-boat snack and get a bit more in touch with the local culture, should you want to.

JUST FOR PARENTS

If your ship is docked overnight on a Sunday in Antigua, don't miss the weekly party across the island from St. John's atop Shirley Heights. The former military encampment high above sea level offers breathtaking views of the island until dusk, when the steel-drum band kicks up to celebrate the sunset. The locals keep the party going late, with plenty of drinking and dirty dancing.

Every year in late April or early May, sailboats flock to Antigua to take part in Antigua Race Week. It's considered the top regatta in all of the Caribbean, and among the top five in the entire world. You can sit atop the island's hillsides and watch the hundreds of boats hoist their sails, or perhaps catch a glimpse from your personal balcony as your ship cruises into and out of Antiguan waters. It's a marvelous sight, reminiscent of the great races of yesteryear from New England and Europe.

Barbados

Barbados is far off the beaten Caribbean path, so far east that many cruise itineraries skip it altogether. That's a shame, given the island's history- and nature-filled attractions, not to mention its beautiful beaches.

One excursion that is great for the entire family on Barbados is a trip to the Andromeda Botanical Garden, started in the 1950s by a local horticulturist and now home to orchids, bougainvillea, pools, and waterfalls. It's a serene day trip, very pretty and relaxing, and a nice way to calm down after a few days of more hectic fun in the sun.

If you prefer time travel, try the Sunbury Plantation House, built around 1660 and for many years devoted to the transatlantic sugar trade. Or spend part of your day ashore at the Francia Great House, which includes Barbadian antiques such as a map dating to 1522. The kids might not enjoy this one, though, if they need a lot of stimulation. If your tykes are that type, consider leaving them on the ship.

If it's modern events that you love, grab a chair at the waterfront cafes and keep an eye peeled for famous people. With Barbados being so far off the beaten Caribbean path, Hollywood A-list celebrities often flock here for a bit of peace and quiet. You might even catch a glimpse of them walking up the passarelles to their private yachts.

FAST FACT

Bougainvillea is ubiquitous in the Caribbean islands, and each colorful version of the flower has its own name. Look along the local streets for dark pink blossoms called Juanita Hatten, pink-and-white petals known as Surprise, and clusters of smaller pink blooms known as Texas Dawn.

Grenada

Grenada is home to sugar and spice plantations, as well as rum distilleries. Cruise ships dock in the quaint town of St. George's. Excursions include trips to the village of Marquis to see pandanus grass weaving and to Soubise to see brightly colored fishing boats being built. If you're a photographer, these are great opportunities to get some action shots of the locals. If you're a do-it-yourself type, they're the place to learn something new about working with your hands.

Like Barbados, Grenada is an off-the-beaten-path cruise-ship destination. This is a good place to visit if you prefer a day away from the crowds that flock to more built-up locations such as St. Thomas and St. Maarten. If beaches aren't your thing and you want to be in the hub of bustling civilization, you might consider a different itinerary.

Guadalupe

Guadalupe is part of the same French archipelago that includes its better-known siblings St. Maarten and St. Barthelemy. Like the other Caribbean islands on cruise-ship itineraries, it has lovely white-sand beaches—but it also has towering waterfalls and tropical rainforests that can make for exciting days of exploring ashore. It's unfortunate that more cruise lines don't stop here, but the lack of traffic makes it all the more precious. If you see Guadalupe on your itinerary, consider yourself lucky.

 **TRAVEL TIP**

Don't expect to do any midday bargain hunting ashore in Guadalupe. In keeping with French culture, its shops shut down to allow for leisurely afternoon meals including plenty of red wine and conversation.

Guadalupe is actually two islands connected by a bridge over the Riviere Salee. Grand-Terre, to the east, has resorts and the island's economic hub, Pointe-a-Pietre. To the west is Basse-Terre, home to the rainforest and waterfalls. You can plan your excursions according to your tastes for being in town or in the heart of nature—an unusual combination that makes this island all the better if you tend to book your excursions at the last minute based on your daily mood.

Martinique

Cruise ships dock at Fort-de-France on Martinique, a French-speaking island that's home to some 400,000 people. Though the local currency is the euro, most shops will accept U.S. dollars or travelers' checks. Such is the benefit of civilization, and you'll be hard-pressed not to spend a few bucks on souvenirs at the Museum of Banana or the Museum of Rum. Skip the T-shirts here and stick with the local souvenirs, which will seem much more special as your cruise continues.

If it's city life you like, stick to the 100,000-resident Fort-de-France. It has a spice market, where you can get some exotic tastes to bring back home, as well as the Museum of Archaeology and Prehistory, which houses more than 1,000 artifacts from the time before Christopher Columbus landed here.

Should you prefer to get away from the crowds, consider an excursion to the rainforest via the Route de la Trace, an impressive path that Jesuit monks carved out of the mountainside. You might also inject a bit of recent history into your visit with a side trip to Habitation Clement, a beautiful house where President George H.W. Bush and French President Francois Mitterrand held a summit after the end of the Gulf War.

≡FAST FACT

Fort-de-France, where cruise ships dock, did not become the capital of Martinique until May 1902, when Mount Pelee erupted. The volcano destroyed the former capital of St. Pierre and killed 30,000 people in just three minutes. Mount Pelee is now dormant, and you can visit it during a cruise ship excursion.

Mustique

In stark contrast to the many Caribbean islands that have built up substantial tourism districts to accommodate cruise-ship passengers, Mustique (pronounced muss-TEEK) remains an unspoiled island that touts its luxuriously quiet pace. It is part of the Grenadines, a forty-five-mile-long archipelago that boasts some of the bluest, cleanest water in the world. Relatively few American travelers ever make it as far south as the Grenadines; most prefer the shorter plane rides and itineraries that come with trips to the Bahamas and the Virgin Islands. In the case of Mustique, their loss will be your gain.

Mustique itself is just under two miles wide and, at its tallest point, less than 500 feet tall. Because of its size, it is often seen during daytime excursions from the larger cruise-ship port in nearby Kingstown, St. Vincent. If you enjoy wandering at a slow pace and stopping to chat with the locals, a side trip here is worth your time. Once in a while, you can even catch the locals playing a morning round of volleyball. Bring your game face—these guys are good.

═══FAST FACT

If you like singing the blues, be sure Mustique is on your cruise itinerary between late January and early February. That's when the island hosts the only annual blues festival in the Caribbean, in partnership with nearby Bequia and St. Vincent.

Nevis/St. Kitts

A channel that's two miles wide separates St. Kitts and its little sister to the south, the island of Nevis. Basseterre, on St. Kitts, is where your cruise ship will dock, but if you're like most visitors, you'll quickly take to the mountains. The island boasts dormant volcanoes and rugged hillsides, making hiking one of the most popular daytime excursion activities. Sneakers will do, but if you have hiking boots, you might want to bring them along. You'll work off enough calories to let you indulge later in the chef's chocolate creation after dinner back on the ship.

TRAVEL TIP

The local currency on St. Kitts and Nevis is the eastern Caribbean dollar, which is good only here and in Antigua, Barbuda, Dominica, Grenada, Montserrat, St. Lucia, St. Vincent, and the Grenadines. Most merchants will accept U.S. dollars and travelers' checks, but try to pay with small bills and minimize the foreign change you receive.

For a change of pace, consider an excursion via the St. Kitts Scenic Railway. Built a century ago, it circumnavigates the island with double-deck cars. The tops of the cars have open-air observation areas, allowing for extraordinary views. The lower levels are air-conditioned, which will be important for your comfort during midday journeys under the hot Caribbean sun. You may even want to bring a light jacket or long sleeves, to prevent any discomfort that might occur as your body adjusts to the heat and then the cold when you move outside and in.

St. Barthelemy

Long the playground of the rich and famous, St. Barthelemy— or St. Barth's, as the locals call it—is widely regarded as the St. Tropez of the Caribbean. It claims twenty-two beaches, dozens of luxurious boutiques, and (especially during Christmas and New Year's) the opportunity to catch a glimpse of movie stars living the high life. Even more than Barbados, this is the island to see and on which to be seen.

Not to mention the island to enjoy. As part of the French empire, St. Barth's is the place where you'll be able to spend your cash on delicious food and excellent red wine. True, your cruise ship's package may include all meals, but how can you resist a freshly baked baguette in the middle of paradise? Be sure to say *merci beaucoup* if you receive service you especially enjoy.

 TRAVEL TIP

Restaurants on St. Barthelemy typically add a service charge to the bill, so be careful when calculating your waiter's tip. If you take a taxi, expect to tip the driver 10 percent of the fare. It's the local standard.

Because of its proximity to other eastern Caribbean Islands, St. Barthelemy is sometimes a stop on shorter cruises that hop from place to place within a small overall distance. (One example is the four-night round-trip itinerary from San Juan, Puerto Rico, with

Radisson Seven Seas Cruises.) You may not be able to visit St. Barth's during longer itineraries that choose only one of the islands in its region before moving on, so if this island is an important port for you, you might choose a shorter cruise and add a few nights ashore to create a weeklong vacation.

St. Lucia

The big draw during a cruise to St. Lucia is the Pitons: dramatic twin peaks that tower startlingly some 2,000 feet above the water. This is neck-craning country, the place to get out the video camera and aim sky high. Consider, for example, that the nearly 1,500-passenger Carnival cruise ship *Celebration* is 733 feet long, and the sheer mass of Petit Piton and Gros Piton becomes clear. You'd need about three *Celebration* ships piled bow to stern up toward the sky to reach the tops of these peaks.

Your ship will dock in Castries, a lovely town with good shopping. It's within excursion distance of Sulfur Springs, the world's only drive-through volcano. Sulfur Springs is not quite as dramatic as it sounds, but the pockets of steam you'll see bursting through cracks in the earth's surface are definitely an interesting sight—and fodder for plenty of dinnertime conversation with the kids about geology and the Earth's molten core.

St. Maarten

With a French side and a Dutch side, St. Maarten (a.k.a. St. Martin, if you're on the French side) is a bustling island. It boasts a terrific shopping district, a casino, and even a golf course for duffers who need a day of wandering somewhere other than the beach. The restaurants on the French side of the island are excellent. If you want to get even more of a taste of European life, you can wander down to the nude section of Orient Beach. It's segregated at the very end of the crescent-shaped harbor, so you need not worry if you want to restrict your kids to sections of sand where people are covered up. If you do head down to the nude sunbathing area, leave your camera behind. They're not allowed, and you will be asked to put it away immediately or leave.

═FAST FACT

The governments of France and the Netherlands signed a treaty in 1648 that divided the island of St. Maarten, leaving each side to preserve its distinct cultural characteristics. Cruise ships dock in Philipsburg on the Dutch side, which is often spelled Sint Maarten.

St. Maarten has become a mega-yacht port of choice in recent years, and some cruise-ship itineraries provide you with a chance to live as the private boat owners do. Royal Caribbean, for example, offers excursions aboard the famous racing yacht *Stars and Stripes* that include an actual race on a shortened version of an America's Cup course. Combine this excursion with an itinerary that takes you to Antigua during that island's famous race week, and you've got yourself one of the finest boat-lover's vacations on the planet.

CHAPTER 8

Western Caribbean, Virgin Islands, Bahamas, and Bermuda

IF YOU LIKE THE idea of the tropics but aren't pulled by any of the destinations in the highly popular eastern Caribbean, maybe you should consider an itinerary that brushes up against the eastern coast of Mexico and continues on to include the various islands sprinkled throughout the western Caribbean. Or you can go north from the eastern Caribbean and focus your itinerary on the Bahamas or Bermuda, which also have plenty of great ports of call.

Western Caribbean

The islands of the western Caribbean are more segregated than their eastern Caribbean counterparts, which translates into a bit more time spent cruising on open water during most cruise-ship itineraries. Grand Cayman and Jamaica stand virtually alone to the south of Cuba, while Aruba, Bonaire, and Curacao—known as the "ABC islands"—are about 500 statute miles to the southeast, just north of the Venezuelan coast.

Yet what the western Caribbean islands lack in proximity, they more than make up for in unique character. Each has its own personality, and some have been enchanting visitors as far back as recorded history.

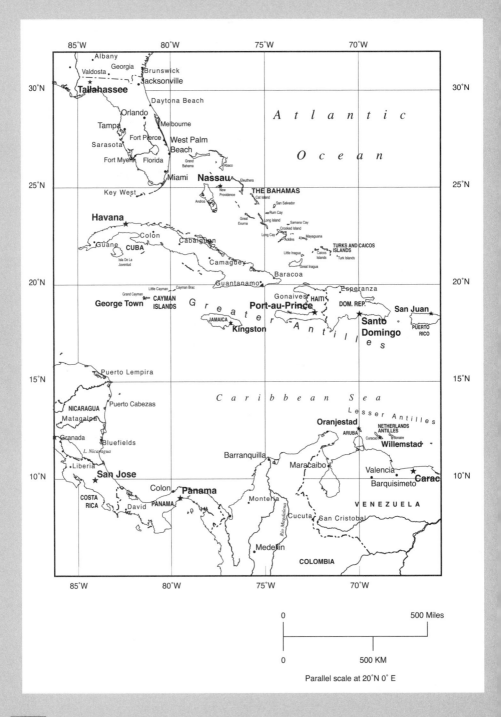

≡FAST FACT

The windward sides of the Caribbean islands generally receive much more rain than the leeward sides. Eastern Jamaica's Blue Mountains, for instance, get about 223 inches of rain annually, while the city of Kingston, on the island's southeastern coast, sees only 160 inches or so.

Stops on the Mexican mainland, far to the west, and in the British Virgin Islands, far to the east, are often included on western Caribbean itineraries, with an additional stop in between at the Dominican Republic port of Santo Domingo. These itineraries cover a lot of geography and allow for interesting peeks into very different cultures along the way.

Aruba

Aruba is the best known of the ABC islands in terms of general tourism, though scuba divers from around the globe have raised the profile of Bonaire and Curacao in recent years as havens for that sport. Your cruise ship will dock in Oranjestad on Aruba's southern coast, providing you with the opportunity to explore the island's schooner harbor, outdoor food and craft markets, and Dutch-colonial buildings. Golfers can hit the links farther inland on a course designed by Robert Trent Jones, Jr., while shoppers can look for great finds on designer jewelry and more.

TRAVEL TIP

If photography is your hobby, be sure to carry your best lenses up the steps of Aruba's old stone California Lighthouse, named for the ship *California* that sank just offshore. The lighthouse affords panoramic views from high above the island, the best perch for photographers of any skill level.

Several cruise lines offer an exciting excursion aboard an air-conditioned submarine. Guests typically must be at least four years old and at least three feet tall to participate, so you may have to leave the kids behind. (Check with the excursions manager on your ship for details.) In some cases, the submarine descends to 150 feet below the water's surface for a view of either a shipwreck or a crashed airplane. That's fifteen stories down, much of it teeming with coral, tropical fish, and maybe even a ray or shark along the way. The ride is like being inside a giant aquarium tank, only with a knowledgeable tour guide and a comfortably dry seat.

If you're a recreational scuba diver, you know you're not supposed to go quite as deep as those submarines, but you can explore the wreck of a 440-foot German freighter that's now encrusted in coral and a favorite haven for fish. Many other dives are available in the area if shipwrecks aren't to your liking; again, check with the excursions manager on your cruise ship.

The snorkeling off Aruba's shores is also quite good. You might even catch a glimpse of the spectacular blue parrotfish, which is much less frequently seen than its stoplight and rainbow cousins.

Cayman Islands

Your cruise ship will dock off the shore of George Town at Grand Cayman, a high-end resort island that tailors itself for luxury travelers with plenty to see and do (and purchase duty-free). You arrive at the island by smaller boat from the big ship, which is important to note if you're traveling with anyone who uses a wheelchair. It may be difficult getting ashore in the smaller boats (instead of just being wheeled onto a dock), and you thus might prefer to schedule onboard activities for the days when your ship is at this port.

Grand Cayman is one of the most meticulously manicured of the Caribbean islands, luring big-money businessmen with its generous taxation policies and keeping them there with its paradisiacal setting. The island offers plenty to keep you and the kids busy, too, but if time allows, don't let Grand Cayman be all you see of the Caymans. The smaller, less-often-visited Little Cayman and Cayman Brac are much quieter and worth exploring on day trips, especially if you are a scuba diver or nature lover. Some of the world's finest underwater walls of coral are here and should not be missed. Non-divers can enjoy some of the stunning underwater views and wildlife with snorkels or in glass-bottom boats on Grand Cayman or the smaller islands.

If you and your family have already enjoyed the classic excursion to Grand Cayman's Stingray City, the next item on your excursion itinerary should be the island's Turtle Farm, an interactive nursery where green turtles and hawksbill turtles are raised—some for food processing, and some for release into the wild. The tour guides explain all of this, so be sure your kids don't start naming their new friends after the Ninja Turtles right before they learn that one or more of them are going to end up being somebody's supper.

≡FAST FACT

Grand Cayman Island allows a maximum of 6,000 cruise ship visitors to come ashore each day. That's about the same number of people that New York City's famed Radio City Music hall holds (not counting the Rockettes).

Before the day is done, try to get to the town of Hell, where you can have a letter mailed with a postmark bearing the same name. A terrific souvenir is to mail a few letters to yourself back home, so they will be waiting upon your return. The envelope can make for a nice keepsake if you plan to fill a shadow box with photos and other fun finds from your vacation.

If Hell is too fiery a proposition for you, consider a stroll to decidedly more gentle-sounding George Town's Conch Shell House. A great photo opportunity, this building is made entirely from mollusk trumpet shells. It'll give the kids some terrifically creative ideas to occupy their time the next day at the beach, when you'll have to be sure to remember your sandcastle-building supplies.

Curacao

Curacao is the middle island in the ABCs, with Aruba to its west and Bonaire to its east. The island has jutting cliffs with caves tucked inside that you can explore by canoe—always a great opportunity for storytelling with the family and much closer to nature than the typical excursion vessels on most other islands. A canoe is pretty much the closest you can get to being in the water without actually getting wet, and a half-day's paddle along the scenic coastline can make for a nice, quiet respite after a few days of hearing the cruise ship's mammoth engines and generators humming as background noise.

As in Aruba and Bonaire, scuba diving is popular off the shores of Curacao, so much so that some of its reefs are reportedly becoming over-dived. That shouldn't prevent scuba enthusiasts from dropping to depth and having a look around, or even from visiting the natural tidal pool that's fenced off by windows. There, you can feed and photograph stingrays, sharks, and turtles without having to search for them in seventy feet of open water. Snorkelers, too, will find plenty to fill their mask views beneath the waters off Curacao.

≡FAST FACT

While most people associate the Caribbean with the Roman Catholic religion, Curacao boasts the oldest Jewish cemetery and the oldest synagogue in constant use in the Western Hemisphere.

If keeping your feet dry sounds better than hand-feeding sharks, consider spending a day touring the capital city of Willemstad, arguably the prettiest in all of the Caribbean, with plenty to see and do along its streets.

Willemstad looks like a Dutch streetscape splashed with Caribbean color, a stout vanilla cupcake with some mighty tasty icing. It's a lovely enough scene to keep budding photographers wandering for hours, but if your mind needs more structure than that—and if your children are on the older side—consider a visit to the

Kura Hulanda Museum. Among other things, the museum traces the searing history of the African slave trade in a profound way that will leave you eager to learn more. It's an educational opportunity of the highest order that older kids can use as a basis for class projects and reports long after your cruise ship returns you back home.

TRAVEL TIP

Don't forgo a side trip to Willemstad, Curacao, and a walk across the Queen Emma Bridge. Built in 1888 and named after Holland's Queen Emma, the bridge floats atop sixteen pontoons—something you'll probably never see or get to set foot on again.

Willemstad is a World Heritage City, chosen in honor of its uniqueness in the eyes of multiple leaders across the globe. Its historic districts include architecture in the style of the Dutch, Spanish, and Portuguese people who have inhabited its streets throughout the centuries, and its charm continues all the way down to the waterfront, where boats still sail into St. Anna Bay to create a floating market of fish, fruits, and vegetables. If you like to meander and simply soak in the culture, the floating market is an ideal spot.

Dominican Republic

The Dominican Republic, which shares the island of Hispaniola with Haiti to its west, has transformed itself from a sleepy nation full of sugar cane and ranches into a popular retreat for those who want to see and be seen. From the spectacular Casa de Campo Resort to the charming medieval Spanish village of Altos de Chavon, you'll find plenty to suit tastes that lean toward the extravagant and the humble alike.

The capital city of Santo Domingo, in and of itself, is an exciting place to explore after your cruise ship docks there. But be prepared—this is no little island town.

Christopher Columbus is known to have sailed to this oldest city in the New World, as did fellow explorers Ponce De Leon and Hernando Cortes. Today, Santo Domingo is the Caribbean's biggest metropolis, home to more than 2 million people. Don't expect quaint little shore-side shacks here—Santo Domingo is more like a small city in the United States. Keep your bag's strap around your neck, and hold your children's hands while walking around. The guided group tours you can sign up for while aboard your ship are an excellent way to see the city without having to worry about inadvertently walking down a questionable alleyway.

≡FAST FACT

The oldest cathedral in the Americas is the Cathedral of Santa Maria le Menor. It still stands and can be toured as part of many cruise-ship excursion packages in Santo Domingo, Dominican Republic.

You can tour sections of Santo Domingo by bus or on foot, but either way, the Old City is not to be missed. This is where the first street, monastery, hospital, and cathedral were built in the Americas, and a tour provides an excellent educational opportunity. The sense of historical significance is palpable as you explore the sites, and each will provide for plenty of chitchat as you make your way through the nearby restaurants, shops, and bars. The place simply *oozes* history. You'll likely have more questions than answers about the city's timeline and architecture, so if your children are particularly inquisitive, consider grabbing a local guidebook from one of the nearby shops before you begin your walk. It's an inexpensive way to enjoy an educational, enchanting afternoon.

Haiti

The continuing political unrest in Haiti makes it less of a paradisiacal icon than the islands that surround it, but the Royal Caribbean

Explorer of the Seas does promote a stop here after departure in Miami. In reality, the ship stops at Labadee, a private (and perfectly beautiful) 260-acre wooded peninsula that Royal Caribbean owns on the northern coast of Hispaniola. Kayaking, parasailing, and other water-based sports excursions are available.

Explorer of the Seas is a massive ship that carries 3,114 passengers who get to use its onboard rock-climbing wall, street fair, and ice-skating rink. So even if Haiti isn't on your must-see list and you choose to stay aboard at the Labadee port of call, you'll have plenty of things to keep you busy until the ship sets off to more traditional Western Caribbean docks.

Virgin Islands

The Virgin Islands are divided into two territories: St. Croix, St. John, and St. Thomas are the major U.S. Virgin Islands, while Tortola, Virgin Gorda, and the far-flung Anegada are the largest of the British Virgin Islands. Your cruise ship likely will be based at the main regional port of Charlotte Amalie on St. Thomas, the most developed island in the group. Though ringed by beautiful blue waters, it actually looks a bit like the United States when you disembark, with fast-food restaurants and even a Hard Rock Café. It can make a nice transition from the U.S. mainland into the Caribbean, sort of a step from the hustle and bustle of "real life" toward the peace and tranquility that await in the outlying islands. Just don't expect quaint, homespun charm when you first arrive. St. Thomas is definitely a major tourist waypoint.

≡FAST FACT

Two-thirds of St. John, in the U.S. Virgin Islands, is protected parkland—much of it underwater. It is arguably the prettiest of all the Virgin Islands that cruise-ship passengers typically get a chance to see.

The Charlotte Amalie shopping district on St. Thomas has developed to meet all your desires as you step ashore, so be sure to bring plenty of spending money. You can collect as much as $1,200 worth of duty-free merchandise on your cruise—and you'd be hard pressed to find a bigger group of stores ready to cater to you anywhere else in the Virgins.

If you're willing to forgo the bargains and would rather get away from the crowds, consider an excursion to St. John or Tortola. They're much less developed, much quieter, and only a short ferry ride away.

St. Croix

St. Croix's cruise-ship options have dropped dramatically in recent years because of reports of increasing crime and decreasing tourist services, but the island is working hard to get itself back into the tourism game. Crime, in particular, seems to be coming under control, with significant enough improvements that Royal Caribbean has decided to send several of its ships into the port city Frederiksted for short stops. No doubt the cruise company will be monitoring events carefully, so it wouldn't hurt to call and ask a few pertinent questions about the local goings-on before booking your trip.

Also consider looking up the latest news about St. Croix on the Internet as your trip's date approaches, so you can get independent verification of where the current situation stands. Major Florida newspapers, such as the *Sun-Sentinel* and the *St. Petersburg Times*, cover St. Croix and the other Virgin Islands regularly. You might search their Web sites for recent articles.

St. John

St. John is arguably the loveliest of the Virgin Islands, with two-thirds of its acreage above and below the water set aside as protected parkland. This is an island where you can still find a white-sand cove without a single footprint after a day of hiking through the trees. A nap in a hammock here is about as far away as you can get from

A t l a n t i c   O c e a n

**British
Virgin Islands**

Great
Camanoe

Guana Island

Jost
Van Dyke

Beef Island
Airport

Virgin Gorda
(U.K.)

Spanish Town

**Road
Town**

Hans Lollik
Island

*Virgin
Passage*

Tortola
(U.K.)

Sir Francis Drake Channel

Ginger Island

Cooper Island

**Charlotte
Amalie**

Savana
Island

Harry Truman
Airport

Coral
Bay

Cruz
Bay

Pillsbury Sound

Peter Island

Norman Island

**Saint
Thomas**
(U.S.)

**Saint
John**
(U.S.)

A n e g a d a   P a s s a g e

U.S. Virgin Islands

C a r i b b e a n   S e a

Buck Island

East Point

Saint Croix
(U.S.)

Christiansted

Frederiksted

Southwest
Cape

Alexander Hamilton
Airport

civilization, even though you'll be just a twenty-minute ferry ride from St. Thomas and its busy port. This is the place to feel your lungs fill with fresh air, sense the sun's rays on your skin, and listen to the wind as it rustles through the swaying palms.

 TRAVEL TIP

The ferry ride from St. Thomas to St. John takes only about twenty minutes. You can easily leave several hours' worth of time for other activities on either island before or after your excursion.

Excursions from St. Thomas to St. John are available by ferry, with tours that focus on the island or, specifically, its beaches. Trunk Bay on St. John has been rated many times over as one of the top beaches in the world, a place where you and your family can snorkel, hike along guided trails, or just enjoy the view. (Check the travel magazines in your local bookstore, and you're likely to find a current article extolling the beauty of the place.) If it's fun in the sun that you're after, consider planning for as much time here as possible. This is not an island to bypass while you stay aboard and swim in the cruise ship's pool. This is the place to live it up in one of the most beautiful destinations on Earth.

St. Thomas

In addition to shopping, Charlotte Amalie on St. Thomas has plenty of nightlife and restaurants. Helicopter tours can be fun for the family here, and golfers can hit the links at a Tom and George Fazio-designed course that has several holes overlooking the water. Parasailing, snorkeling, and scuba diving are also available here, as they are in other major Caribbean tourist hotspots.

Again, St. Thomas is not the place you should expect a quiet nap among the coconuts, but you can keep yourself and your kids happily busy there for a day or two. If you can find a cruise itinerary that makes St. Thomas its first stop, that's a good idea—the island feels more relaxed than the United States, but it's still far busier than the rest of the Virgins. On your way to the fun and sun, it will feel like a step in the right direction. On your way back home at the end of your cruise, it might feel a bit too much like being slapped back to the realities of civilization.

Tortola

Tortola is the largest of the British Virgin Islands, and most of it remains undeveloped with beautiful scenery. As you cruise past, you will see lush trees bursting from the land like bunches of broccoli, a view that makes it nearly impossible for you to stop yourself from heading ashore and taking a peek beneath the waxy green leaves.

═FAST FACT

The highest peak in the British Virgin Islands is 1,700 feet above sea level, in Sage Mountain National Park on Tortola. You can walk the trails there through the rainforest during excursions on some cruise-ship itineraries.

You can often take an excursion from Tortola for a dip at the famed Baths off nearby Virgin Gorda—a geographical oddity of gigantic boulders hurled atop one another by a volcano to create wading pools inside rock caves. The Baths are repeatedly named one of the most beautiful swimming experiences in all of the Virgin Islands, but in truth, they have become far more touristy than they used to be. (There's even a T-shirt stand outside the entrance these days.) The Baths are interesting to see, but if you want to stay away from the crowds, you might consider scuba diving or hiking around Tortola instead, or checking out quaint shops and restaurants on the island's main harbor of Road Town.

The Bahamas

The Bahamas are often overlooked in favor of Caribbean cruising, a mistake you will not make twice after you visit this crystal-water paradise for the first time. Sailors from Florida have long flocked to Bahamian islands, which are surrounded by blues so clear in some areas that you can literally stand up to your neck in water and still see all ten of your toes. Sadly, cruisers from the United States often forgo a trip to the Bahamas because it seems too close to home to be a vacation destination. The truth is, when you're in the Bahamas, things can be so peaceful and friendly that you seem an entire world away.

If you take excursions aboard smaller boats, you will find yourself on islands surrounded by such shallow water that nothing bigger than a canoe could ever get close to shore. The sands and shells are pristine, and the clean water and quiet atmosphere are unparalleled. A good number of the smaller islands are uninhabited, if you don't count the iguanas that skitter all over Allan's Cay or the family of pigs that call Big Majors home.

≡ FAST FACT

Holland America offers excursions to Half Moon Cay, a private fifty-five-acre island and bird sanctuary the company owns in the Bahamas. Princess Cruises also has its own island, a two-mile-wide strip off southern Eleuthera called Princess Cays, and Norwegian Cruise Line has its own two-and-a-half-mile-long island in the Berry chain called Stirrup Cay.

There are several island groupings within the Bahamas, including the Berries, the Exumas, and the Abacos. Most cruise ships dock in Nassau, home of the famed Atlantis Resort & Casino that rises from the island like a castle of cotton candy pink. This is a busy port, for sure, but snorkeling, scuba diving, and glass-bottomed boat tours are all available. Nassau also makes a great jumping-off point for day trips down to the untouched beaches and snorkeling holes in the Exumas.

Freeport

Freeport is a city on the northwestern corner of Grand Bahama Island, just sixty-eight miles east of West Palm Beach, Florida. During four-day Bahamas-only cruises, it is likely to be a stop on your itinerary. You'll find snorkeling here along with scuba diving and golf—more than enough to keep the whole family having fun in the sun. If your children are on the younger side, consider a trip to the Pirates of the Bahamas Theme Park on the beach. It has swings, seesaws, mini-golf, Ping Pong, and more—all with adult supervision.

TRAVEL TIP

The Bahamian dollar is linked to the U.S. dollar at an even exchange rate. You can use either throughout the islands without having to figure out a conversion rate, a nice tourism perk.

The city of Freeport was specifically designed to appeal to tourists, so you'll also find plenty of shops and restaurants to enjoy, as well as nightlife after the sun goes down. Walking around is intentionally made easy so that you'll stay ashore and enjoy yourself as long as time allows.

Nassau

Nassau is the capital of the Bahamas, located on New Providence Island. You will have countless excursion options here, including every kind of water sport plus day cruises on smaller local sailboats and high-speed powerboats. Expect crowds here, as Nassau is the jumping-off point for trips all over the rest of the Bahamas. The Atlantis resort alone draws thousands of visitors at a time.

If your cruise line offers an excursion down to the Exumas part of the Bahamas south of Nassau, sign up immediately. The beaches are exquisite, the water is as clear as a baby's conscience, and you can find interesting wildlife—including those uninhabited islands full of pigs and iguanas. Many of the photo shoots for Bahamian marketing and tourism are done here or in other parts of the "out islands," which tells you something very special about their pure beauty.

Bermuda

Bermuda is a mid-Atlantic island group east of Charleston, South Carolina, but is traditionally included on maps of the West Indies along with other vacation destinations close to North America. The positioning is more mental than geographical, since Bermuda offers many of the same fun-in-the-sun moments to remember as the islands to its south.

Because Bermuda is so much farther north than, say, the Virgin Islands, cruise lines can offer short Bermuda-only itineraries leaving from the northeastern United States. Royal Caribbean, for example, offers round-trip vacations from New York City and Baltimore, Maryland. These are great getaways if you live in the Northeast corridor, without the hassle of having to fly all the way to Florida and back on either end of your cruise.

There are other ways to cruise to Bermuda: Baltimore is the starting point for an eleven-day Crystal Cruises trip through Bermuda to the Bahamas and ending in San Juan, Puerto Rico. Crystal Cruises also makes Bermuda a stop on its one-way cruise from Lisbon, Portugal, to Fort Lauderdale, Florida.

═FAST FACT

Bermuda shorts are still fashionable, at least in Bermuda, where businessmen even wear them to meetings with a tie and jacket. Hey mon, nice pants!

Golf is always a major draw for vacationers in Bermuda, but don't overlook deep-sea fishing as an option. The big blue marlin can be quite exciting when they're pulling at your reel, leaving everyone aboard screaming "Fish on!" well after the day is done.

CHAPTER 9

Western Mediterranean

THE MEDITERRANEAN SEA HAS long been a favorite summertime cruising destination, since well before the United States even existed. And the western Mediterranean is the most popular cruising ground of all, thanks to the romantic cultures of France, Italy, and other Old World nations. From sipping a fine Bordeaux in a quiet vineyard to walking with your children through a stadium where gladiators once raged for cheering crowds, western Mediterranean cruises offer exhilarating opportunities for discovery.

Portugal

The coastal country of Portugal is often forgotten in the shadow of her big sister to the east, Spain, but this nation of 10 million proud citizens packs an awful lot into its geographic boundaries. World Heritage sights are as ubiquitous as freckles on a redhead's cheeks, winemakers are working to compete with the more established vineyards in France and Italy (and have already established themselves as premier makers of port), and folk festivals abound that can make you feel like you've stepped back in time to a simpler, more relaxed way of life. If olive oil is a key ingredient in your personal culinary happiness, you'll find more than enough Portuguese brands to tempt your palate as souvenirs.

You can sail to Portugal either as part of a round-trip cruise from a port in Europe such as Southampton, England, or during a one-way transatlantic cruise, usually heading to or coming from Florida. Keep in mind that the transatlantic cruises typically include four or five straight days at sea, and that you'll want to be aboard a ship with plenty to do during this time. You'll also encounter open-ocean waves—sometimes many stories tall—so be prepared with seasickness remedies. Often, simply getting into the fresh air on deck and watching the horizon will ease your stomach in such seas, with the added bonus that you'll be among the first to catch sight of civilization. After a few days at sea, you'll be surprised at how you can sometimes smell the land before it comes into view.

 TRAVEL TIP

If you simply want to enjoy cruising past European landscapes, a round-trip cruise that starts and ends in the same port is the way to go. If you are more of an explorer who wants to see as much of the Mediterranean as possible, consider a one-way cruise, say from Venice, Italy, to Barcelona, Spain. You can tack a day or two onto either end of your trip to explore the different countries by land.

In addition to the ocean cruises that include Portugal, there are locally based river cruises aboard smaller boats that you can take into the heart of the country. Uniworld, for instance, offers one such cruise up the Douro River to the Spanish border. In some cases, you can extend river cruise packages for a few days' worth of land-based touring in Lisbon. The charming capital city is also the port where cruise ships dock.

Lisbon is a beautiful city of picturesque hillsides and cobblestone streets. Of course, these features can make it a challenge to tour on foot if you are with small children or elderly grandparents, but most cruise lines offer bus tours that enable you to see many of the sights from the comfort of an air-conditioned seat. The city boasts more than twenty *centuries* of history—more than enough to keep the historically minded busy for an entire lifetime, let alone the day or two that will probably be part of your itinerary.

As a port city, Lisbon saw towns sprout up all around its borders, like dandelions spreading across a field. Cruise-ship excursions can include visits to places like Sintra, which has three architecturally stunning national palaces as well as marble quarries and handicraft shops. Also available are excursions to smaller towns such as Sesimbra, a fishing village in the shadow of a castle that is full of colorful local working boats.

Just remember to bring a good pair of sneakers or walking boots—the ground is hilly and the streets are of mixed materials in most of these places, filling your day with cardiovascular challenges beyond what you'd expect during a day at the beach. If you're traveling with elderly grandparents, this might be a good port for them to stay aboard the ship and take part in an onboard activity instead.

Spain

When you think of visiting Spain, the first idea that often springs to mind is the capital city of Madrid or the former Olympic city of Barcelona. Both are terrific stops worth seeing, packed with daytime treats and nightlife to be sure, but if you dig a little deeper into cruise-ship itineraries you will find ports in the Canary and Balearic islands.

Unlike the major cities, these are places much less traveled, haunts where the pace of life harks back to the days of old. You're bound to find craftsmen still making souvenirs by hand for you to take home, be it pottery or leather goods. In the Balearics, for instance, you can often stroll into a shop that has strips of leather ready to be turned into belts. You choose your style and then sift like a miner through countless baskets sitting on the floor full of gold, silver, and designer buckles. The shop owner will build your belt right before your eyes,

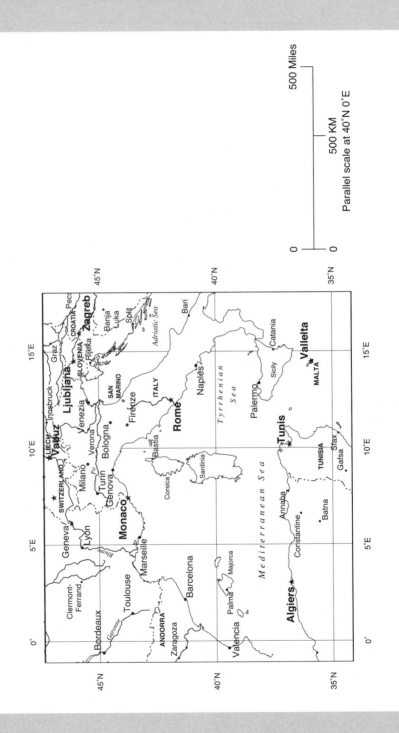

500 Miles

500 KM

Parallel scale at 40°N 0°E

so you can wear it out of the shop—perhaps while carrying a brand-new matching leather handbag or wallet.

Truth be told, Spain offers varied destinations that will appeal to all kinds of travelers, from some of the largest art museums in the world to some of the most cutting-edge discotheques ever created. On many itineraries, you can find a combination of Spain's biggest and smallest ports along with a few other stops in France, Italy, and even Greece.

 TRAVEL TIP

When you purchase souvenirs in the European Union, you are required to pay the member state's value-added tax, or VAT. The minimum VAT is 15 percent, but some countries charge more. American citizens are entitled to refunds on these taxes, so when you buy an item, ask about the member state's refund policy. Your cruise ship's information desk can also be of help.

Barcelona

Archaeological remains put the date of Barcelona's creation sometime in the first century A.D., with the first buildings erected by Romans. Its evolution has continued into the modern day, when in 1992 it hosted the twenty-fifth Olympic Games—and startled television viewers around the world with the city's beauty. Tourism has been strong in Barcelona ever since, with shops and restaurants popping up like cloudbursts to cater to visitors who arrive by land and by sea.

Art lovers will delight in this city, which has been home to Pablo Picasso, Joan Miro, Salvador Dali, Antonio Gaudi, and more. There is even Museo Picasso, devoted entirely to the master of cubism.

Other cultural excursions can include flamenco shows, where dancers in colorful costumes stomp heels, snap fingers, and clap hands the way Gypsies used to in the 1700s. If you're traveling with children and want to enjoy some of Barcelona's rich artistic traditions, this is a nice alternative to museum tours. The kids will be dancing all the way back to the ship.

RAINY DAY FUN

The well-worth-seeing Museo Picasso in Barcelona, Spain, has more than 3,500 works by the master in its permanent collection, including most of the artist's early creations, which he donated to the facility himself.

Cadiz

Known to far fewer people around the globe than the bigger cities of Barcelona and Madrid, the 160,000-resident city of Cadiz sits on a long, narrow peninsula in Spain's southwest corner. It used to be a major port, from which Christopher Columbus launched two voyages. Today it draws tourists mostly from within Spain's borders—which means it hasn't yet succumbed to the cookie-cutter rows of shops that often develop in more international vacation destinations. You will be sure to find the real flavor of Spain in this city's old quarter, whether by walking down the narrow alleyways or watching the faces as people stroll about the plazas.

Excursions here include a horse show at the Royal Andalusia School of Equestrian Arts, a tasting at a local sherry shop, and day trips to Seville, the city from which Don Juan himself set out to capture the hearts of beautiful women worldwide and where the Andalusian culture of bullfighting and flamenco still reigns. Your biggest challenge in Cadiz will be deciding which excursion to choose and which to forgo. The city has so much to offer, you can't possibly take it all in during a single day's visit.

Canary Islands

The Canary Islands, though under the Spanish flag, are located off the northwestern coast of Africa at the southern tip of Morocco.

The archipelago has seven main islands—La Palma, Hierro, Gomera, Tenerife, Gran Canaria, Fuerteventura, and Lanzarote—and some cruise ship itineraries stop at ports on almost all of them. Because the Canaries are a popular European vacation destination, many of the beachfront areas are built up and crowded, but it is still possible to find charming hamlets on hillsides during day trips ashore. Don't expect privacy on the sand, but do expect to have a good time.

 **TRAVEL TIP**

Though the weather is inviting in the Canary Islands year-round, swimmers (especially children who like to play in the water) will have a better time visiting during the summer months. In the wintertime, the Atlantic Ocean can kick up some nasty swells.

Be sure to take home a bottle of the dessert wine Malmsey, the best-known style of the Canary Islands. If your tastes lean more toward the dry than the sweet, you can tour the wineries during excursions on Tenerife, the largest of the Canaries.

If nature is more your style, be sure to go ashore on Lanzarote, where more than 300 volcanoes dot the landscape. You can even visit a volcanic crater that's been overrun by seawater from underground and perhaps take a stroll along its black lava-sand beach. Remember to bring your beach shoes for this one—lava rocks can be much sharper underfoot than regular sand.

Ibiza

What New York City's Greenwich Village is to punk rock, Spain's Ibiza is to lounge clubs. Located in the Balearics archipelago to the south of the French-Spanish border, Ibiza is one of the world's best places for using the word "club" as a verb. This is where your excursion should entail nothing more than sipping drink after drink and clubbing at places like the world-famous Café del Mar. You would be hard-pressed to find better DJs and nightlife that rages into the wee hours anywhere else on the planet. You can buy compact discs from many of the clubs at the tourist shops and often at the clubs where the artists play night after night. These CDs make a terrific souvenir that you can use to recreate the atmosphere of Ibiza long after you return back to your home.

JUST FOR PARENTS

The discotheques on Ibiza, in Spain's Balearic Islands, are world-renowned for their fabulous lounge music. Be sure to drop in to sample the nightlife, but leave the kids behind after dark. The clubs are for adult eyes (and hips) only.

You'll also find beautiful beaches on Ibiza, so if you're traveling with children, you will have options beyond the neighborhoods where the young, beautiful, belly-button-displaying crowd is in control. Ask your cruise-ship director for details about the easiest routes away from the discotheques.

Malaga

Malaga is on Spain's Costa del Sol, on the country's southern shore just east of the much better-known Gibraltar. This is the place to plant yourself on a towel and vegetate on the warm sand along the lapping Mediterranean waters, perhaps wandering up to a local open-air restaurant to indulge in some *tapas* or gazpacho when your belly grumbles for a midday meal.

TRAVEL TIP

When dining in Spain, be sure to order *tapas,* small portions of local dishes that enable you to sample as many as a half-dozen new kinds of food in one sitting—without committing yourself to eating any one dish as an entire meal.

If you prefer to pamper your mind instead of your body, consider an excursion to Castillo de Gibralfaro or to the ancient palace Alcazaba. Both are high off the coastline and offer great views—today for tourists with panoramic cameras, but centuries ago for watching possible invasions from the African coast. The Alcazaba even has ruins from a Roman theatre, a sight that will make you feel like you've stepped into a well-preserved Italian or Greek archaeological dig.

Mallorca

Mallorca, like Ibiza, is in the Balearic Islands chain. The heartbeat of the island is bustling Palma de Mallorca, whose main drag does its best to compete with Ibiza for the hearts, minds, and scantily clad bodies of young clubbers from all across Europe.

Still, there is much to do in Palma besides boogie the night away. Its Gothic cathedral is its greatest landmark, fantastic to see both outside and in. The nearby Royal Palace is also an architectural masterpiece, with lovely shop- and restaurant-lined streets all around. Walking in Palma feels much like walking through a city on the European mainland, but with far less congestion and tourism than, say, Madrid. Even walking around for a dinner about 10 or 11:00 P.M., as the locals do, you will feel safe. And if you want to blend right in, be sure to stop and sit down at a street-side table and order a coffee every hour or two. Such is the relaxed pace of life in this delightful city.

If you have time for a day-trip excursion during your itinerary, don't miss the charming northern town of Valdemossa on Mallorca's northwestern tip. The village towers high above sea level inside the stone walls that were built to protect it centuries ago, and life continues amid its narrow stone streets with the charming appeal of yesteryear.

Valdemossa has gardens you can wander through where local musicians strum guitars and croon mellow melodies, plenty of open-air cafes for a midday espresso, and the same kind of romantic ambience that lured composer Frederic Chopin and his female writer friend, George Sand, for a love affair in the winter of 1838. There are shops that cater to tourists, but if you poke your nose around a few corners, you can also find local artists drawing and painting original pieces. They'll even sign them before rolling them up for you to take home if you ask politely.

≡ FAST FACT

Actor-director Michael Douglas has an estate on the Spanish island of Mallorca near Valdemossa. This town so enchanted him that he opened a cultural center there called Costa Nord. A visit to the center can be part of cruise-ship excursions.

Gibraltar

Though located at the tip of Spain, Gibraltar is actually a British colony. It may be a giant rock, but its geographic location makes it one of the most fought-over pieces of land in all the world's history. Gibraltar guards the entrance to the Mediterranean Sea for all ships coming from the Atlantic Ocean and from the African mainland less than nine miles away. Soldiers trampled its shores for centuries, but today it is tourists who descend from near and far in an effort to climb high above sea level and take in the views.

Excursions will take you by cab (often without air conditioning) or on foot up to the top of the rock, where you can take keepsake photographs of Catalan Bay.

TRAVEL TIP

If you plan to walk to the top of Gibraltar, bring a solid pair of hiking boots. The climbing can be difficult, with rough surfaces in places. You will surely survive, but your favorite old sneaker soles might not.

Hikes to the top of Gibraltar typically include a stop at the Ape's Den, which Barbary apes and tailless monkeys call home. An officially designated Officer of the Apes feeds them each day at 8:00 A.M. and 4:00 P.M., if you want to watch. This is definitely a great excursion if you have kids—as long as you are prepared to field questions about why they can't get their very own pet monkeys to bring back to the ship.

France

There is perhaps no other country on Earth that embodies romance the way France does. The country seems to ooze pleasure in everything it offers visitors, from fine wines to luscious cheeses to mesmerizing works of art by none other than the master of impressionism, Claude Monet, who painted his famous series of water lilies at a house outside of Paris in a town called Giverny.

The smell of fresh-baked baguettes fills the air in France like deliciously starchy oxygen, and the pastry confectioners challenge even the finest chocolate chefs in Switzerland. (Dr. Atkins and his low-carb cronies must have loathed the French!) The Cote d'Azur on the country's southeastern shore, from St. Tropez all the way to the Italian border town of Menton, has perhaps some of the most famous see-and-be-seen beaches in all the world. Indeed, if you're looking to pamper your body and soul, France is the place for you.

River Barge Cruises

An increasingly popular cruise option in France is aboard small barges on inland rivers. Germans have been vacationing on river cruises for decades, but only in recent years have companies started reaching out to lure English-speaking travelers off the coasts and into the heartland of Europe. It's an enticing option if you prefer smaller crowds and towns that have not yet completely sold themselves out to the tourist masses.

In France, the river barges offer trips to the world-famous wineries of Bordeaux; up the Rhone and Saone rivers to the charming cities of Lyon and Dijon; through the famed Loire valley; along the Seine to Paris; and several combinations that take you through these places and beyond into Germany and the Netherlands. Medieval castles and Roman monuments are often part of the scenery, often less crowded than those along the coast where bigger cruise ships visit. Many river-barge trips are all-inclusive (except for airfare) and provide local wines and cheeses aboard, along with guided excursions.

TRAVEL TIP

If seasickness has been a problem for you when cruising in the past, consider a barge cruise through the rivers and canals of France, where the water is much calmer. Though there will be no shows or shops aboard your boat, you will still have plenty to see and do ashore.

These barges are much, much smaller than traditional cruise ships, taking as few as six or as many as fifty passengers. The cruises, therefore, take on a much more personalized feel—if you're traveling as part of a family reunion, for instance, your party may be the only one on the boat. The prices can be comparable to those aboard premium cruise ships, with some of the inclusive barges running from about $1,700 to $5,000 per person for a week's vacation (again, not including airfare). If you travel during the shoulder seasons in April or late October to early November, you can save as much as $1,000 on the higher-priced cruises.

Many barges offer themed itineraries, with everything from murder mystery cruises to golf trips and antiques vacations. European Waterways Limited advertises "painting and art" barge cruises through Burgundy and Provence, where passengers receive easels, art supplies, and instruction both aboard and at local artists' workshops along the river. Wine-themed cruises are, of course, a mainstay of barging companies in France, including Uniworld and Viking

River Cruises. Check with the companies' Web sites or with your travel agent for other options.

As with regular cruise ships, river-barge companies allow you to select either round-trip schedules or one-way itineraries that begin in one city and end in another. The latter is best if your goal is to see as much of the countryside as possible. Many people say that the most picturesque river cruises in France are on the Nivernais and Briare Canals in the Burgundy region, and the Canal du Midi in the South of France.

Bordeaux

Bordeaux, long considered the wine capital of the world, is on the Garonne River. It is accessible during river-barge itineraries and as part of traditional cruises run by companies including Crystal Cruises, Oceania, Radisson Seven Seas, Seabourn, and Swan Hellenic.

Bordeaux is a big city, with 650,000 residents, and in places is sagging visually under the pressure of the metropolitan grind that cities all over the world seem to fall beneath from time to time. Still, the local businesspeople understand the value of tourism's dollar, and they are working to spruce up the city through renovations and cleanup efforts.

⹀FAST FACT

The countryside that surrounds the city of Bordeaux in France is said to produce more than 70 million new gallons—and to sell close to a billion new and aged gallons—of wine each year.

Many of the chateaux around the city are open for tours and tastings. Families often run the smaller wineries, where you can expect five-star taste but not five-star service. This is not necessarily a bad thing—what better way to appreciate a fine red wine than by discussing it with the man who actually grew the grapes?

The bigger, more famous wineries are worth a visit but have a more touristy feel. Examples include Chateau Mouton-Rothschild, Chateau Lafite-Rothschild, and Chateau Margaux. You'll be among the crowds here, for certain.

If you'd rather stay closer to the boat, you can often find local wine shops that have collected the best of the region's bottles for you to sample and take home. This is a nice alternative on rainy afternoons, when you might be more comfortable hosting your own private tasting back on the ship instead of tramping through the soggy vineyards.

Calais

Calais is in northwestern France, just across the Strait of Dover from England. It used to be a medieval walled town with a moat and canals surrounding it, but the action it saw in both World War I and II flattened many of its historical buildings. Still, you can enjoy glimpses into the past, such as a thirteenth-century watchtower that stills stands as if on guard. Today, of course, the many ships and ferries that call on this port have no pirates or soldiers aboard; they are full of commerce, eager to make their way inland and up the Rhine River.

Honfleur

Up the northwestern French coastline from Calais is Honfleur, also on the English Channel. It's a fishing village that tourism is quickly beginning to usurp, but a walk through the cobblestone streets will make you feel like you're in Old Europe as it existed decades ago.

The harbor is arguably the prettiest part of town, though the center is also charming—if ever more crowded. A nice option here is a horse-and-buggy ride around town, a way of seeing the place that you may not find at other ports on your itinerary.

Le Havre

Le Havre is yet farther up the northwestern French coastline, a gateway to many exciting excursions in France including the D-Day beaches of Normandy and Paris, the City of Lights itself. Most cruise ships recommend using Le Havre as a jumping-off point for inland exploration. You can take day trips to Giverny and see the lily ponds that Claude Monet so famously painted, or climb to the top of the landmark Eiffel Tower in Paris, or catch a glimpse of the *Mona Lisa* at the sprawling Louvre museum.

 RAINY DAY FUN

Calling this excursion "fun" is probably a stretch, but "fascinating" sure fits the bill: The Landing Museum at Normandy tells the story of the historic D-Day assault that paved the way for Allied victory in World War II. It's a great way to spend the day with older kids who are open to learning a little during vacation time.

Le Havre is at the mouth of the Seine River and does offer some interesting sights of its own. The Granville Abbey and St. Adresse Fort keep visitors busy, and there are several museums in town. If you only have one day here on your itinerary, though, skip the local sights and head inland. If you're traveling with someone who has trouble walking or traveling on land, this would be a good port for her to stay aboard and enjoy some of the ship's services and activities.

Nice

There is more to see and do in Nice than you could ever accomplish in an entire month—nineteen museums and galleries, thirty-two historical monuments, and acre upon acre of parks, gardens, ornamental lakes, and fountains. That's not including the sea and sun, wild nightlife, and palaces that epitomize luxury on the French Riviera. And—if you happen to be cruising during the wintry off-season in the Mediterranean—the famed Carnival of Nice draws a million visitors with concerts, parades, fireworks, and more. Oh, yes, and there are also day trips to nearby Monaco and Cannes, home of the Grand Prix and annual film festival, respectively. Whew!

Nice is a busy city, even on the beaches. Expect crowds and occasionally long waits for tables near the harbor. If you're traveling with children, you'd be wise to pack a snack from the ship to tide them over.

St. Tropez

Like many other cities on the French Riviera, St. Tropez pulls in celebrities and billionaires with more force than the best Hollywood agents and sweetheart deals. You'll want to bring your best nightlife outfits to wear to the clubs, and don't be shy on the beaches—skin is definitely in. Actually, that's good advice for after-hours, as well. Dress to impress if you're getting off the boat to mingle ashore.

A nice daylong excursion away from the fashionistas in St. Tropez is to Port Grimaud, which is full of picturesque canals and homes with terra cotta roofs. It was built atop 160 acres about thirty years ago by architect François Spoerry, who was born there. Grimaud offers all the charm of Provence with much fewer crowds. This is a nice option if you're on a honeymoon, for instance, and would prefer a romantic stroll to a walk in the more crowded city.

Villefranche

The full name of this town is Villefranche-sur-Mer, so named because its harbor is perhaps one of the most beautiful in all of the Mediterranean. It's just two miles east of Nice, but a world away in terms of crowds. Yes, Villefranche sees its share of tourism, but it's nothing like Nice in the high season of July and August.

The colorful buildings that line the harbor are a vision in pastel, postcard-perfect if photography is one of your hobbies. You can sometimes come upon a flea market in the streets, with everything from family china to brand-new throw rugs.

For more organized adventure, check out the Citadel. It was built to protect the harbor in the late 1500s, and it is still a popular place to explore. It contains two art museums and some works by Picasso and Miro.

≡ FAST FACT

The harbor at Villefranche is one of the deepest in the Mediterranean, as much as 3,300 feet deep in some places. That's more vertical space underwater than a lot of mountains take up in the sky, and it makes maneuvering easy for cruise ships.

From Villefranche you can take an excursion to Saint-Jean Cap Ferrat, where a villa decorated with more than 5,000 artworks of Baroness Béatrice Ephrussi de Rothschild is open to the public. It's like stepping into the world of aristocracy, straight from the beach, and makes for a nice air-conditioned excursion during cruises in the hot summer months of July and August.

Monaco

Ah, to be one of the beautiful people. That is the thought that will cross your mind after you step ashore in Monaco, one of the world's foremost playgrounds for the rich and famous. Consider that the docks here boast private yachts that are longer than U.S. football fields, and you'll begin to get the picture of just how elegant and moneyed the place is. The Grand Casino is like a magnet for men who have made their fortunes elsewhere and headed off in search of new and exciting competition among their peers from the rest of the world. Oh yes, not to mention a place where they have to pay no income tax should they choose to settle down and stay.

On your cruise-ship itinerary, Monaco will often be called Monte Carlo, a name that sparkles with Mediterranean chic like the world's most flawless diamonds. Excursions here can include a day trip to Eze, a beautiful stone-walled city whose former living spaces have been converted into shops and restaurants. Eze is definitely self-aware when it comes to its tourism charm, but not so much that you feel the place has been "Disneyfied."

JUST FOR PARENTS

> The Grand Casino at Monte Carlo is the place to learn the difference between English and European roulette. The English version uses color-coded chips for each player, has additional ways to bet, and limits the number of seats at the table.

If you want a little less tourism and a little more authenticity, consider the excursions that take you farther away from shore to the old fortified town of St. Paul de Vence. Here, too, merchants cater to the tourists, but there are enough artisans still struggling for originality that you'll be able to find a truly one-of-a-kind souvenir to take home. Silk scarves, pottery, and burled-wood cheese boards (with matching knives) are good choices that you may not find elsewhere.

Italy

Italy is like a cultural bridge between Paris and Athens, offering as much romance and culinary delights as France plus all the history and archaeological treasures of ancient Greece. Its landmarks are known the world over, from the Colosseum in Rome to the Leaning Tower of Pisa, and its foods are adopted favorites in many American restaurants. (What would Super Bowl Sunday be without pizza?) To indulge in a bowl of fettuccine bolognaise with a room-temperature, no-label house wine after a sunny day of people-watching and shopping along the streets that surround Rome's famous Spanish Steps— it's an experience you will remember for a lifetime. Or, at least, until you cruise on to Venice and see the colors and reflections that have inspired artists there for centuries.

Ravenna

Ravenna, south of Venice in northeastern Italy, is the gateway to the region's capital, Bologna. It's often the first port of call on cruises that depart from Venice, or the next-to-last destination on cruises that end in Venice. Though Venice is better known the world over for its beauty, Ravenna has architectural points of interest that you will find nowhere else on the planet. Don't skip your chance to go ashore here. It's a terrific day of touring.

The mosaics that adorn Ravenna's Byzantine tombs and churches are heralded as being among the most beautiful in all of Italy, with colors that will mesmerize you and histories that will intrigue you if you take the time to learn about them at each site. Some date from the fifth and sixth centuries. If your cruise ship offers excursions with local mosaics experts, take them. You will find much more beauty and meaning in the pieces you see ashore.

≡FAST FACT

The reason that the mosaics in Ravenna have survived so many centuries is because they were built using *smalti*—small, glossy, multicolored, opaque glass and marble cubes that were cut individually and laid atop an underlying design.

A lesser-known attraction in Ravenna is jazz. Though musicians play this style of music in Ravenna year-round, the second half of July is when worldwide jazz aficionados arrive in Ravenna for jam sessions. If you happen to be cruising during that part of the summer, it will be worth your time to stay ashore and catch a little music after dinner.

Rome

Rome in a day, as the saying goes: You can do it when your ship docks here, as long as you have a good pair of walking shoes and a hearty appetite.

The place to start—as soon as it opens to avoid the crowds—is the Colosseum, the sports stadium inaugurated in A.D. 80. Built on the site of Nero Caesar's private land, it was created to give a bit of Rome back to the people, with seats for more than 50,000 spectators who could watch gladiators—the star athletes of their time—do battle *a la* Russell Crowe in the recent feature film. You can walk around the Colosseum alone simply by paying the entrance fee, but you'll have a far better experience if you pay the extra couple of euros for the guided tour. They start frequently to keep groups small, and they are led by archaeologists who bring to life all the history that is literally crumbling from the walls and arches. You will learn as much about construction as you will about civilization's past on this tour. It's mesmerizing.

If you're a fan of keepsake photographs, leave a little extra time for your family to wander around the perimeter of the Colosseum. You'll run into paid actors dressed as gladiators who will hold their swords high and pose with you for pictures.

After the Colosseum, the next can't-miss spot in Rome is Vatican City. Even if you're not religious, you will be awed by the sheer grandeur of St. Peter's Basilica. It took 150 years to complete, with input from none other than the master artist Michelangelo himself. The Sistine Chapel is also here, but be aware that the frescos Michelangelo painted on the barrel-vaulted ceilings are a massive tourist draw. The last admissions to the chapel and to the Vatican museums are midday at the latest, so get in line before lunchtime if you want to get inside.

TRAVEL TIP

If you want to blend in with the locals in Rome, dress up a bit. Wear shoes instead of sneakers, slacks instead of shorts. Italian people are well known the world over for being among the best dressed, even when simply making a quick run to the corner store.

Finally, after a leisurely afternoon full of pizza, pasta, and wine, finish your day with some people-watching at the Spanish Steps. The fountain beneath the steps is a traditional meeting place for Romans, and the streets around it are lined with shops that give Manhattan's Fifth Avenue a run for its high-end money. Versace, Gucci, and all the other designer names you would expect are here, often with sales clerks who appear to be guarding the store entrances from the masses. If you can take a little time to look around, you will find more affordable keepsakes such as scarves and boots—a full season before they will arrive in the United States and become available to your friends and neighbors.

Sicily

Sicily is the island that the Italian mainland appears to be "giving the boot"—providing for an endless array of Mafia jokes. Messina, just three miles off the mainland on Sicily's northeast corner, is the port where cruise ships tend to dock. An earthquake in the 1900s killed 84,000 people and destroyed much of the Old World architecture, but the reconstruction of the past century has created a charming blend of classic and new styles. There has always been a strong Greek influence here, adding to the charming ambience.

Mount Etna, Europe's largest active volcano, is two hours from the pier. You can get 8,500 feet above sea level—the mountain itself is more than 11,000 feet high—and even walk around some of the craters. Be careful here if you are prone to altitude sickness; some people find it difficult to breathe so high above sea level. Also be careful if you chose scuba diving as an excursion during a previous day on your cruise. The altitude change, without a proper rest period after your dive, can lead to a painful—and possibly fatal—case of the bends.

Mount Etna's most recent eruption was in 2003, preceded by eruptions in 2001 and 1991 through 1993. Though scientists are of course watching, there is no way to tell when Etna will again spout lava and steam—making your visit all the more exciting.

Messina itself was built with a typical city grid system, so it is easy to get around if you want to enjoy a day of leisurely walking versus hiking up the mountain. The Norman cathedral, rebuilt painstakingly after the earthquake, is arguably one of the most beautiful on the entire island.

 TRAVEL TIP

> If you plan to take an excursion to Mount Etna, pack layered clothing and rugged shoes. The temperature drops substantially as you make your way upward thousands of feet, and the terrain of dried lava can be so harsh that it will chew through sneaker soles.

A charming day trip from Messina is to the town of Taormina, to the south on Sicily's eastern coast. With just 11,000 residents, this is a sophisticated resort town that woos everyone from authors to royals, especially during its annual summer film festival in July and August.

The shopping and sunbathing are terrific, as are the medieval sites where architectural treasures are beautifully preserved. You will feel you have found a quiet little gem of a town in this place, and so it is very much worth stepping ashore for a look around.

Venice

Venice, forever treasured in the hearts and works of romantic artists and writers, is a city best visited on foot. You will find nooks and crannies and buildings and views by walking around that you would never see during a bus tour—visions that have inspired every-one from Byron to Cezanne. The port city itself is looking its age, but the decay only adds to its charm, like wrinkles on a beautifully aging face.

St. Mark's Cathedral is a popular excursion here, with extensive discussions outside the building because guides are not permitted to lecture after they step indoors. The glass showrooms never disappoint, with craftsmen you can watch and samples of beautiful Venetian art that you can take home as souvenirs.

≡FAST FACT

The city of Venice, Italy, has 150 canals and an incredible 409 bridges. The city itself is built on 117 small islands, making it unique and one of the most beautiful in all the world.

Gondola rides are also in order in Venice. If romance is part of your vacation plan, this is the place. You can even ride aboard boats where you will enjoy a serenade under the starry night sky. Thinking of proposing marriage? There is no better backdrop!

CHAPTER 10

Eastern Mediterranean and Northern Europe

FAR FROM THE ROMANCE of Rome and the diamonds of the Cote d'Azur, you will find an entirely separate version of Europe. The eastern Mediterranean is a world unto itself, with its strong Greek heritage and Arab influences, while the cruising areas around northern Europe boast long-standing, history-rich cities, and towering fjords as enchanting as any you'll see in Alaska. If you've been to the Mediterranean Sea and believe you've seen all there is of Europe, think again.

Croatia

Croatia has become quite the boating hot spot in recent years. Cruise ships and even private yachts are flocking to its shores, with guests enjoying the yet-to-be-fully developed coastline and the virtually endless island groups alongside it. Now that the region's political situation has stabilized, Croatia is a pleasure to visit during a summertime vacation.

On many cruise-ship itineraries, Croatia is sandwiched between visits to Italian and Greek ports—which is perfect, because then you get to see a bit of something different between the lands that tourism has been building up for years. Much of Croatia and its port city, Dubrovnik, was shelled during the early 1990s when the Bosnians, Croats, and Serbs were at war, but buildings and shops are being rebuilt and restored to the point where the atmosphere is downright cozy on many of the narrow city streets.

Bigger ships usually dock at Gruz Harbor, a Dubrovnik suburb that's about a fifteen-minute cab ride from the old city, while smaller ships can drop anchor in Old Harbor, right at the center of the old city.

Dubrovnik

Dubrovnik is a medieval city, still encircled by a wall. The wall is more than eighty feet tall in some places and runs a full mile and a half around, with stairs at two different points that you can climb on your way to walking the wall itself. Be sure to bring your camera; the views of the Adriatic Sea are simply spectacular. If you should slip and stumble while making your way toward one of the sixteen towers along the wall, don't worry—you can buy an over-the-counter pain reliever at the pharmacy next to the Franciscan Monastery. The drug store opened way back in 1391 and is still dispensing aid today.

≡FAST FACT

While Croatia has many lovely beaches, the locals tend to sun themselves and go swimming from the flat rocks along the city's wall. You can try this yourself during an excursion on some cruise lines.

The most talked-about beach in and around Dubrovnik is called Sunj, and it is accessible during excursions on some cruise lines. Seaside cafes line the waterfront, making for a lovely day off the boat in the sun and surf, and a nice alternative to the architectural tours for families traveling with hungry children.

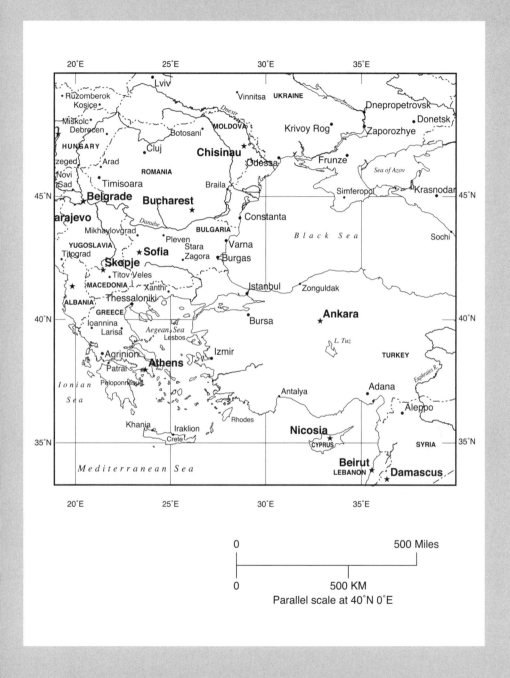

0   500 Miles

0   500 KM

Parallel scale at 40°N 0°E

Greece

History, archaeology, mythology—all of it is embodied in Greece. From the sprawling city of Athens to the island chains that dot the Aegean and Ionian seas, Greece offers an unparalleled opportunity to explore the foundation upon which human civilization was built.

Cruise ships stop in several portions of this sprawling country, from the major port city of Piraeus at the foot of Athens to the Turkish-influenced Rhodes all the way east, and back again to the deep blue waters of Mykonos—smack in the heart of the Aegean Sea between Greece and Turkey. Some itineraries are focused almost entirely on the Greek Isles, while others make Greece one among many stops during a round-trip European cruise from as far away as, say, Barcelona, Spain.

No matter how you cruise to Greece or which parts of it you explore, each of its many islands is as enchanting as the next, and life throughout the sea-sprawling nation is about slowing down and exploring every bit of it that you can, starting with Athens.

Athens

This sprawling, dusty, congested city got a seaside makeover in 2004, when the Olympic Games returned to their birthplace. The local trains that assist bus lines in moving the millions of residents and tourists around also received an update, making public transportation a good way to get around town nowadays. Walking is fine, too, but if you are a woman traveling alone, it's wise to walk with crossed arms. Groping is not uncommon on the streets near the port of Piraeus.

Most visitors to Athens begin at the famed Acropolis, which has something in common with Seattle's Space Needle or the St. Louis Arch: it's always crammed with tourists trying to get to its top. Scaffolding will scar your view of the Acropolis more often than not, with seemingly constant work required to keep the ancient ruins from becoming, well, ruined. You can actually get a better view (and better pictures) of smaller—and often beautifully preserved—acropolises on the outer islands. The one on Aegina, for instance, known as the Temple of Aphaia, is an hour-and-a-half ferry ride from Piraeus, the port of Athens. If you have the time and don't want to mix with the crowds, it's a good bet.

 TRAVEL TIP

In Greek, the word *yassos* (YAH-sos) means both hello and goodbye, like *aloha* in Hawaiian. Use it when entering and leaving souvenir shops, and you'll be sure to see the proprietors crack a smile.

If you do visit the Acropolis in Athens, leave extra time to walk the grounds of the nearby Greek Agora, an ancient communal gathering place, as well as the nearby district known as Monastiraki. This is the old Turkish quarter, which still has a bazaar where you can find everything from silverware to old coins displayed in flea-market style. It's a wonderful place to get lost in a daydream while sifting through treasures that have graced local homes for years, and that you can bargain down to a good price if you fancy them as souvenirs. If you're a golfer, you can find old Turkish, Greek, and Romanian coins here for a few U.S. dollars that will make excellent ball markers (and conversation starters) out on the links back home.

Rhodes

Rhodes is one of the most charming of the Greek Isles, nestled south of the Turkish coastline and renowned as the capital of the Dodecanese chain. The beaches are beautiful and the island is majestic in its history—including the Palace of the Grand Masters, built by the twelfth-century Order of the Knights of St. John of Jerusalem, who took oaths of poverty, chastity, and obedience and then set out to help the sick, defend the church, and struggle against infidels.

The Old Town on Rhodes has a Turkish Quarter with an Asian atmosphere and many Byzantine churches that have been converted to mosques. Nearby is the Jewish Quarter, which also feels

Asian and where you can stop at the Square of the Jewish Martyrs, named in memory of several thousand Jews who were deported from Rhodes.

Thessaloniki

Thessaloniki is the capital of Macedonia, the sprawling northern part of mainland Greece that borders Albania, Yugoslavia, and Bulgaria. Thessaloniki prides itself on its cosmopolitan shops and restaurants, but it also has an interesting Old City, with Byzantine churches that are every bit the architectural equals of their counterparts in more touristy cities.

JUST FOR PARENTS

Ouzo is the favored drink in Greece. It's clear like vodka but has a strong aftertaste that many people associate with black licorice. If you want to enjoy it without enraging your taste buds, ask for a glass of ice water on the side. Even the locals often mix a little water into their ouzo to dilute its potency.

Excursions in Thessaloniki can include a day trip to the ancient city of Pella, where Alexander the Great was born. This is a terrific educational opportunity if you are traveling with children in Greece, which is often called the cradle of civilization.

Other Islands

You could spend a lifetime in Greece and still not see all of its islands, but cruise ships are now stopping at a few that offer glimpses at the evolving cultures on either side of the mainland. Two examples are Corfu, off northwest Greece in the Ionian Sea, and Mykonos, which is part of the Cyclades chain between Greece and Turkey.

Corfu

Corfu is known as the Emerald Isle, with stunning gardens at its Achilleion Palace and a virtually untouched landscape that you can tour during off-road excursions. A day in a rented four-wheel-drive vehicle will take you through the gorgeous mountain terrain to villages that tourists frequently don't even know exist. Have your camera ready for the zigzagging turns up Pantokrator Mountain, know as Little Switzerland for its steep climbs and breathtaking views.

Mykonos

If you only get one day to visit the beach during a trip to the Greek Isles, make it the day that your ship stops at Mykonos. Go a step further and bring yourself a small basket of local treats such as olives, pistachios, and cheese; there's nothing like a Greek beach picnic to get you into napping mode during your vacation.

 TRAVEL TIP

Pack a snack when taking a day excursion from Mykonos to Delos. The latter is uninhabited, with only one cafeteria where you can find food. Having your own snack will help you avoid the lines on the busiest tourist days.

Should you want to get more culture than skin color from your visit, consider a thirty-minute boat excursion to Delos, the birthplace of Apollo, god of the sun. The site includes a museum with a scale model of the entire city, and beautiful mosaics and wall paintings that once graced the villas of the city's richest inhabitants.

Northern Europe

Southern Europe and its Cote d'Azur drip with white-sand beaches and beautiful people that lure snowbirds like a lighthouse beacon, but across the continent to the north is a cruising destination that offers something different—rich history, magnificent fjords, and Old World grandeur. The names of the cities alone on the port-of-call roster inspire a feeling of nostalgia for a bygone era: Copenhagen, Stockholm, Amsterdam, Berlin. A cruise to northern Europe may not be right for sun-worshippers, but it's an unparalleled delight for anyone who wants to sample some of the greatest ports in the history of civilization itself.

Cruises in this region run on a variety of itineraries. Some are entirely within the confines of the Baltic Sea, whose boundaries include Denmark, Germany, Sweden, and Russia, while other itineraries include travel through the North Sea off the coast of England and even the Norwegian Sea, which separates Norway and Iceland.

Of course, your experience will vary depending on which area you choose. The Norwegian Sea, for instance, includes scenic cruising alongside dramatic natural fjords, while the city of St. Petersburg, Russia, offers extraordinary man-made historic opportunities ashore. You can drink a few rounds and sing along with the locals in the pubs in Ireland, or enjoy the breathtaking views of northern Germany as you cruise through the massive Kiel Canal and its locks.

RAINY DAY FUN

If you're cruising with kids to Copenhagen, Denmark, take some time aboard the ship to read them stories by Hans Christian Andersen, such as "The Ugly Duckling," "The Emperor's New Clothes," and "The Princess and the Pea." When the ship pulls into port, you can take a family excursion to the Andersen Museum.

No matter which itinerary you select, you are likely to have a stop at one or more of the region's treasured cities. Don't miss the chance to go ashore and explore; you'll find more interesting architecture and history here than almost anywhere else in the world.

St. Petersburg, Russia

Talk about being built on the foundations of history itself. St. Petersburg, Russia, began its existence in 1703 as a fortress created by none other than Peter the Great. You can feign royalty in this western Russian city while touring palaces constructed under the watch of Catherine the Great, or you can be one with the people as you stand in the Palace Square where citizens gathered to rally during the Russian Revolution in 1917. It's hard to escape the sense of history all around you in a nation that has undergone such dramatic political changes—and that is still making headlines as it continues its transformation. If you're hoping to expose your older children to a little bit of history as it relates to current events, this port of call is an excellent choice.

An excursion not to be missed in St. Petersburg is the Hermitage Museum. It is in the heart of the city on the River Neva and comprises six buildings and more than 3 million works of art. That's not a typo: 3 *million* works of art. You can see pieces from collections that date to prehistoric times, the early nomads, and ancient Greece and Italy, as well as paintings from masters such as Leonardo da Vinci, Henri Matisse, and Pablo Picasso. As with the Louvre in Paris and the Metropolitan Museum of Art in New York City, the Hermitage offers far more than you could ever expect to see in a single day. Ask your ship's excursion coordinator for a museum brochure so you can plan in advance which collections you will focus on during your limited visiting time, and so you can see which touring exhibits happen to be open while you're there.

☂ RAINY DAY FUN

The Hermitage Museum in St. Petersburg, Russia, offers special programs, seminars, and tours for preschool-age children through young adults. Check for details with your ship's excursion coordinator, or get the details in advance of your trip from the museum's Web site at ✐ *www.hermitagemuseum.org.*

Other possible excursions in St. Petersburg include city tours that walk you through the political history of Vladimir Lenin and his Bolshevik party, an evening of watching the St. Petersburg ballet, or tours of palaces with beautiful gardens and fountains. If you're military-minded, don't miss the St. Petersburg Artillery Museum and the memorial ship *Aurora*, a 418-foot floating museum that, during her service days, fired the shot that signaled Russians ashore to begin storming the palace in the nation's revolution.

Stockholm, Sweden

The buildings of Stockholm stretch across more than a dozen islands, earning this waterside landscape the nickname "City of Bridges." If you are able to book a cabin with a private balcony, you'll surely use it during the approach to Stockholm. More than one visitor has been known to compare the scenery to a more populated version of Alaska's spectacular Inside Passage.

Once you make landfall, the excursion options will seem nearly endless. Museums are plentiful in Stockholm, including the interesting and unique Nobel Museum, which showcases the ideas of Nobel Prize winners. It's a great stop right in the middle of the Old Town, known as Gamla Stan, which has cobblestone streets lined with restaurants, cafes, and shops.

Some cruise ships will allow you to cruise the waterways that link Stockholm's islands as a half-day excursion aboard smaller boats. Other possible day trips include a visit to the Ice Bar in the

Nordic Hotel, where everything—even the seats—is made of ice. It's a great photo op for your souvenir scrapbook, and you don't even have to worry about being cold. Warm fur ponchos and mittens are available on request.

Amsterdam, Netherlands

Amsterdam is a city where several cruise-ship itineraries start or end, which is nice because it has a major international airport and plenty of hotels. You'll need both if you want to see more than the top layer of what this fantastic city has to offer during your usual single day in port. If you really want to see the best of the city's attractions, consider adding an extra twenty-four or forty-eight hours in an Amsterdam hotel on either side of your cruise vacation.

≡FAST FACT

You might be surprised to find yourself in the tropics during your visit to Amsterdam—that is, if you take a few hours to explore the Tropenmuseum. Its focus reflects Holland's longtime ties to (and lordship over) Caribbean and Indonesian islands.

You can take advantage of plenty of excursions in Amsterdam, including windmill and cheese-making tours (it doesn't get much more homegrown than that!) and more museums, such as the one devoted to Vincent van Gogh. If you're willing to leave the organized tours behind, consider arranging a private trip on your own to the Anne Frank House. No organized tour groups are allowed in this tiny home, so you'll be on your own, but the visit is as powerful as the diary of the scared young girl who captured the world's attention after World War II.

Eastern Europe

While you may find Greece and Croatia on the itineraries of western Mediterranean cruises, they are sometimes considered part of the Eastern Europe cruising experience—which extends to the Turkish city of Istanbul and beyond into the Black Sea. Far fewer cruise ships travel to these spots than to northern and southern Europe, but there is plenty to discover here, as well.

Istanbul, Turkey

Culture, culture, culture. It's hard to think of anything else when you're in Istanbul, the Gateway to the East, whose influences include Christians, Muslims, Turks, and Persians alike. Perhaps the most significant historical landmark is the Hippodrome, which the Romans built for chariot races around A.D. 200, and most of which is now, unfortunately, gone to parkland and buried beneath a paved road. You can see what's left before going next door to tour the famous Blue Mosque, which is named for an interior wall treatment that comprises more than 20,000 blue tiles. You can sometimes see the mosque's minarets from your cruise ship porthole; they're the high, slender towers with balconies where criers used to stand and call down prayers to the people below.

Another don't-miss excursion is to Aya Sofya, a museum that was once considered one of the greatest cathedrals in the world. Its marble and mosaics are exquisite, but what really will drop your jaw is Aya Sofya's nearly 100-foot dome.

═FAST FACT

Before the Ottoman empire overtook the city of Istanbul in 1453, it was known as Constantinople, the capital of the civilized region that stretched from Europe all the way into Asia.

Istanbul (like Athens, Greece) is often used as the beginning or ending port on an Eastern European cruise, so if these sights are more than you care to fit into one day of exploring about town, consider staying an extra night or two at a local hotel before or after your cruise.

Sevastopol, Crimea

The Black Sea doesn't have the size or cache of the Mediterranean Sea to its west, but this body of water on the nape of Russia's neck is surrounded by interesting ports that are worth a look. One is Sevastopol, whose biggest attraction is the Panorama, a 5,000-square-foot painting called "The Defense of Sevastopol" that occupies the majority of an entire circular building. Created in 1905, the Panorama depicts the Russian perspective of the battle of Malakhov Hill, which took place during the Crimean War in the mid-1800s. Most of what you will view is the original artwork, though some sections had to be restored from photographs after the painting caught fire during a German bombing run in 1942.

CHAPTER 11

Alaska, the Panama Canal, and Costa Rica

WHEN THE NEARLY 600,000-SQUARE-MILE territory known as Alaska became the forty-ninth state of the United States in 1959, it brought with it about 6,600 miles of spectacular coastline to explore. Icebergs, glaciers, and fjords that climb thousands of feet toward the sky combine to create a landscape that is among the most breathtaking in the world, all just two and a half hours by plane from Seattle, Washington. If you like the idea of adventurous sightseeing but would rather head south to a warmer locale, consider the Panama Canal or Costa Rica. There, instead of icebergs, you'll find towering rainforests full of monkeys and sloths.

Alaska

The cruise market in Alaska has exploded in recent years. On a typical Saturday and Sunday in August, when temperatures are at their seasonal high in the 60-degree range, no fewer than fifteen ships set sail for Alaskan ports that stretch from Ketchikan all the way north to Anchorage. Some leave from western U.S. cities on round-trip itineraries from San Francisco and Seattle, while others start inside Alaska's borders and head northbound or southbound on one-way trips. All are packed with tourists hoping to catch a glimpse of humpback whales, spawning salmon, and icebergs whose peaks peek out of the water like blue-tinted diamonds.

Your first bit of business in planning an Alaskan cruise is to decide just how much time you actually want to spend in Alaska. If you prefer to spend a few days at sea enjoying the restaurants, casinos, and other amenities that cruise ships offer, your ideal itinerary is probably round-trip from the mainland United States. A ten-day cruise from San Francisco, for example, typically includes two full days at sea with a stop in between at the Canadian city of Vancouver, British Columbia, on your way to Alaska, and then two back-to-back days at sea cruising on your return to San Francisco after you leave Alaska. In total on an itinerary like this, you'll get about four days in different Alaskan ports, less than half your total time aboard. A typical seven-day itinerary from Seattle is similar, with only three of the cruising days actually in Alaska. The rest of the cruise is devoted to activities and dining aboard your ship, perhaps with a stop in Victoria, another city in British Columbia.

═FAST FACT

Southeast Alaska, where cruise ships operate, is the feeding ground for the North Pacific's largest concentration of humpback whales. Nearly 400 of them come to feed between May and early October. You can watch them breach high into the air before slapping their tails into the sea with a thunderous clap.

Other itineraries are one-way, usually embarking up north in either Whittier or Seward, Alaska, or down south in the Canadian city of Vancouver, British Columbia. These trips will afford you more time off the boat in Alaskan ports. A seven-day itinerary from Vancouver north to Seward, for example, includes five full days in the Great Land state. Compared with the ten-day round-trip itineraries embarking from Seattle or California, this typical seven-day cruise is shorter, with more days actually spent in Alaskan destinations—and less time spent enjoying the amenities aboard your ship.

It's an important distinction that will help you decide which cruise ship is right for you. If you'd rather spend more time aboard relaxing and enjoying the scenery from a deck chair, choose a round-trip itinerary aboard a ship with the most amenities you can afford. If your goal is to see as much of Alaska as possible, with excursions on a daily basis, you can save money by considering a one-way trip aboard a cruise ship that lacks extra game rooms and the like, since you won't have long periods of downtime at sea to use them anyway.

≡FAST FACT

During the cruising season in July, the average temperature in Anchorage, Alaska, is 58 degrees. That average temperature drops to just 16 degrees each January—when you'd be hard-pressed to find a cruise ship anywhere near the city.

No matter which type of itinerary you choose, most of your Alaskan cruising likely will take place along the Inside Passage, which is more than 1,000 miles long and part of the Gulf of Alaska. The Inside Passage, which includes the cities of Ketchikan, Sitka, and Juneau, is so named because it allows ships to pass north and south "inside" the Alexander Archipelago instead of "outside" in the open waters of the Pacific Ocean. Cruising between the mainland and this archipelago is important for comfort under way, with calm waters instead of massive waves rolling into your ship from across the Pacific Ocean in Asia.

Gulf of Alaska

Perhaps the most exciting thing about the Gulf of Alaska is that it contains many of the world's biggest glaciers. One that cruise ships often get close enough for guests to see is Sawyer Glacier, in the part of the Inside Passage known as Tracy Arm, southeast of Sitka. Though the water is very deep, big cruise ships can't get very close to Sawyer Glacier because it is almost constantly calving, or breaking off into chunks. The biggest chunks are, of course, icebergs, but far more pieces break off that are much smaller and end up littering the water like debris on a highway. To get around these "bergie bits," cruise ships load you and other passengers into much smaller excursion boats, which can make their way around the frozen floating obstacles the way a slalom skier would maneuver around a course of buoys.

To see and *hear* a glacier calve is a humbling, awe-inspiring experience. The ice in Sawyer Glacier, for example, is made of water that froze a good thousand years ago. Gravity and time have compressed the ice into a sprawling block the length and width of a river and the height of a city building. The ice is so compact that it is without air bubbles, like a flawless diamond. Only instead of being clear, the ice looks like opaque blue glass—so dense in some places that it cannot absorb the color spectrum's indigo rays and thus reflects them back with all the glitter of a sapphire jewel.

≡FAST FACT

The fjords that you can cruise through in Alaska are sometimes more than a thousand feet deep, with mountains towering several thousand feet above the water's surface on each side. In some places, you can actually see skid marks along the sides of the mountains where glaciers carved their way through the land.

You can imagine the geological stress that must be required to break off a chunk of such a spectacular natural creation—and you will be able to hear it from your cabin's balcony or the ship's deck as you make your way toward Sawyer Glacier. It sounds like the roar of a lion projected over thousands of stereo speakers, and it is one of the greatest memories most people have after a cruise through the Gulf of Alaska.

Yet all this wonder is still just one part of most cruise-ship itineraries. You will also get to enjoy stepping ashore to see some of the local towns such as Ketchikan, Juneau, Sitka, and Skagway. Some of the culture is so void of the commercialism that stretches from California to New York that you may have to remind yourself you are still in the United States.

Ketchikan

Ketchikan is the place that more Tlingit, Haida, and Tsimshian people call home than any other town in the state. The native culture here is superbly preserved, with the world's largest collection of totem poles as well as cultural centers and museums where you can learn about the history of the area and its residents. Excursions here can be a wonderful opportunity to explore the evolution of a specific region with your children.

If you want a little more adventure, excursions in Ketchikan also include watching black bears feed in the salmon-rich streams of Tongass National Forest. During spawning season in August, salmon literally jam themselves into the rivers like sardines, sometimes to the point that they cannot swim over riverbed rocks during low tide. The black bears know this and gather by the sides of the rivers like hungry diners in line at a buffet, scooping up armfuls of the fish at a time to satiate their hunger.

 TRAVEL TIP

Be aware that the animals you can view in Alaska are in their natural habitat, not in a zoo environment. Leaving your group to follow bear tracks, while perhaps an intriguing idea, is actually very dangerous. You could end up scaring a bear and being mauled or even killed.

Other excursions in Ketchikan include a coastal drive to a rainforest sanctuary, where you might catch a glimpse of a bald eagle swooping down to collect scraps of salmon that bears have left behind, or get a chance to go crabbing for the local breed, Dungeness, and enjoy a feast of your catch later in the day.

Juneau

Ships have been cruising into Juneau regularly since 1881, when a steamship brought supplies once a month to the quickly expanding gold-mining camps. Alaska's capital city, Juneau, is named for Joseph Juneau, one of two prospectors who discovered gold here in 1880. The gold-mining town grew into the city that today includes a bustling port lined with everything from fur shops to salmon canneries. Whether you want to shop, eat, or explore, you'll be able to find a day trip that suits your tastes in Juneau.

You can tour what was once the world's largest gold mine during an excursion from your cruise ship—you even get to wear a hard hat and pan for gold yourself. Or, if you prefer to take in more of the scenery and get away from the crowds, you can use Juneau as a base for hikes, helicopter rides, and whale-watching cruises aboard smaller boats.

The hikes usually include views of towering waterfalls, soaring eagles, and majestic valleys carved out by glaciers, while the helicopter rides can include actually landing on a glacier where you can walk around and take pictures.

 JUST FOR PARENTS

Be sure to check with your cruise line about excursions that include helicopter rides to glaciers where you can walk around. Often, children younger than eight or ten years old are not permitted to accompany you on these day trips.

Whale-watching is a hit-or-miss excursion; the locals joke that it's more like "water watching with a few whales thrown in if you get

ALASKA, THE PANAMA CANAL, AND COSTA RICA

lucky." If you take the chance, you may be rewarded with a glimpse of these spectacular creatures, which can grow to about fifty feet long and weigh thirty to fifty tons. Capturing a photo of a humpback breaching is incredibly difficult, even for professional photographers, so don't be shy about buying existing souvenir photos if you want a keepsake from this type of excursion.

If you're an angler—or have an interest in becoming one—you should pass on all of the above and instead take a seaplane excursion to a stream or estuary for an afternoon of fly-fishing. Depending on the season, you will be casting for salmon or trout. Either way, you will be away from the crowds in a quiet, private piece of the countryside. Alaska law requires you to get a fishing license for a nominal fee, and usually this detail is taken care of as part of your cruise-ship excursion. If you don't notice a reference to the license in your cruise-ship materials, be sure to ask about it.

Sitka

Sitka, the former capital of Russian Alaska, is the only big city on Baranof Island, and it still reflects the culture of its former parent nation. The area was actually home to a community of Tlingit Indians before Alexander Baranof, manager of the Russian-American Company, built an outpost there in 1799 and helped his employer become the planet's most profitable fur trader.

Today in Sitka you can enjoy Russian folk dances and see the icons at St. Michael's Russian Orthodox Church, or you can get to know more about the wildlife that has brought humans here for centuries. Along with fur seals, this includes birds—and the Alaska Raptor Center in Sitka is Alaska's foremost bald eagle hospital and educational institution. It treats as many as 200 birds each year and helps to educate visitors about the birds' needs and environment.

Other excursions in Sitka include riding in a semisubmersible craft to see the wildlife beneath the ocean's surface, exploring a salmon hatchery to see how the fish are raised, and mountain biking for experienced riders along rolling terrain and up to spectacular views that are well worth all the pedaling.

☂ RAINY DAY FUN

In Sitka, ask the shore excursions director aboard your ship about the Alaska Raptor Center's "Passport to Raptors" program. It was created to enable children to learn about eagles, falcons, hawks, and owls. Kids can touch and compare bones and feathers, and make their own booklet with a keepsake photo of themselves.

No matter which excursions you choose, keep an eye out for black and grizzly bears. They have plenty of wilderness land to call home and usually stay away from people, but it's wise to be aware of your surroundings, especially if you head into the island's unpopulated interior.

Skagway

Skagway is tucked up at the tip of the Lynn Canal in the northern part of the Inside Passage. This is where the Klondike Gold Rush took place, eventually bringing enough people to the area that it required the creation of the Yukon Railroad. Today, just 800 or so people live here year-round—but you'll be among the more than 700,000 tourists who stop in for a visit.

The big draws are the Klondike Gold Rush National Park and the historical district's false-front buildings, which date from the gold rush days that took place during the last millennium turn of the calendar. Some of the excursions play into the history of the place, with guides who regale you with tales of the local barflies and prospectors as if they were still walking on the streets today.

≡ FAST FACT

The White Pass and Yukon Route is one of the world's only narrow-gauge railroad systems. The railcars run on tracks that are only three feet apart.

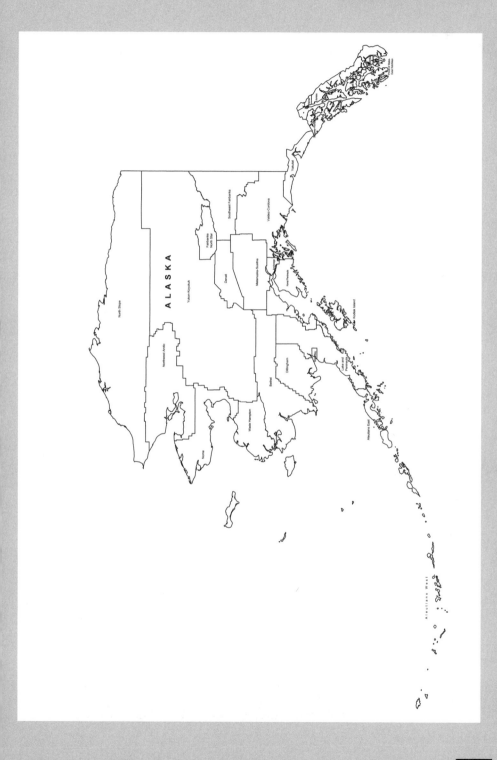

Exploring the road less taken was a hallmark of gold prospectors, and if you're twenty-five or older with a passport, you can do the same during excursions in Jeep Wranglers that head up into the Yukon Territory across the Canadian border. If you'd rather move at a slower pace, horseback excursions are available in Skagway's valleys. (Be sure to check age requirements here, too; children younger than fourteen are usually not allowed.)

The really fun transportation of choice here is the railway itself, which you can ride all the way to White Pass Summit on the United States/Canada border. Your train will curl like a snake around impossibly tall mountains, leaving you breathless from the view. Some of the train excursions are all about sightseeing, while others incorporate stops at historic mining camps and towns. If you are traveling with children, the latter is likely to be more interesting for them.

Panama Canal: Gateway to Central America

The Panama Canal is one of the world's dream boating destinations. It is simply fabulous to be able to say that you have cruised through the eighth wonder of the world—a canal that took the United States ten years to finish carving across the Continental Divide, at a shared cost with the original developer of more than 30,000 lives and nearly $400 million. That's a hefty sum, considering the project began in 1904.

If that's not enough, a trip to the Panama Canal usually includes even more than your chance to learn about this historical route. As you cruise from the Atlantic Ocean to the Pacific Ocean, or vice versa, you usually will have port stops that enable you to explore a bit of Costa Rica, a country full of beautiful beaches and monkey-filled rainforests that, because of its lack of a standing army, is often dubbed "the Switzerland of Central America."

Central America

Let's face it. If the news presented by the U.S. media is anything even close to accurate, Central America isn't exactly what you might consider a typical vacation destination. From the streams of poverty-stricken immigrants surging across the southern U.S. border to the seemingly endless military skirmishes in Nicaragua to the covert operations during the 1980s between the U.S. government and Panama's General Manuel Noriega, you've likely given very little thought to how pretty, interesting, or enchanting parts of Central America might be.

In fact, there are many lovely vacation destinations there, from the scuba diving resorts in Belize to the white-sand strips along the shores of Costa Rica. You would be more than safe to think of these places as the good neighborhoods in what is often portrayed as a bad town by many evening newscasts.

The Panama Canal is one of those good neighborhoods, one that knows it can do well for itself by appealing to tourists from around the world. It is as unique and impressive as the Grand Canyon, in some cases more so when you consider that it was not entirely created by nature. True, the towns around it are not wealthy or built up like resort destinations, but the views along the canal are spectacular and well worth seeing from aboard a ship where you will feel safe about yourself, your family, and your belongings. The Panama Canal is easily one of the top ten destinations in the world, where there is no better way to enjoy the view than by boat.

≡FAST FACT

The nation of Panama did not officially regain control of the Panama Canal until 1999. Former U.S. President Jimmy Carter attended the ceremony even though, in a continuation of historically chilly relations between the two countries, no senior U.S. officials joined him.

Cruises to the Panama Canal generally come in two varieties. The first are round-trip and usually ten-day itineraries from Florida, during which you'll likely stop at Caribbean islands, including Grand Cayman and Jamaica, and possibly a port such as Cozumel on Mexico's Atlantic coastline. During these cruises, you may not actually transit the entire length of the Panama Canal. You will get to cruise inland and stop at a port (likely Colon, a relatively poor city on the Atlantic side), so you will definitely get a feel for the canal's beauty and be able to say that you have been there. You can also book excursions aboard smaller boats to get farther across the canal than your cruise ship goes if it does not complete the crossing.

Your second Panama Canal cruising option is a one-way itinerary—say, from Fort Lauderdale, Florida, to Los Angeles, California, or vice versa—during which you will transit the entire length of the canal and stop at ports in both the Atlantic and Pacific Oceans such as the Bahamas, Aruba, Curacao, Jamaica, and Mexico's Acapulco and Cabo San Lucas. These itineraries must be at least fifteen days long to accommodate the expansive distance you will travel, and the bulk of your trip will be spent in destinations outside of Panama or at sea. The main characteristic that sets these one-way itineraries apart from round-trip cruises is the complete crossing through the canal versus a peek inside before you turn around and head back to your ship's port of origin.

On either style of itinerary, it's worth considering an upgrade to a cabin with a balcony or perhaps booking aboard a cruise ship that offers more balcony-style cabins than others at reasonable rates. Perhaps the most exciting part of cruising through the Panama Canal is the scenery. It goes on and on and on—unlike the scenery you see, for example, during the hour or so when you cruise into a port and dock. You will want a comfortable perch from which to watch the sides of the canal go by with an unobstructed view, as the odds are good that you would get tired of craning your neck to see around the crowds that gather along the main deck railings.

💼 TRAVEL TIP

If you have a solid month to spend at sea and want to transit the Panama Canal, consider Holland America's thirty-day itinerary from Los Angeles, California, to Tampa, Florida. You'll see parts of Mexico, Grenada, Brazil, Barbados, and scenery along the equator. Rates for 2005 start at $5,700 and run to more than $14,000 per person.

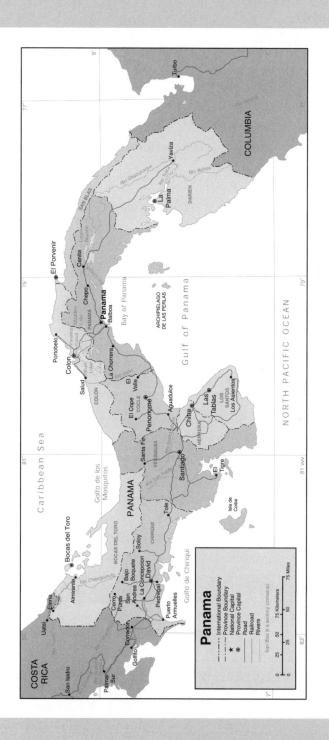

Panama

International Boundary
Province Boundary
National Capital
Province Capital
Road
Railroad
Rivers

San Blas is a territory (comarca).

0   25   50   75 Kilometers
0   25   50   75 Miles

COSTA RICA

COLUMBIA

Caribbean Sea

NORTH PACIFIC OCEAN

Gulf of Panama

Bay of Panama

Golfo de los Mosquitos

Golfo de Chiriqui

ARCHIPELAGO DE LAS PERLAS

Isla de Coiba

BOCAS DEL TORO

CHIRIQUI

VERAGUAS

COCLE

COLON

PANAMA

SAN BLAS

DARIEN

HERRERA

LOS SANTOS

Turbo
Yaviza
La Palma
El Porvenir
Canita
Chepo
Panama
Balboa
Portobelo
Colon
Salud
La Chorrera
El Valle
El Cope
Penonome
Aguadulce
Chitre
Las Tablas
Los Asientos
Santa Fe
Santiago
El Tigre
Tole
Soloy
Bajo Boquete
David
San Andres
La Concepcion
Cerro Punta
Pedregal
Puerto Armuelles
Corredor
Golfito
Palmar Sur
Uatsi
Elena
Almirante
Bocas del Toro
San Isidro

Panama

Excursions when you get to Panama are varied. There are tours that will have you hiking up steps for bird's-eye canal views before a trek through lush rainforests, as well as walkabouts into the heart of Panama City's Old City and day trips in dugout canoes to an Embera Indian village. If you prefer to ride with more modern comforts, you can take an aerial tram above the rainforests or a journey aboard the Panama Canal Railway.

The transcontinental is actually a pretty interesting option if you are traveling with children or elderly grandparents who might have a tough time negotiating the steps on the walking tours. Built in 1855 and restored in 2001, the railway has air-conditioned cars and dome ceilings with observation windows. During your train ride, you will see the same rainforests as other cruise ship guests who choose to walk, but you will do so while sitting down and listening to a tour guide. Not a bad deal at all.

☂ RAINY DAY FUN

If it happens to rain during the day your ship docks at the Panama Canal, consider a tram ride or an excursion on the Panama Canal Railway. You'll still get to see the scenery, and you'll stay dry along the way.

If you're an angler, consider a bass-fishing excursion on the man-made Gatun Lake, which serves as a freshwater connector between the Atlantic and Pacific oceans. The species you'll be hoping to hook is the peacock bass, known locally as *sargento*. The name derives from the word "sergeant," so chosen because the canal variety of peacock bass has four stripes instead of the usual three. (Why it's not called "captain bass" with those four stripes is a mystery of designation that you'll have to sort out with your cruise ship's skipper.)

Your fishing excursions in the Panama Canal will likely be catch-and-release, so don't get your hopes up about bringing dinner back to the ship. Still, you can expect a really fun day on the water. The species is known to put up a good fight after it chomps down on the bait.

A cruise to the Panama Canal will include stops at many other ports. Most of those are covered in other chapters of this book, except for a jewel of Central America known as Costa Rica.

Costa Rica

Costa Rica is to Central America what the Apollo Theater was to Harlem, New York, in the neighborhood's older, more notorious days—a place so packed with culture and beauty that you simply don't want to miss it, no matter what's going on all around its borders.

For starters, the nation boasts a countryside that is simply gorgeous. Rolling green mountains, rivers churning through tropical rainforests, beachside tropical dry forests filled with capuchin and howler monkeys—this isn't a Disneyland built for tourism. This is a countryside into which you can venture after spending a morning soaking up some rays on the beach. It is unlikely you will ever forget hiking along the dry dirt paths just off the coast and coming face-to-face with white-faced capuchins like the one in the classic Indiana Jones movie *Raiders of the Lost Ark*. To hear another species called howler monkeys off in the distance, roaring even louder than theme park roller coasters, is both unsettling and fascinating. And the rivers that cut through Costa Rica, such as the Pacuare, are fantastically full of rapids. A ride downstream is pure thrills and excitement in a towering setting of waterfalls and lush forests. With a good guide, the experience can be the thrill of a lifetime.

Cruise ships typically dock at Puntarenas or nearby Caldera, which are on Costa Rica's Pacific Ocean side, tucked into a protected harbor called the Gulf of Nicoya. Your ship will likely pull into one or the other, but not both.

Caldera

Though Caldera and Puntarenas are only about ten miles apart geographically, the cruise lines seem to differentiate them by offering different styles of excursions at each port. In Caldera, Costa Rica's biggest Pacific Ocean port, the day trips tend to include coffee plantations, an active volcano, and a biological reserve where you might get a chance to see parrots, toucans, and even a three-toed sloth in the canopy of trees.

≡FAST FACT

Forget about shopping for knickknacks and furniture back in the States. Costa Rica's artisans carve everything from bowls to doors from a variety of woods so beautifully different they are like a rainbow of colors on a palette. Some souvenirs, such as kitchen cutting boards, are crafted from a combination of local woods, making them appear striped.

Excursions to the reserve tend to be less physically taxing than those to, say, Poas Volcano, where you can see one of the largest craters on the entire Earth and learn about the different kinds of lava that flow during an eruption. If you are prone to altitude sickness, skip the latter trip and perhaps opt for a day of touring the sprawling valley city of San Jose, Costa Rica's capital. You'll feel better and will get to see a good deal of the pretty countryside during your ride inland from the port.

Puntarenas

The port of Puntarenas traces its modern history to the mid-1800s, when oxcarts filled with coffee made their way from the inland mountains to the shore in preparation for shipping abroad. Today, some of Costa Rica's most tourist-friendly beach resorts are here offering sun, fun, and (no doubt) a really good cup of joe first thing in the morning.

If you want to get the airline portion of your vacation over in a hurry, consider starting your Panama Canal cruise in Puntarenas or Caldera in Costa Rica. You'll see more than you would on a round-trip itinerary from the United States, and your cruise ship's last port of call will probably be in the States—home sweet home.

Excursions in Puntarenas lean toward ecotourism, with horse-back riding and river rafting among the highlights. The rafting is a must-do activity if you have even so much as a pinkie full of adventure in your bones. Serious whitewater rafters come from all over the world to run Costa Rica's rivers. Because the country is one of the world's rafting capitals, tour operators are first-class, with fun-loving, knowledgeable guides. Even if you're a first-timer who doesn't know when to paddle, you'll have the time of your life crashing through rapids and floating quietly beneath waterfalls for an entire afternoon. It is truly an activity not to be missed for those who enjoy a bit of excitement and an unpredictable ride.

JUST FOR PARENTS

You can enjoy Costa Rica's whitewater rafting excursions on rivers that range from class one (for beginners) to class five (for experts). If you are traveling with children, do not expect them to be able to handle the upper classes. In many cases, safety restrictions will preclude them from even stepping aboard the rafts.

If you'd rather stay dry, there are rainforests to explore—some by air-conditioned tour bus and others on foot while crossing suspended cable bridges. The lushness of the scenery can't be overstated. You'll rarely find such deep, thick greens outside of a 1970s shag carpet, and many of the rainforests are home to spectacular waterfalls that induce more neck craning than anything you've experienced at your local air show. The smell in these forests is one of the finest memories you'll have. The air is so clean and fresh, it makes you wonder exactly what you're breathing in back home.

CHAPTER 12

The Rest of the Americas

BEYOND ALASKA, THE CRUISING grounds of North, Central, and South America offer unparalleled opportunities to see everything from lava-spewing volcanoes to colonial history's roots to the finches that led Charles Darwin to articulate his theory of evolution. That's quite the gamut, of course, especially when you consider that your airline flight to the ship might be far shorter than one to a more exotic locale that offers less to see. Don't overlook the Americas as a great cruise destination—they have something for everyone.

Hawaiian Islands

Hawaii is like Alaska in that it offers all the benefits of being on U.S. soil yet has all the exotic atmosphere of a faraway land. It is, quite literally, a faraway land—about 2,500 miles southwest of mainland North America at its closest point. Though there are dozens of islands in the entire archipelago, six main islands host the vast majority of tourism business: Oahu, Maui, the Big Island (Hawaii), Kauai, Lanai, and Molokai.

Unless you want to focus on a single location in the islands, a cruise ship is actually the best way to explore Hawaii. While you can take short hopper flights from island to island while staying at resorts on shore, you will see at least as much and spend quite a bit less if you follow the same itinerary by boat (and you'll only have to unpack once). Even better, you can scout out your favorite places in case you decide to return someday for a land-based holiday.

 **TRAVEL TIP**

It's much easier to get around Honolulu, Hawaii, by foot than it is by car. If you arrive a few days before your cruise and want to take in the sights, skip the rental car. You'll find your way to the best tourist spots faster.

Pearl Harbor is the most famous attraction in these islands. The Arizona Memorial Visitors Center commemorates the 1941 attack by Japanese warplanes, and you can visit the U.S.S. *Missouri*, aboard which the Japanese eventually signed surrender papers and ended World War II.

As interesting as Pearl Harbor is, most people visit Hawaii for its natural beauty. You'll find plenty of it, whether you enjoy fun in the sun, ecological tours of volcanic craters, or views of verdant mountains that tower higher than skyscrapers. Most cruise lines offer a variety of such excursions from island to island, so if you want to see it all before saying your final *aloha,* that's definitely an option.

Canada and New England

Charming lighthouses, craggy shorelines, buttery lobster (or "lobstah," as the locals say), and major points of U.S. historical interest—these are the things that make a cruise through New England and its northern neighbor, Canada, so enticing. The weather here during the summertime months is downright delightful, and nowhere else on Earth will you experience firsthand a better on-the-water view of working lobstermen and commercial fishermen returning from sea.

Classic ports in the heart of New England include Boston, Massachusetts, and Bar Harbor, Maine, but some cruise lines will begin or end your itinerary as far south as Philadelphia, Pennsylvania, or as far north as Quebec City in Canada. There are often stops in New York City, as well, or across the Hudson River in New Jersey within a short ferry ride of Midtown Manhattan and the Statue of Liberty.

RAINY DAY FUN

If your cruise ship docks at Cape Liberty Cruise Port, across from Manhattan on the New Jersey side of the Hudson River, you can take the kids to the nearby Liberty Science Center. Exhibits include everything from demonstrations of how light moves through the eye to a look at the science behind the creation of ice cream.

Cruising in this part of North America is a pleasure because you'll enjoy a nice mix of picturesque shoreline landscapes and bustling cities. You can do round-trip itineraries, but you'll see far more sights on shore if you book a one-way cruise. In some cases, one-way weeklong cruises go all the way from Quebec City down to Fort Lauderdale in Florida, with one or two New England stops along the way. This obviously isn't a good choice if you want to see as much on land as possible, but it is a fantastic option if you are from Florida and want to be dropped off practically at your doorstep when the cruise itinerary ends.

There are many well-known and beloved New England ports of call, including the summertime retreat of Martha's Vineyard in Massachusetts and the charming cobblestone city of Portland, Maine, but three of the best stops that you should make every effort to see are Boston, Bar Harbor, and Quebec City.

Boston, Massachusetts

Get out your 2004 World Series Championship baseball cap and prepare for the time of your life—Bostonians are flying high now that the Curse of the Bambino is finally over, and the city will likely ride for years on the ecstatic feeling. There has never been a better time to visit the Cradle of the American Revolution, where you can become one with the Red Sox Nation at Fenway Park and learn a whole lot about your own nation's history, to boot.

Boston is awash in historical significance, much of which you can learn about as you walk the Freedom Trail from Boston Commons to the home of Paul Revere, which throughout its long existence has served as a tenement, candy factory, and grocery store. Just think about the people who have called this ocean-side city home: Samuel Adams (son of a brewer), John Quincy Adams (son of a president), and Henry Cabot Lodge (known as a son-of-a-you-know-what for the way he hounded corrupt politicians). Few places in the world have given birth to so many important historical figures.

If you get the chance, choose an excursion that includes a tour of the city by way of a DUCK—a refurbished amphibious World War II landing vehicle. You can cruise through the streets of town without missing an inch of Bunker Hill or Copley Square, and then hold on tight as your guide drives right off the road and into the Charles River for a cruise along the Boston and Cambridge skylines.

≡FAST FACT

The DUCK amphibious vehicles that are now used to give land-and-water tours in Boston, Massachusetts, are the same variety of machine that delivered fully 40 percent of supplies to soldiers on the beach during the Normandy invasion during World War II.

If you prefer a quieter afternoon, consider an excursion to Boston's Museum of Fine Arts. In addition to works by Claude Monet and Pierre-Auguste Renoir, the museum boasts a fine collection of paintings by Winslow Homer, who is best known for his seascapes of Maine's coast. You can decide for yourself whether the area has changed as your cruise ship makes its way from Boston up north to the Pine Tree State.

Bar Harbor, Maine

The first thing you need to do is learn how to pronounce the name of this charming Maine town: It's "Baah Haabuh," unless you want the locals to sniff you out as a tourist based on your accent. Surrounded by the beautiful Acadia National Park, Bar Harbor has long been a destination of choice for well-heeled New Englanders in search of summertime homes. Folks by the last name of Rockefeller, Astor, and Vanderbilt still walk the streets today, and the harbors are always filled with classic sailing yachts heading in and out from luncheon cruises. The sights and sounds along the coast may just be enough to inspire you to take up oil painting.

Acadia National Park itself is arguably the best excursion in town, with its natural rock formations and hand-cut stone bridges. Then again, if you're not into nature, the charming boutiques in town will call to you like ranchers herding sheep. You'd be hard-pressed to find more unique clothes and quaint knickknacks anywhere else along the New England coast.

Quebec City, Quebec

Au revoir, New England, and *bonjour* French Canada! Quebec City is often the first or last stop on a one-way New England-Canada cruise, since it marks the meeting point of the St. Charles and St. Lawrence rivers. It's a spot the city has grown into beautifully during the past 400 years, making it one of the oldest cities in all of North America. Given its age, Quebec City has much history and culture to offer, but it also has a hip, younger side—with music and arts festivals that continue from spring straight on through to late fall. No matter when your ship docks here, you're bound to discover something special going on ashore.

Excursions here include a ride to the top of the 2,600-foot-tall Mont Ste. Anne, sometimes aboard a horse-pulled sled; a look at the nearly 300-foot cliff that spills the Montmorency River over and into the St. Lawrence below; and a walk through the cobblestone streets and alleys in the Old Town—a World Cultural Heritage Site and the only fortified city north of Mexico that still has standing walls. With so much to see and do in this charming Canadian city, you might consider staying in a hotel for an extra day or two if your cruise-ship itinerary starts or ends here.

≡ FAST FACT

On July 3, 2008, Canada's Quebec City will celebrate its 400th anniversary. It is one of the oldest cities in all of North America, having survived from the days when its influence stretched all the way down to what today is known as Louisiana on the southern United States border.

Mississippi River

It's hard to imagine a modern cruise ship plying the Mighty Miss; it just doesn't feel right having anything but a white boat with a red paddlewheel cruising past the landmark Gateway Arch in St. Louis, Missouri. Luckily, steamboats are still in action, just as they have been since the early 1800s here on the Midwest's greatest waterway. If Huck Finn were alive and sitting on the shores of the Mississippi River today, he might not even notice a difference in the cruising ships beyond the fact that they've gotten bigger.

The Delta Queen Steamboat Company promotes itself as having the only genuine paddle wheelers available for three- to eleven-day trips here (or anywhere else in America), and reviews from previous ship passengers are good. The company's boats run from all the way north in Minneapolis, Minnesota, down the Mississippi River to St. Louis, Memphis, New Orleans, and the Gulf of Mexico. Also available are cruises along the Ohio River, with ports of call in Pittsburgh, Pennsylvania, all the way through Cincinnati to the Mississippi River. Shorter river cruises branch out to Chattanooga, Tennessee; Nashville, Tennessee; and Little Rock, Arkansas.

 TRAVEL TIP

If you enjoy theme cruises, you can find them on the Mississippi River. The Delta Queen Steamboat Company offers everything from a bluegrass jamboree to a Civil War week to a Charles Dickens holiday cruise complete with costumed characters.

Prices for the riverboat cruises are typically a bit higher than they are for lowest-rate cruise ships elsewhere, and airfare is extra. On the other hand, the boats are well maintained, the crew is all American (making communication easy), and the service repeatedly gets high marks. Chalk it up to the "You get what you pay for" theory of travel.

U.S./Eastern Seaboard

If you're a snowbird who likes to head south for the winter, you'll adore the itineraries that run from, say, New York down to the Bahamas during two scenic weeks in the fall. No other stretch of coastline in the United States compares with the Eastern Seaboard in terms of well-developed ports of call that are full of unique character and things to do, and it's hard to beat the pleasure of leaving winter in your wake along the way.

Cruise lines probably designed these itineraries with pure business in mind. They have to reposition their ships down to the southern latitudes during the winter, so they might as well get you aboard to help them cover the expenses of the trip. Nevertheless, the ships that run these routes have created a cruising experience that is perfect for people who shun the sun in favor of culture-filled city excursions. You don't need a bikini to eat a Philadelphia cheese steak; no sunscreen is required for a plate of Baltimore crab cakes, you won't get a snorkel full of water on a golf course in Charleston; and you certainly won't get sand in your toes at midnight in Savannah's garden of good and evil.

Philadelphia, Pennsylvania

Philadelphia was actually the largest city in America during the early 1800s, and it remains a major metropolitan hub on the banks of the Delaware River. The man who designed Philadelphia's streets, William Penn, still stands watch over the residents in the form of a statue atop City Hall. If you're like most visitors, you'll take a quick look up at Billy Penn before heading straight to the more famous Liberty Bell for a picture near its famous two-foot-long crack—which occurred on February 26, 1846, as it was rung in honor of George Washington's birthday.

The waterfront in Philadelphia is adjacent to the historic district, a place so packed with important U.S. sites and trivia that it could become its own Smithsonian Institute. You can visit the home of Betsy Ross, who famously sewed the U.S. flag; or Congress Hall, where the U.S. Senate and House of Representatives met in the late 1700s when Philadelphia was the capital of the United States; or Declaration House, where Thomas Jefferson drafted the Declaration of Independence after renting not one, but two rooms (hey, it was an important document). And don't forget Benjamin Franklin—you could spend a week in Philadelphia tracing his roots alone, or even flying a kite in the park in his honor.

≡FAST FACT

The bronze statue of William Penn atop Philadelphia's City Hall is said to be the tallest statue on any building in the world. Billy Penn, as the locals call him, is thirty-seven feet tall and weighs twenty-seven tons. A single strand of his hair is four feet long.

If history's not your style, you can listen for the tell-tale heart in the floorboards at the former home of Edgar Allen Poe, or take the kids for a tour of a World War II submarine at the Independence

Seaport Museum, or see what food and music has center stage during festivals at nearby Penn's Landing.

The point, of course, is that there is so much to see and do in Philadelphia that you'll have to pace yourself and make a plan of attack in advance. If you don't, you might become exhausted and miss out on all the good stuff just down the coast in Baltimore.

Baltimore, Maryland

Visiting Baltimore by ship is an experience you should have at least once—that is, if you want to be like everyone else who came to and stayed in this area during the 1700s and 1800s. The city got its start as a major port for handling grain and tobacco, and shipbuilders had more work than they could handle from the Revolutionary War all the way through to World War II. If you lived and worked in Baltimore during the first century of its existence, the odds are good you had something to do with ships.

The famous Inner Harbor has undergone a lovely restoration and now bustles with all kinds of shops and restaurants—even an ESPN Zone with more video games than kids could play in a whole day. You can climb aboard the U.S.S. *Constellation*, the last floating ship from the Civil War, or take in the rotating exhibits at the towering Maritime Museum, or see who's performing at the outdoor amphitheater right on the waterfront.

If you visit during the warmer months, don't miss a chance to see the boys of summer in action at Oriole Park at Camden Yards. The baseball stadium is less than a fifteen-minute walk from the Inner Harbor.

Charleston, South Carolina

Civil War historians mark Fort Sumter in Charleston, South Carolina, as one of the most significant sites of the devastating conflict. The state was the first to secede from the union after the election of Abraham Lincoln in 1860—with five other states joining the Confederacy during the following six weeks—but Fort Sumter, at the entrance of Charleston Harbor, remained under federal command. It would be the place where states rights versus union control became more than a battle of words, with the first shots of the Civil War being fired just off the city's shore.

Today, Fort Sumter is a national monument that you can see as your ship pulls into Charleston Harbor. You can take an excursion to walk on the grounds where the soldiers waged war and visit the museum there to collect books and other memorabilia (as nearly a million people do each year).

Charleston also offers opportunities for you to learn more about what the North and South were fighting over, at places such as the Slave Mart Museum, where slave auctions were held until 1863. Also worth a visit is the Charleston Museum, which has exhibits about the city's history as well as its maritime roots—including the skeleton of a whale.

Savannah, Georgia

It's not every day that you get to cruise into the homeport of the first steam-powered ship ever to cross the Atlantic Ocean. Savannah holds that distinction—with great thanks to the S.S. *Savannah*, of course—and stands in more ways than one as a testament to what can be achieved through thoughtful planning. The city is actually credited as being the first planned city in the United States, conceived by General James Oglethorpe after he and 120 fellow Britons made landfall from their ship, the *Anne*, and named the colony of Georgia in honor of their king back home.

Oglethorpe's careful attention to open streets and public squares makes Savannah an easy city to explore today. Heck, you don't even need to be going anywhere special to enjoy this town; the graceful examples of Southern architecture all along its streets are as pretty as any vistas you might find in other parts of the world. If you're someone who needs a bit more structure to your walking, mark your maps for a look at the King-Tisdell Cottage, the Juliette Gordon Low Birthplace, and the Davenport House.

🧳 TRAVEL TIP

Fall is a great time to cruise to Savannah, Georgia. In the month of October alone, the city usually hosts a Greek festival, a film festival, a Jewish food festival, and—of course—a bratwurst-filled Oktoberfest celebration.

Other things to do in Savannah include golf excursions, museums, and clubs that host blues, jazz, and bluegrass musicians. You can find a little bit of everything at the City Market, including art galleries, restaurants, and boutiques full of handmade souvenirs.

Pacific Northwest

The Pacific Northwest embodies a rugged spirit of individualism, whether you're talking about hikers in the San Juan Islands or brainiacs creating new computer software in Seattle. A lot of people bypass this area as a cruising ground and instead head farther north to Alaska, but this section of North America where the United States and Canada meet offers a lot in terms of wildlife and scenic views. True, you won't see towering glaciers here as you will farther north beyond Vancouver—the gateway to the Inside Passage—but the forest greens smell even fresher than they look.

Itineraries here can be as short as three days, but like Caribbean trips of the same length, you'll likely leave the boat wishing you'd had more time to explore. A week here will both put you in proximity of moose and give you an opportunity to discover the shops and sights in the lovely Canadian cities of Vancouver and Victoria in British Columbia.

Vancouver

Captain George Vancouver visited here in 1792, and even though the Spaniards had beaten him to the place, the British captain's name stuck. It's unlikely he could envision all that the city has become today, with its massive summertime festivals, suspension bridges that sway in the treetops, and terrific maritime museum—complete with children's discovery center. The major international port that exists today is guaranteed to offer you a lot more than Captain Vancouver found back in the eighteenth century.

≡FAST FACT

Before Vancouver was called Vancouver, part of the land it sits on was known as, among other things, Gastown. The origin of Gastown— still the name of the city's oldest neighborhood—is reportedly a man called Gassy Jack, who ran a local saloon in the mid-1800s.

Excursions in Vancouver include a trip to Granville Island, a small peninsula that has a huge marketplace and even a special kids' shopping section. If that doesn't get your children excited, you can take them to the nearby water park with movable cannons.

If your kids are a little bit older (or if there is an adventurous kid inside of you), skip the shopping and head to the 450-foot Capilano Suspension Bridge, which you can cross at an altitude of 230 feet in the air. That's twenty-three stories high, for you city dwellers who thought only buildings could get so tall.

Victoria

Victoria is a smaller city than Vancouver that has many charms all its own. One of the best excursions available here is to Butchart Gardens, a meticulously maintained fifty-five-acre display of colorful flowers, fragrant trees, and picturesque paths. Even if horticulture isn't your favorite pastime, you are likely to be awed by the beauty of this place.

If you're just not the type to swoon over blooms, you can stay in the city and enjoy high tea at the Empress Hotel, an Edwardian structure that has entertained celebrities for decades. (Rita Hayworth, Roger Moore, and John Travolta have all been guests.) Or you can forget the shore-side attractions altogether and head out on a whale-watching tour. There are orcas, also known as killer whales, living in these waters. Though you won't always see them, you'll have just as good a chance here as anywhere else in the world.

Mexico

The entire western coast of Mexico, from the southern tip of California all the way down to the northern edge of Guatemala, is known as the Mexican Riviera. It's been a popular cruise-ship destination for decades, at least since the 1970s, when Captain Steubing, Isaac the bartender, and the rest of the *Love Boat* crew brought Pacific ports such as Puerto Vallarta into the homes of television viewers across the United States. Other popular western Mexico destinations whose names you might recognize in your cruise-ship brochure include Acapulco, Baja, and Cabo San Lucas—the last of the three having been immortalized in the Van Halen rock song *Cabo Wabo*. Whereas in some exotic destinations you have to worry about the condition of the available ships, you need not fret here on the Pacific side of Mexico. The market is well developed, if less crowded than the one on the country's eastern coast.

While most cruise ships focus on September through May as the best season to visit the Mexican Riviera, you're likely to experience good weather and temperatures around the 80-degree mark all year round. If you don't mind a little extra heat and humidity in the middle of the summer—say, with the thermometer up in the 90s—you might even be able to find a good off-season bargain on a few of the half-dozen cruise lines that have operations here. For a family bargain during the off season, this is as good a choice as any.

Your cruise to the Mexican Riviera is likely to start in California, and you can book everything from three-day trips to itineraries that are two weeks long. The length of your trip will, of course, determine how much of the coastline you get to experience, but possible ports of call in addition to those already mentioned include Mazatlan, Manzanillo, and Ixtapa.

 ## JUST FOR PARENTS

If you're a fan of the rock band Van Halen and have an itinerary stop in Cabo San Lucas, Mexico, be sure to visit lead singer Sammy Hagar's Cabo Wabo Cantina in the heart of the city's downtown. The "Red Rocker" plays a fair amount of shows there each year with his backup band, the Waboritas, and you can sing along while sipping his personal brand, Cabo Wabo Tequila.

Mazatlan

Mazatlan is the largest port on the Mexican Riviera, and it offers everything you would expect to find by way of excursions in a warm, sunny, waterfront location—fishing, snorkeling, scuba diving, sunbathing, sailing, and even just wandering around the beach collecting shells, if that suits your fancy. If you want to get out of the sun during the hottest part of the day, Mazatlan also has a section dubbed "The Golden Zone" where you can shop for silver jewelry, belts, and other local crafts to take home as souvenirs. The shops won't all be air-conditioned, but they will offer a shaded respite from the heat.

If you have time to hop into an open-air taxicab, you can take a ride up the mountainsides and enjoy a broader view of the area from up on high—a jaunt that is especially worthwhile if photography is one of your hobbies. Other excursions in Mazatlan can include a round of golf at a championship course designed by Robert Trent Jones, Jr., or a visit to small villages where you might encounter a local baker and fresh bread from a brick oven.

Manzanillo

The town of Manzanillo gets its name from trees of the same name that were a popular choice for shipbuilding many years ago.

Today it is the busiest commercial port in the entire country, and it's a hot spot for fishermen who like to troll for wahoo, sailfish, swordfish, marlin, mahi, and giant tuna. Most cruise ships offer excursions aboard fishing boats here, and you'll rarely find more catch during a day on the water in any other part of Mexico.

≡FAST FACT

Some cruise ships offer an excursion for a round of golf at La Mantarraya Golf Course in Manzanillo. Don't be surprised if you hear about fungus overtaking many of the greens there. It happened in the mid-1990s, and by all reports the grounds crew has things well back in order—especially on the stunning island green at the eighteenth hole.

If you'd rather keep your feet on shore, Manzanillo has open-air markets called *tianguis* where you can often bargain for better prices on souvenirs than you'll find in the shops at other ports of call. Just remember that when you see dollar signs on items in these markets, they refer to pesos, not the U.S. dollar, which historically is worth far more than a single peso.

Ixtapa

Ixtapa is just four miles north of Zihuatanejo on the Mexican Riviera. You may see the port of call listed as either name on your itinerary, but for the most part, you can enjoy similar excursions no matter which local dock your ship chooses as its port of call.

Ixtapa is much more commercialized than Zihuatanejo, with luxury resorts and gourmet restaurants that were built up as part of a successful government plan to lure tourists. The resorts themselves are so nice that you can actually tour them as an excursion with some cruise lines.

The beaches are beautiful in both places, but they are arguably a bit less crowded and hectic in Zihuatanejo, a traditional fishing village that offers an almost identical view of the sunset. If you want to see and be seen, Ixtapa is the place; if you're hoping for a little solitude, head to Zihuatanejo. The split is actually somewhat ideal for parents who want a quiet day at the beach while their teenagers want to strut around in the surf.

TRAVEL TIP

In Mexico, it is considered rude for a waiter to bring you a restaurant check before you've requested it. Unless you want to sit at your table until dawn, be sure to ask for your bill well before you need to get back to your ship for departure.

Plenty of restaurants and small eateries line the beach areas in both towns, so you need not worry about getting back to your ship for meals. As a precaution against Montezuma's revenge, stick to bottled water with whatever you order (not forgetting that ice is made with local water), and skip the homemade soups.

South America

South America has interesting ports of call along virtually every part of its coastline, from the easternmost part of Brazil to the southern tip of Chile. You can start and end your entire cruise on this continent or, in some cases, cruise from Fort Lauderdale on one-way routes. Either way, you will see a continent that boasts everything from bustling cosmopolitan cities to dense tropical jungles to towering icy fjords.

Itineraries run from a few days to more than three weeks. You can choose to spend the bulk of your time at sea—say, cruising round-trip from the eastern coast city of Buenos Aires, Argentina, with a few nights' visits in Brazil—or you can see far more shore-side sights by cruising from, say, Buenos Aires down south through the Straits of Magellan and around Cape Horn, then up north along South America's western coast to Valparaiso, Chile, or even farther north to Guayaquil, Ecuador.

Some of the better ports along the way are Argentina's Buenos Aires, Brazil's Rio de Janeiro, and Punta Arenas in Chile.

Buenos Aires, Argentina

Buenos Aires is one of those cities that seem to attract the world's most beautiful, most sensuous people like a magnet. This is a city that tangos, a city that sways, a city where passion has been known to run just as deep for games of soccer as for entanglements of the heart. It is a place special enough that you should consider spending an extra night or two in a hotel if you have the opportunity and want to drink it all in.

 JUST FOR PARENTS

A fun excursion in Buenos Aires, Argentina, is to the wine-producing regions of Cafayate and Mendoza. You'll find common names on the labels, including chardonnay, merlot, and pinot noir, but also some names that might be new to you, such as chenin blanc, Torrontes, and ugni blanc.

This capital city is known as the Pearl of South America, with beautiful European-inspired architecture, including fountains and a massive clock tower. Tango and jazz bands still play at the old coffeehouse known as Cafe Tortoni, and street artists often work along Florida Street performing whatever they can to attract the interest (and tips) of shoppers and tourists. Whether you want to wander and ponder or get into the music and movement of the city, you will find excursions to your taste in Buenos Aires.

Rio de Janeiro, Brazil

If you need an even sexier stopover than Buenos Aires to satiate you, Rio de Janeiro is the place. Consider that the favorite dance here is the samba—a sort of bump-and-grind evolution of the anticipation-filled tango—and you quickly understand that Rio is called the Marvelous City for a reason.

One of the top excursions here is to the beach. The spectacular waters and soft sands are a huge draw for tourists from all over the world, many of whom come to show off their bodies in a style not unlike the parade of bikinis in Miami Beach, Florida. If you prefer substance to skin, you can hop in a tour bus and ride about a half-hour away to Petropolis, home of the Imperial Museum and the crown jewels, which are on display. There are also nature excursions for sightseeing amid the waterfalls outside of the city.

Punta Arenas, Chile

Punta Arenas is at the southern end of Chile. While the downtown offers more than enough to keep you busy for a daylong excursion, you're more likely to join the crowds and use this city as a jumping-off point for more exotic excursions beyond.

Some cruise lines offer specially organized flights from Punta Arenas to Antarctica for sightseeing amid the glaciers, penguins, and sheets of snow and ice that seem to stretch right into the horizon. You can also visit the nearby colony of tens of thousands of Magellan penguins if you'd prefer to stay on land and stick to wildlife sights alone.

═══FAST FACT

Magellan penguins are the most common species in South America, and tens of thousands of them live at a single colony near Punta Arenas. It's hard to believe that with all those birds around, the males mate for life and can recognize one another by voice.

Other excursions from Punta Arenas include a day of watching sheep-shearing at a working farm or a tour of the Torres del Paine National Park, which includes three breathtaking granite towers more than 10,000 feet tall.

Galapagos Islands

The Galapagos Islands are one of those dream destinations, a place you hear people talk about visiting just once before they die. Darwin's "laboratory of evolution" lies about 600 miles west of its parent country, Ecuador, smack in the middle of nowhere in the Pacific Ocean. Its islands are more than 90 percent protected parkland, which means many of them are nothing but black lava patches, white sand, and meticulously monitored tourist trails. In many cases, your cruise ship's dinghy will unload you directly onto a bunch of rocks—most of the islands don't even have docks, since building them would harm the environment. Keep this in mind if anyone in your party has a physical limitation; Galapagos is not the place for people who need assistance walking.

 **RAINY DAY FUN**

Before you visit the Galapagos Islands, watch the movie *Master and Commander* starring Russell Crowe. The portion of the film that takes place in Galapagos was actually filmed there, and you will recognize some of the sights, including the famous landmark Pinnacle Rock.

The reason for all this environmental conscientiousness, of course, is the animals—those giant tortoises and belching sea lions and blue-footed boobies that so fascinated the father of evolution. Nowhere else in the world can you get so close to animals in the wild, be they flamingoes or finches or three-foot-long land iguanas. With no natural predators to hunt them, and with tourists kept strictly on the trails, these animals have no fear and act as if nobody is ever watching them. You will see mothers feeding babies, mating behavior, and sometimes hatchlings being born. Ornithologists, in particular, will appreciate the innumerable birds here in their natural environment.

The difficulty with cruising in Galapagos is that its biggest cruise ships hold only 100 passengers—good for the animals and the environment, but sometimes bad for the conditions aboard. Ships based in Galapagos have a history of packing as many people as possible into limited spaces, so don't expect cruising amenities that are anything like what you'd find in Europe or the Caribbean. You will be safe, well fed, and comfortable, but there won't be any art auctions or water slides on deck. Remember that Galapagos is about seeing what's on shore; the boat is merely your ride to the action.

CHAPTER 13

Africa, Asia, and The Far East

THE CONTINENTS OF AFRICA and Asia are vast, sprawling together along the edges of the Atlantic, Indian, and Pacific oceans. The experiences you can enjoy in these places are mind-boggling in their uniqueness, from rhinoceros treks in authentic preserves to educational tours of an A-bomb museum built on the very soil where the world's largest explosion ever occurred. Whether you want the wildest of wildlife or the most potent history of human civilization, a cruise to one of these places will provide it.

Africa

There are some big-name cruise lines operating on both coasts of Africa, including Crystal Cruises, Princess, Silversea, and Seabourn. The itineraries tend to be more than a week long as a minimum (and sometimes a solid thirty days in total). This is a good thing. You'll be flying halfway around the world to begin your cruise, and you will need every last day you have to experience as much as possible.

Some Africa itineraries are almost entirely within that continent, while others hop from there across the Indian Ocean to destinations as far away as Singapore and Australia, with stops at places like the Seychelles Islands in between. Most itineraries run from Cape Town, South Africa, north along the east coast of the continent—though Silversea, for one, also offers a cruise up the western coast of Africa.

Virtually all of the cruises offered are one-way, which is again a good thing because you will get to see more ports than you would on a round-trip route.

Given the way the American media portray Africa, it's easy to envision the nations there as nothing but arid deserts full of starving, warring people. While it's true that there are some desperate areas in great need of help, plenty of African ports are well developed and eager to please in exchange for tourism dollars.

Remember, Africa is a sprawling continent several times larger than the entire United States, so it is unfair and inaccurate to paint the whole of the land with one broad brush. Cape Town, South Africa, for instance, is widely regarded as one of the most beautiful cities in the world.

JUST FOR PARENTS

The South African town of Stellenbosch, which you can visit during an excursion from the port in Cape Town, boasts more than two dozen wineries producing everything from sauvignon blanc and chardonnay to merlot, shiraz, and cabernet sauvignon.

Cape Town, South Africa

Cape Town is arguably the mariner's gateway to Africa, with cruise ships and private yachts alike pulling into port from all over the world. Table Mountain towers like a beacon from the land, where the architectural and cultural offerings are a blend of influences from native tribes and visitors from Indonesia, Germany, Britain, France, and the Netherlands. Pretty much any boat-building civilization has found its way to Cape Town, often as a last stop before casting off across the Atlantic Ocean in search of rum and sugar in the Caribbean. Today, cruise-ship itineraries often start or end here.

Excursions in Cape Town include a visit to the vineyards just outside of the city, strolls along the sandy beaches (where surfing is often quite good), a cable-car ride up the more than 3,500-foot-tall Table Mountain for a bird's-eye view of the city, and a number of museums, parks, and gardens.

The center of the city is packed tightly together, so you can easily explore all it has to offer on foot. If you have a chance, visit the Waterfront Craft Market. You'll find everything from precious gems to tacky souvenirs, along with restaurants, taverns, and cinemas—a sort of throwback to the days when the Dutch East India Company used the area as a port for its merchant ships bringing interesting goods to sell from all over the world.

Mombasa, Kenya

About midway up Africa's eastern coast from Cape Town is the nation of Kenya and Mombasa, its leading port. Mombasa is actually on a coral island that's linked by causeway to the mainland, meaning you will be able to enjoy any of the beautiful beaches and blue ocean waters that strike your interest.

If you're like most visitors, though, you'll hightail it onto the mainland and off the coast to the overland game preserves and safari lodges. This is big game country, with lions, leopards, buffalos, elephants, hyenas, cheetahs, and even warthogs. Talk to your cruise ship's excursion coordinator about day trips in open-air Jeeps and remember to bring your camera. If you have been saving up to buy a telephoto lens, now is the time. When will you be able to get so close to a rhinoceros again? (No, the zoo doesn't count.)

Asia

Asia—as defined separately from the Far East nations of China and Japan (described later in this chapter)—is slowly beginning to emerge as a popular cruising ground. Cruise lines are launching new services in this part of the world, catering in part to a new generation of American travelers who are willing to give tourism a chance in places that, for their parents, represented war and the struggle against Communism just a few decades ago. Holland America, for instance, offers cruises that pass through the Philippines as they make their way from Australia to Hong Kong, and Celebrity Cruises has plans to begin servicing itineraries in 2006 that will include Singapore, South Korea, and Vietnam. Radisson Seven Seas already has ports of call in Danang and Ho Chi Minh City in Vietnam, as well as in Laem Chabang (Bangkok) in Thailand.

═ FAST FACT

The most celebrated landmark in Cebu, Philippines, is a large wooden cross that the explorer Ferdinand Magellan left there in 1521. It commemorates the islands' first encounter with the West—and for many visitors today is one of their first encounters with the East.

Because some of the Asian itineraries are still evolving along with the ports of call, it's difficult to say exactly where your cruise through Asia might take you. You can, however, make a safe bet that you'll end up at least one night in Vietnam, Thailand, or both.

Danang, Vietnam

American troops landed in Danang in 1965 and began building a military complex that would serve troops throughout the Vietnam War. A full decade later, in the mid-1970s, the city finally began to crawl out from beneath the devastating remains of the war, and renovations hit a new stride during the 1980s. Today, the city is home to about 750,000 people and boasts two ports that make it a strong shipping hub in the region.

Excursions here focus on far more than the recent history of war, of course. Danang was actually the heart of the central Champa kingdom, which dates back 2,000 years. There are still Chams living in the region today, carrying on the Hindu and Buddhist traditions. You can visit the Cham Museum, which explores the culture, as well as view historical monuments. You also can take an excursion outside the city through the pine forests to Hue, the Imperial City of the

Nguyen emperors. There are several opportunities for scenic photography along the way.

 **TRAVEL TIP**

Be prepared to be patient when listening to your tour guide in Danang. Many of the guides learn English as a second language while living in Vietnam, and their accents can be thick and difficult to understand at times.

Ho Chi Minh City, Vietnam

Ho Chi Minh City, the largest city in Vietnam, was known as Saigon until 1975, when the Vietnam War ended and the name was changed. Today, the streets are filled with bicycles instead of soldiers, and Chinatown and its surrounding areas are abuzz with marketplace bargaining and pagodas.

Excursions in Ho Chi Minh City can include day trips to the Mekong Delta, which has a canal system designed to help sustain the farming of soybeans, rice, peanuts, and more. Some ship excursions offer you a chance to cruise in a smaller boat on the Mekong River among the local boats and everyday goings-on. If you're lucky, you might get to see rice paper and coconut candy being made.

Laem Chabang (Bangkok), Thailand

Nearly 10 percent of Thailand's residents are squished into the capital city of Laem Chabang, better known as Bangkok, which experienced startling growth well into the 1990s, including skyscrapers rising from the plots adjacent to historic buildings. The city thus has a mixed atmosphere of ancient and modern, with a heavy Buddhist influence. Canals that wind through the city led to Bangkok being dubbed the Venice of the East.

There are tropical monsoons in this part of the world, and you'd be smart to plan your vacation to avoid the flooding that often occurs.

November through February is the safest time of year in terms of weather, while June through October is the rainy season. August and September are usually the worst.

If you visit when it's dry, you'll find a lot to do ashore. The Grand Palace is a popular excursion site, with its white façade and stunningly intricate terra-cotta-red roofing. The Temple of the Emerald Buddha on the palace grounds is Thailand's holiest of shrines and includes a Buddha that's a bit more than two feet tall and made entirely of translucent green jasper (a type of opaque quartz). It sits atop a gilded altar and is changed into a different costume for each of the three seasons.

≡FAST FACT

The enshrined Emerald Buddha in Bangkok, Thailand, is believed to have been associated with several miracles since it was discovered in 1434—when a bolt of lightning struck a pagoda. Even though it's only about two feet tall, it is far more revered than the city's Golden Buddha, which is solid gold and weighs five and a half tons.

Other excursions in Bangkok include a visit to the Rose Garden on the city's edge, or a tour of the renowned Shangri-La Hotel Bangkok and its tropical gardens. The hotel is home to Chi, the largest, most luxurious spa in the country. It has a holistic focus and offers treatments such as Himalayan bath therapy, milk honey wraps, and a yin yang couple's massage.

Far East/Orient

When you think of the Far East, you think of Japan and China. Indeed, there are cruises that focus on these two countries alone, but you sometimes will get to see them as part of itineraries that include Indonesia and the Philippines, or even eastern Russia as a stopover destination between Japan and Alaska. Many cruises that include the Far East are at least two weeks long, a function of the long distance you must fly to the starting points and your need to adjust to the time zone for a few days before you can really settle in and relax. Don't think for a minute that you could do all of the Orient in a single week; you honestly couldn't do all of it in a lifetime. Two weeks to eighteen days on a cruise ship is a good first step.

Far East cruises that include Indonesia and the Philippines often start in Australia and head one-way to the northwest instead of cruising northeast to the South Pacific islands. Such trips typically include many more days at sea than on land, so be sure you book your cabin aboard a ship that offers a lot of amenities such as a health spa and nighttime shows. Unlike the more scenic destinations, you'll be happier if you invest your vacation fund in an interior cabin aboard a busy ship than in a balcony suite aboard a quiet cruiser with few social activities. By day three or four at sea, you'll be much happier having something to do instead of having a private view from your bedroom.

Interestingly, the cruises that begin in Japan and cruise one-way through Russia and across the northern Pacific Ocean to Alaska tend to have fewer days at sea than the Philippines routes. On these, the opposite logic applies: Invest in the balcony view instead of the onboard activities if you're forced to make the choice. You'll be happy you have a private veranda to sit on in your bathrobe and wool socks with a warm mug of hot chocolate once you get to the stunningly gorgeous icebergs and glaciers.

If you stay in the cruising area that includes only China and Japan, you'll have plenty to do ashore and won't have to worry so much about what kind of ship you're aboard. Popular ports of call include Beijing, Hong Kong, and Shanghai in China, as well as Nagasaki and Tokyo in Japan.

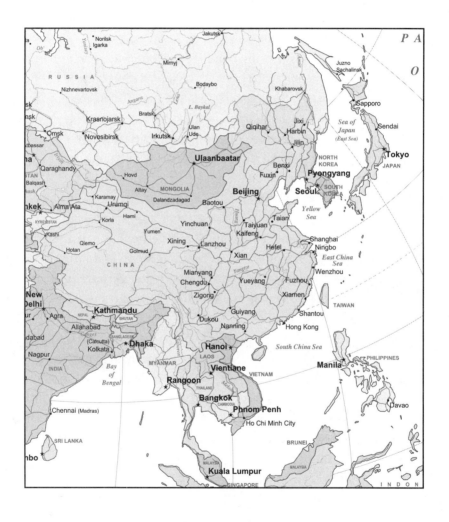

Japan

The cruising industry in Japan is far less sophisticated than its counterparts in the Caribbean and Mediterranean, but this island nation is a fascinating place to visit and is luring more and more tourists on cruise ships every year. The cities where ships make their ports of call are very modern and bursting with technology and gadgets, but some of the excursions are designed to introduce you to the culture of the less-populated regions.

Spring and fall are the best times to visit in terms of weather, though if you choose the spring, you'll likely find yourselves sharing the tourist attractions with locals who are on vacation themselves. On the other hand, the June-through-September typhoon season has been known to stretch into October, so if you visit in the fall you might end up with less-than-pleasant weather. The autumn storms, of course, are not as constant as the springtime crowds, but you should be prepared for the circumstances no matter which season you choose.

TRAVEL TIP

Japan is one of the world's most expensive vacation destinations. If you're traveling on a budget, save your shore-side dining allotment for one or two great meals instead of getting nickeled and dimed (or "yened," as it were) on snacks that you could just as easily have back on the ship.

Whenever you decide to travel, be prepared to pay retail prices when you shop and dine at restaurants—bargaining is uncommon in Japan. On the plus side, tipping is also a rarity, so you needn't worry about adding 10 or 15 percent to the bill, no matter how good the service.

Ports of call are likely to include Nagasaki, on the island of Kyushu, and Tokyo, on the southern coast of Honshu.

Nagasaki

The name Nagasaki conjures horrible memories in the mind of the world, with the city's residents having been the second victims of atomic bombing during World War II. The Nagasaki Atomic Bomb Museum is a harrowing reminder of the horror of that 1945 day—and of the psychological and physical effects that continue a generation later. Just as in the United States, the men and women who survived World War II are elderly, so the A-Bomb Museum takes very seriously its mission of preserving their recollections and experiences. A visit here feels almost morally imperative no matter how little time you have in port.

≡FAST FACT

At Peace Park in Nagasaki, Japan, you can visit the humbling Monolith at the Hypocenter—the spot where the atomic bomb fell in 1945, exploding into a fiery wave of debris that killed about 74,000 people and injured about 75,000 more.

Thankfully, the city has recovered from the physical destruction and offers charming excursion options, such as a visit to Arita for a look at local ceramics techniques. You can also take a day trip to Sakai National Park and cruise aboard a smaller boat throughout the park's ninety-nine islands, or stand atop Sakai Bridge and watch the tidal swirls as the current smashes into the nearby channel.

Tokyo

About 12 million people live in the city of Tokyo—a solid 4 million more than live in New York City. Think about the crowds at Grand Central Terminal during rush hour and multiply accordingly, and you'll quickly realize that Tokyo is about as bustling a place as the world has to offer. The neon signs that choke its landscape make the billboards in Times Square look like fanciful glints in a child's eye, and the bumper-to-bumper backups would push even the calmest taxi driver into a rage.

Nonetheless, Tokyo is a mesmerizing blur of energy, a place with a buzz so frenetic that you can't help but get sucked up into its action. For this reason, cruise-ship excursions often include general tours of the city itself, including stops at the Eiffel-like Tokyo Tower and the dominating Imperial Palace Plaza, where the Japanese emperor resides.

Other excursions include trips to the Edo-Tokyo Museum, charged with preserving the city's heritage and history, and the Ota Memorial Art Museum, which contains lovely Japanese art. If you prefer less culture and more couture, head over to the Ginza shopping district, where you can find everything from high fashion to pet robot dogs.

China

With a climate similar to Japan's, eastern China also makes an excellent destination for spring or fall cruises. There is so much to see and do that some cruise lines offer extended stopovers in cities such as Beijing and Shanghai, to give you enough time to get acclimated and take in a better percentage of the sights. If you can afford the extra time in your itinerary, take this option. Once you see all China has to offer, you'll likely want to stay even longer.

Shanghai

Depending on which source you consult, Shanghai boasts somewhere between 11 million and 16 million residents, with either number making it the largest city in all of China. It is the gateway to the Yangtze River delta, which also makes it China's leading port in terms of trade and industry. The blending of personalities and cultures is reflected in the city's offerings, which include myriad shopping styles and restaurants that serve everything from spicy Sichuan to plain ol' French fries.

Excursions from your ship will likely include a standard half- or full-day tour of the city. If your cruise line offers private tours, you should book one—and book early. It's easy to feel lost in a city this size where you don't know the language or the culture, and being in a smaller group with a guide can be as comforting as your pillow back home.

TRAVEL TIP

Trains designed specially for tourists run between Shanghai, China, and the nearby provinces Jiangsu and Zhejiang. If you have a few days in port and want to escape the city's hustle and bustle, you should ask about them at your cruise ship's excursion office.

Other excursions in Shanghai include a trip to the Jade Buddha Temple and its six-foot-high, jewel-covered centerpiece. Also popular is the Arts and Crafts Research Institute, which has more than 160 craftspeople working at any given time on traditional Chinese needlepoint, jade carving, and lantern making. If you need a spoonful of activity in your cultural sampling, you can also watch shows by legendary Chinese acrobats.

Beijing

China's capital city is gearing up to host the summer Olympic Games in 2008. Until then—as was the case in Athens, Greece, in 2004—you should expect to find a lot of sprucing up, which means scaffolding and construction.

Nevertheless, the city will continue to offer plenty of interesting sights and experiences. Beijing is, after all, the literal birthplace of the Chinese nation, where *Homo erectus* (exemplified in the fossilized Peking Man) is believed to have originated about 500,000 years ago. It has been growing more interesting every day since, and today has a cultural depth almost unparalleled anywhere else in the civilized world.

An excursion to the 250-acre Forbidden City is not to be missed. The array of temples and palaces—the most sprawling complex on the planet—was originally built for the Ming and Qing dynasties and served as the secluded imperial palace for five centuries. The Forbidden City is surrounded by a nearly twenty-foot-deep moat and a wall that's thirty feet tall. Today, the Forbidden City is a World Cultural Heritage Site that you could spend days touring without seeing even a fraction of all the treasures it holds.

≡FAST FACT

Ming emperor Yongle is often cited as the man who created China's capital city, having moved his government to Beijing in 1421. Westerners had trouble pronouncing the word "Beijing," so the city was known as Peking for many years.

What trip to China would be complete without an excursion to the Great Wall, one of the Seven Wonders of the World? Just don't expect to walk the whole thing; it stretches for more than 4,000 miles across the country.

Hong Kong

The Ocean Terminal where cruise ships dock in Hong Kong is a sight unto itself, with a pier about 1,250 feet long (the length of four football fields) and a five-story building that houses 700 shops and fifty restaurants. The terminal is within walking distance of Tsim Sha Tsui, the heart of the city and home to shops, restaurants, museums, cultural centers, and more. Bring your spending money here. You'll rarely find a better spot to dole it out for souvenirs.

Other excursions in Hong Kong can include a morning of tai chi (great exercise that won't leave you aching the next morning) or a visit to a traditional Chinese herbal shop where massages are offered. If you have two days at this port, you might consider the workout on day one and the pampering on day two.

Some cruise lines offer multi-day excursions that include a visit to the terra cotta warriors in Xian. A farmer digging a well in 1974 unearthed this virtual battalion of about 6,000 life-size clay statues that are believed to have been created as guardians for Emperor Qin Shihuang after his death. It's a mind-blowing vision that's worth the trip if you have the time in your itinerary.

CHAPTER 14

Exotic Itineraries

IF YOU'VE BEEN SAVING every penny, clipping every article, and dreaming every night about an exotic dream cruise, this is the chapter for you. Outside of the traditional cruising grounds in the Caribbean and Mediterranean, and far beyond the shores of even far-flung coastlines in Asia and Africa, there is a big and exciting world to explore—some of it without ever stepping ashore. Perhaps a transatlantic crossing is your dream vacation, or a stop in Fiji, or a cruise through the Indian Ocean. It's all available if you're willing to think "exotic" as you plan your cruise vacation.

Transatlantic Cruises

Transatlantic cruises are more about the ship itself than the destinations on either side of the Atlantic Ocean. You'll spend almost an entire week at sea, out of sight of land, and thus will have to turn inward to your floating hotel for all your dining and entertainment needs. The marketing brochures explain this with phrases like "days free of obligations," but the subtext is clear. Without a good book and a hefty list of on-ship activities, you might get a little bored.

It pays to spend a little extra and get aboard the best ship you possibly can during a transatlantic cruise. You'll have a much better time if you put your money into a ship with countless amenities and facilities—casinos, spas, shows, art auctions, and the like—than you will if you book a balcony suite aboard a vessel that offers fewer things for you to do outside your cabin. Think about it: How much fun will sitting on your balcony really be if the view never changes?

Higher-end cruise ships cater to this idea, creating new and ever-more-impressive venues to keep you entertained aboard. Cunard's *Queen Mary 2,* for instance, boasts an on-ship planetarium and cultural classes with instructors who are affiliated with Oxford University. You may not find anything that grand aboard less pricey ships, but be sure to compare amenities aboard when choosing your home away from home for such a long time at sea.

 TRAVEL TIP

If you want to spend some time in the ports where your transatlantic cruise begins and ends, add a few days onto either side of your vacation and talk to your travel agent or cruise company about booking hotels ashore.

South Pacific

The South Pacific is to Australia what the Caribbean is to Florida—a tropical playground full of islands with crystal blue waters, white-sand beaches, and swaying palm fronds. Most cruises start in the land Down Under (think of Sydney, Australia, as the Fort Lauderdale of the region) and cast off for the spectacular shorelines of Tahiti, Fiji, and beyond. Many itineraries last about two weeks, giving you enough time to leave Australia and explore a good number of islands in Polynesia, plus American Samoa on occasion.

Don't be turned off by longer itineraries in the South Pacific. While two weeks may sound like a lot in the Caribbean, consider that nonstop flying time from California to a ship docked in Australia is more than fourteen hours. By the time you adjust to your new time zone, the first few days of your trip will be over. You'll want that second week aboard to relax.

The summers and winters in Australia and nearby New Zealand occur during seasons that are opposite those in the United States; it's warm in Auckland in January and chilly during July. This, combined with the tropical climates in the islands, might make you think the South Pacific is a terrific alternative to a Christmas cruise through the Caribbean (especially if you've already done your fair share of exploring in that part of the world), but keep in mind that cyclone season typically runs between November and April. Consider cruising the South Pacific in September and October or May and June, when the big countries will be warming up and the islands will have little chance of getting pounded by storms.

If you don't mind exchanging a few days' worth of on-land exploring for a few days at sea, you can book longer South Pacific cruises—some nearly a month long—that start in Australia and end in California after a few stopovers in the Hawaiian Islands. On these or the shorter South Pacific–only itineraries, your ports of call are likely to include stops in the tropics as well as some time in Australia and New Zealand. Your ship may visit more than one destination in these countries, but almost all the cruise lines call on the cities of Sydney and Auckland.

Sydney, Australia

Sydney is a bustling, cosmopolitan city in the southeast corner of the country and continent known as Australia. Perhaps the city's best-known landmark is the Sydney Opera House, a stunning architectural achievement that is displayed in photographs with the Sydney Harbour Bridge in the background on pretty much every tourism brochure the Aussies see fit to create. It's not hard to understand their bounty of pride once you realize not just how interesting the Opera House is architecturally, but that it cost an estimated $100 million to build. That's an awful lot of shrimp on the barbey! The saga of the building's creation was so staggering that there is even an opera about it.

If you'd rather spend your time in Australia seeing what nature created, book an excursion to the Blue Mountains, a rugged strip that marks the line between the coastal region and the outback. You'll see plenty of interesting wildlife, including koalas, wombats, and kangaroos, and you can sometimes arrange for a scenic ride on a train if you would rather sit than hike up for a great view.

═FAST FACT

One of the rarest animals in the world is the hairy-nosed wombat. You may not see one during your Sydney, Australia, excursion to the Taronga Zoo, which has garden-variety wombats, but you can impress your tour guide and fellow travelers by telling them the animal is a marsupial, just like the kangaroo.

From Australia, your ship likely will either head up to the islands or cruise southeast to New Zealand, possibly for a call at the port of Auckland.

Auckland, New Zealand

The north and south islands that combine to form the nation of New Zealand boast some stunning scenery—which much of the world learned after seeing it as the backdrop for the hit movie trilogy *The Lord of the Rings*. While some cruise ships dock at Tauranga on the north island's Bay of Plenty, the city of Auckland on the Hauraki Gulf sees most of the tourism action. It has been known as the City of Sails since long before the Kiwis took the America's Cup firmly in hand, and the gulf is almost always abuzz with ships, private yachts, and sailboats whose jibs flutter in the breeze. The city itself is quite modern, complete with a sky tower reminiscent of Seattle's Space Needle that offers huge window views and even bungee jumping from its tippy top.

If your cruise ship offers an excursion that will teach you about the native Maori culture, sign up immediately. In some places, ancestors of the Maori tribesmen re-enact greetings and other ceremonies by dancing with spears and snarling at the passersby while sticking out their tongues in a show of defiance. It's all for show, of course, but it's a heck of a show. You might also get to see some of the spectacular totem-style carvings done in the Maori tradition.

JUST FOR PARENTS

You might think twice before bringing young children to watch a traditional Maori greeting ceremony in New Zealand. Tradition dictates that the Maori men look as fierce as possible—spitting out their tongues and hissing at the tourists—and the littlest kids might be more afraid than intrigued by the display.

Tahiti

Ah, Tahiti—the land of so many dreams. Yes, the nearby islands of Bora Bora and Moorea have become just as well known to traveling Americans during the past few years, but Tahiti has always been (and likely always will be) a dream destination in the minds of many. It is a particularly popular spot for honeymoons, weddings, and vow renewals, which can be done in the traditional style, with the bride being carried to the groom atop a rattan throne. Now that's something you won't find during a cruise to Antigua!

RAINY DAY FUN

The Paul Gauguin Museum in Tahiti explains all the local spots that inspired the artist's paintings, but it displays the paintings only in replica. If you want to see the original masterpieces created during Gauguin's years in the South Pacific, you have to visit museums in well-heeled cities such as New York and London.

Papeete will likely be your port of call on Tahiti, and it offers everything from sun-kissed beaches to four-wheel-drive adventures to afternoon excursions at the Gauguin Museum. If you enjoy rugged road travel and have only one day on the island, consider the four-wheel-drive excursion. The system of rugged roads on Tahiti is the largest in Polynesia, thanks mostly to the sheer mass of the island compared with others in the region. The sightseeing can take you from deep in the valleys to the highest points on the island, with views that will make you wish you had an even wider-angle camera lens.

Fiji

Fiji boasts sunsets that put even Key West, Florida, to shame. The sky fills with red like a heart full of joy, and orange and yellow streaks wave goodbye to the day as they dip into the ocean below. People who visit Fiji never forget the view overhead, which is a wonder considering how good the view is below on the beaches, as well.

Suva is the port where cruise ships call, the nation's capital on the big island of Viti Levu. Fiji itself is composed of hundreds of islands—from 300 to 800, depending on which source you consult and how you define the word "island." Viti Levu's tourism operators have done a good job of bringing the culture of the outer islands in, so you can enjoy excursions to see fire walks, wood carvings, and the creation of tree-bark cloth.

 ## JUST FOR PARENTS

In Fiji, you may be offered the traditional local drink, kava. While it won't make you feel intoxicated, it will likely calm your nerves—and perhaps even leave your tongue feeling fuzzy. Drinking just a little kava has been known to cause exceptionally vivid, and sometimes unsettling, dreams, so don't be shy about having an extra few sips.

Suva is a particularly good showcase of Fijian history, with the Fiji Museum located in the center of the city's botanical gardens. The archaeological exhibits date back as far as 3,500 years, and you can see the beautiful carvings along dugout canoes that were used for trade and warfare alike.

Indian Ocean

You can experience some Indian Ocean ports of call, such as the Seychelles Islands, during the Africa-based cruises discussed in Chapter 13. But that archipelago, along with Madagascar to its south and, farther to the east, the Maldives and Sri Lanka, are all within the boundaries of the Indian Ocean. This body of water is smaller than either the Atlantic or Pacific Ocean, but it is still pretty big—about five and a half times the size of the continental United States. And there's a lot of great stuff packed inside—from unique animal species to beaches so remote they lack a single footprint.

You can find short Indian Ocean cruise-ship itineraries that include just the Seychelles and Madagascar, while weeklong and longer trips sometimes start as far away as Cochin, on mainland India, and cruise west to the islands near Africa as their ending port. The most popular stops tend to be the Seychelles and Mauritius, a small island just east of Madagascar.

🧳 TRAVEL TIP

Sri Lanka and the Maldives were among the countries hardest hit by the tsunami that swallowed Indian Ocean coastlines in late 2004. The tourist areas have worked quickly to recover (there is, after all, a lot of money at stake), but check with your travel agent about conditions before you book your cruise.

No matter what length trip you decide to make or which ports your ship lists on the itinerary, most of your cruising will take place in the northern Indian Ocean—where seasonal monsoons and tropical cyclones need to be taken into account. In the Maldives, the most sunshine tends to beam down between December and April; in Sri Lanka, the high season is December through March. You can, of course, travel off-season, but if you do you will likely need to bring a raincoat and umbrella.

Fully 40 percent of the world's offshore oil production is said to be based in the Indian Ocean, an industry fact that's difficult to comprehend in the face of the region's picturesque islands, clear blue waters, and sparkling sand beaches. Still, working vessels far outnumber cruise ships in some of these places, and you might have to trust your travel agent to book you a cabin aboard a boat run by a company whose name you don't recognize from U.S. advertisements. That's not necessarily a bad thing, as the industry is always evolving, so have your agent fill you in on the latest ships to add this area to their routes.

No matter what brand of ship you get on, you'll find plenty of great views and interesting excursions in the Seychelles, the Maldives, Madagascar, Mauritius, and Sri Lanka.

Seychelles

The Seychelles are a group of more than 100 islands off Africa's eastern coast. They have long been considered some of the most beautiful spits of sand in the world, and yet their faraway location means less tourist traffic than many other destinations such as the Caribbean and Bahamas. Europeans, given their closer proximity to the Seychelles, tend to vacation here more than Americans do, and their presence means the standards of service are well in line with Western demands.

══FAST FACT

The Seychelles suffered about $30 million worth of damage in the late 2004 tsunami, the first major disaster there since 1868. Check with your cruise-ship operator about the status of reconstruction before booking your trip.

Your ship is likely to dock in Victoria, the capital city on the island of Mahe. It's a quiet place with coconut groves and pretty sunsets, so don't expect too much in terms of shopping and dining ashore.

The lure of the Seychelles is nature in its prettiest, most pristine form. You can enjoy a stroll along the beach at sunset and still have plenty of time to get back to your ship for a late dinner and maybe even a midnight massage.

Madagascar

Madagascar is one of the world's largest islands, with nearly 17 million residents who enjoy its pretty beaches, coral reefs, and forests filled with interesting animals, such as the mongoose and the civet, a type of cat. The varied excursion opportunities make this a great stop for groups traveling together, since people with different likes and dislikes can split up for the morning and enjoy their own adventures before gathering back on the boat to swap stories over dinner.

≡FAST FACT

Madagascar, off the southeast coast of Africa, is nicknamed "the Perfumed Isle" because of all its vanilla, sugar, and pepper plantations. You'll also find civet cats here, which is appropriate—a gland on their underbellies secretes a musklike substance that's used in making perfume.

Some of the most interesting sights you'll see ashore are the animals. There is, for instance, a reserve for lemurs, which are primates found only on Madagascar and in the Comoro Islands (also in the Indian Ocean). Madagascar, by far, has the most species of lemur, with a total approaching sixty-five, though conservationists and animal-rights activists fear that deforestation is destroying their habitat at a rapid pace and threatening endangerment.

Other possible excursions on Madagascar include a trip to Nosy Be, a resort area with good food and nighttime fun where you can enjoy the facilities of hotels that share affiliations with whatever cruise line you choose.

Mauritius

Mauritius is part of the Mascarene archipelago and has an extensive variety of flora and fauna for you to discover during shore excursions. Just consider palm trees alone—a full sixty species are on display at the Pamplemousse Royal Botanical Gardens in Port Louis. Some of the palms are more exotic than others, such as the talipot palm, which flowers only once during its century-long life, right before it dies.

Port Louis, the capital city, is home to restaurants, nightclubs, and even a casino. If you want a bit more culture, consider heading south to the town of Moka, where you'll find the Gandhi Institute's Folk Museum of Indian Immigration and its limited artifact collection. There are also beaches, of course, and all the water activities associated with them.

Maldives

The coral formations that you can see while snorkeling and scuba diving in the Maldives are so gorgeous that they're actually referred to as underwater coral gardens. The nearly 1,200 islands that make up the Maldives are coral themselves, a sort of geological stepping stone that eventually produced the snorkeling and diving sites that have become tourist attractions today. A lot of people cruise to the Maldives simply to don a mask and fins in these warm waters, with their great visibility.

===FAST FACT

Weekends in the Maldives, west of Sri Lanka, officially fall on Fridays and Saturdays. Businesses typically operate from 9:00 A.M. till 5:00 P.M. from Sunday through Thursday each week.

The Maldives are definitely different in terms of culture. Dhivehi is the language spoken most frequently, but don't worry if you can't read the Thaana script (which, like Arabic, is written in characters from right to left). English is widely understood, and some English terms have even become part of the commonly spoken language. The official currency goes by the names *rufiyaa* and *laaree,* with one rufiyaa equal to a hundred laarees. Some of the tourist-friendly restaurants and shops will take U.S. dollars instead, and your credit cards, of course, will translate in just about any culture.

Of course, if you're like everybody else, interacting with shop-keepers will represent the most limited part of your stay in the Maldives. You'll be in the water, exploring the coral and being as one with the fishes.

Sri Lanka

Unlike the Arab-inspired cultures to its west, Sri Lanka maintains an Oriental flair. Of course, this is because of its proximity to mainland India and the rest of Asia, far from the Indian Ocean islands that are closer to the African coast. In Sri Lanka, you're a lot less likely to see a lion preserve than you are to see dancing elephants and colorful bazaars.

Europeans have been cruising to Sri Lanka for years, so even though it sounds exotic to most U.S. travelers, the country actually has a nicely developed tourism infrastructure. The other major group of visiting people is Buddhists. They take pilgrimages to places like Temple of the Tooth, where it is believed that the tooth of the Lord Buddha still rests.

Columbo is Sri Lanka's capital city and the port where your cruise ship is likely to call. Excursions on shore include trips to temples and churches. If you're not into religion or you prefer more secular activities and still like to look at impressive buildings, consider skipping the downtown and heading south to an area called Cinnamon Gardens for a look at the homes of the wealthiest people in the area.

Transpacific Cruises

You don't hear about transpacific cruises nearly as often as you hear about transatlantics. Perhaps this is because transatlantic cruises are a lot alike, usually ending up in London, England, while transpacifics offer a somewhat overwhelming array of final destinations. As with anything, when presented with too many options, you sometimes feel overwhelmed trying to sort them all out and simply stop considering the idea altogether.

In part, the number of days you intend to sail will determine your transpacific itinerary. If you've only got ten days, you're certainly not going to make it all the way from Los Angeles through the South Pacific Islands and on to Australia—though that is an option if you have a month to devote to your vacation aboard. Some itineraries run from California through the Pacific Northwest and Alaska to Japan, while others head south to Mexico before heading west toward Hawaii and, eventually, New Zealand.

≡FAST FACT

The Pacific Ocean is the largest in the world, with more than 64 million square miles of water. You'd better bring at least a few good books if you expect to stay busy while crossing it during a transpacific cruise.

As with transatlantic trips, you should pay extra attention to the type of ship you book for a transpacific. The Pacific Ocean is, after all, the largest of the world's oceans, and it's going to take any ship a good number of days to get across it. Put your money into a boat with the best amenities and facilities you can find so that you'll have plenty to keep you busy while you're out of sight of land.

Antarctica

Antarctica is a unique environment on the planet, and as such it plays host to uniquely built ships. To cruise here through the extremely cold and frozen waters requires a ship that can handle breaking a little ice from time to time, which is not such an easy task. Just think about that iceberg scene from *Titanic*.

Luckily, shipbuilding has come a long way since then, and safety is paramount. You can choose from among several different kinds of well-appointed ships if you want to visit the land of penguin colonies, giant glaciers, and breaching whales. There are research ships that offer economical berths if you want to cruise alone and share a cabin with other solo travelers; there are luxury expedition ships that offer private penthouses and all the amenities you would find aboard the finest cruise ships anywhere else in the world; and there are ships that offer levels of service anywhere in between. As long as you are willing to spend somewhere in the neighborhood of $3,000 to $15,000 per person, plus an extra thousand or two in airfare to the bottom of the world, you'll be able to find a ship that suits your budget in Antarctica.

JUST FOR PARENTS

A cruise in Antarctica might be exciting for the kids, but the flight from south Florida to the world's last great wilderness will be torturous. With two stopovers for refueling and the resulting lengthy layovers, the total one-way flight time from Miami to southern Chile can be more than twenty-nine hours—and that doesn't count the cruise from Chile to Antarctica itself.

Your cruise will be round-trip from a port in southern Chile or Argentina, and your actual destinations in Antarctica may vary with weather conditions. This is an important thing to keep in mind when booking your trip—you will want to invest your vacation dollars with a company whose guides are well-educated and able to help you understand what you're seeing no matter where the ship ends up going. On a trip like this, where nature and wildlife are the biggest attractions, the importance of having the best guides available can't be overemphasized.

During longer Antarctica cruises, itineraries often include stops in the Falkland Islands east of Argentina, and South Georgia Island to the Falklands' south.

Falkland Islands

Port Stanley is where your ship will pull into upon arrival at the Falkland Islands, which remain staunchly British even though the sun does now set on England's once-formidable empire. The weather here is about as welcoming as it is a bit farther south in Antarctica, so the Falklands aren't exactly abuzz with shore-side activities. Still, there are museums, shops, and—of course—pubs, and the port of call helps to bring a little bit of civilization back into this nature-filled cruising ground.

The West Falklands are all about animals, a place that compares with Galapagos in terms of wildlife diversity and the opportunity to get close to creatures in the wild. You'll have a chance to see penguins, albatross, and many species of migratory birds. Also available here are hiking opportunities, so be sure to pack your Timberland boots, along with a few good pairs of wool socks.

South Georgia Island

The great Captain Ernest Shackleton, whose sailing ship got stuck in Antarctic ice before he finally accepted that he had reached man's boundary of navigation, is buried on South Georgia Island. Only a place of such monumental natural power could contain such a spirit; more than half of South Georgia Island is covered in glacial ice, literally impenetrable to man.

The sight of the ice-covered mountains, though, is well within your reach, and it's astounding to learn that the island itself is really part of the Andes chain that is above sea level on the South American continent. Part of the chain is submerged beneath the Scotia Sea, but South Georgia Island demands to be seen, with at least one peak that's more than 9,500 feet tall.

World Cruises

If you have several months available for travel, a true love of adventure, and a vacation fund somewhere in the neighborhood of $40,000 to $300,000, you can literally cruise around the world.

Well, okay—it's not a *true* circumnavigation, but companies such as Crystal Cruises and Holland America offer itineraries that run 105 to 108 days from port to port across many of the world's oceans.

The Crystal Cruise itinerary, for example, starts in Los Angeles, California, and winds its way down to Mexico, Central America, and South America before darting west for the South Pacific, Australia, and South Africa. The ship then turns north and heads for Dubai, United Arab Emirates, and the famed city of Tripoli in northern Africa before entering the Mediterranean Sea and calling on ports in Italy, France, and Portugal. The trip ends in London, England.

Holland America's version, as another example, is a round-trip experience that starts in Fort Lauderdale, Florida, and heads in the opposite direction. The route goes south through the Caribbean and all the way down the eastern coast of South America to Antarctica before turning northeast bound for South Africa. From there, it follows a path similar to the Crystal itinerary, cruising up the eastern coast of Africa to the Mediterranean Sea and over to Portugal before returning to Fort Lauderdale. If you're willing to stay aboard three more days, you can do an extra "little" leg from Florida up to New York City.

≡FAST FACT

The "crystal penthouse with veranda" aboard the 1,080-passenger *Crystal Serenity* is a 1,345-square-foot apartment with flat-screen televisions in the living room, bedroom, and bathroom. To book it for an entire 106-day around-the-world cruise costs a little more than $230,000.

You can book legs of these trips without staying aboard for the entire route, which means opportunities to see places like the Amazon and Antarctica that may otherwise be harder to come by on standard cruise-line routes. Talk to your travel agent for details. Heck, talk to your travel agent just to see a copy of the impressive brochures and route maps (some of which are online at the cruise lines' official Web sites).

CHAPTER 15

Aboard Your Ship

NO MATTER WHAT DESTINATION you choose, life aboard your ship will be a lot like life everywhere else: You need to get the lay of the land and figure out who's in charge of what. Your first order of business will be getting your family situated. You'll need a basic orientation to the ship and its personnel, and you'll need to make some reservations for activities you want to do later in the week. Don't worry—it's almost time for some serious fun. You just need an hour or two to get organized.

First Things First

If you have never before been aboard a cruise ship, your first few moments will be eye-openers. Today's cruise ships are *huge*. It's hard to fully appreciate the size of these small floating cities until you find yourself standing in the middle of one, perhaps clutching your kids by the hands and wondering, "How are we going to make sense of all this and find our way around without getting lost?" The kids, of course, will be screaming with excitement, and you'll find it hard not to look like a tourist as you stare up into a towering atrium full of murals and sculptures. You'll also be hard-pressed to keep your jaw closed during your first ride above the sea in a glass elevator, and your belly might tell you that it's time to start looking around for the welcome-aboard buffet.

Adding a little bit of structure to your first hours aboard won't dampen your family's enthusiasm for any of these things—it will make everyone in your group feel more comfortable as you settle into your home away from home. The worst thing you can do is try to dive right into the experience before you feel certain that every member of your family knows their way around the ship, can find the way to your cabin, and has reserved a spot for the excursions and special dining opportunities that you've decided are most important for the rest of the cruise. Your first order of business is, well, to do a bit of business.

Ship Identification Cards for the Family

Every member of your family will need a ship identification card. You get these during the check-in process, after you present your tickets, driver's license, and/or passport for each member of your family. Make sure your children understand that their ship identification card is not a toy—they will not be allowed on or off the ship without it.

Because of heightened security measures since the terrorist attacks of September 11, 2001, many ship identification cards now include your photograph. Some also include other identifying information, much like your driver's license.

Every time you disembark in a port, you swipe your ship identification card and the departure is noted. The computer will remember you (well, your card, anyway) when it's time to get back aboard at the end of the day. You'll also need your card for booking spa appointments, restaurant reservations, and the like.

Some cruise companies, including Norwegian Cruise Line, require kids who are participating in organized children's activities to wear an identification bracelet in addition to having a ship identification card. The bracelet includes your child's name, cabin number, allergies, medications, and lifeboat station number. If you're not aboard a ship that requires this extra safety measure, make sure the young children with you memorize your ship name and cabin number—or carry the information on a written note in their pocket every day.

🧳 TRAVEL TIP

If you expect to be separated from your kids, either during tours ashore or onboard activities, make sure you and your children all wear something that is quick to spot in a crowd. This can make everyone feel much more secure, such as when a limbo contest ends and you're searching for one another in a crowd.

Shipboard Charge Accounts

After you've got your ship identification card, your next priority is to get shipboard charge accounts for every member of your family. Cash is no good on cruise ships; everything is charged to your cabin. In some cases, these cards will serve triple-duty as ship identification cards and cabin keys. You literally can't leave "home" without them if you want to do anything, buy anything aboard, or get back into your bed at the end of the day.

Every charge account is linked to a cabin number. If you and your kids are sharing a cabin, you will all be using the same account. If your kids are in an adjacent or separate cabin, they will have their own account that is charged back to you (assuming you're the one booking the vacation). You will need to fill out an application form before getting these cards, much as you would fill out an application form to get a regular credit card ashore. You also will be required to put down a deposit in cash or with a regular credit card—and that deposit amount will be the limit on your account unless you add to it during your cruise. If, for instance, you put a $300 deposit down, that is the entire amount that the ship will allow to be charged to your account. Cruise personnel will notify you when your limit has been reached, and you will have the option of adding to your account with cash or a regular credit card.

This makes it easy for you to monitor your family's spending aboard, especially if your kids are in their own cabin, and you won't have to worry about theft of cash or traveler's checks because your children simply won't have a need to carry them.

TRAVEL TIP

If you plan to use a regular credit card to make deposits for your shipboard credit account, remember that a hold will be placed on your regular credit card each time you add to your ship's account. Your regular credit card will not be charged in full until the end of your cruise, but its available balance will go down as the holds become active.

There is usually a minimum deposit required to activate your shipboard charge account, sometimes as little as $100. However, there is no maximum. If you're not worried about overspending or monitoring what your children buy, go ahead and put down a deposit for more money than you think your entire family will need for the duration of your vacation. You will get a refund at the end of your cruise, and you won't have to bother with heading down to the guest relations desk to refill your account every few days.

Once you have your shipboard charge account activated, it's time to start using it on reservations for the activities and specialty dinners you hope to enjoy.

Excursion and Spa Reservations

Hopefully, you and your family have taken some time before arriving at your ship to talk about shore excursions and onboard activities. The most popular ones fill up fast, and it's important that you make your reservations as soon as possible after stepping aboard. While everyone else is trying to find their cabins so they can unpack right away, you can be snagging the last four seats on that helicopter tour you really have your heart set on. After all, your luggage will still be in your cabin waiting to be unpacked after you complete your bookings and get set for the rest of your cruise.

Excursions book up even faster nowadays than they used to because some cruise ships let you reserve spots online many months before the ship even sets sail. Royal Caribbean, for instance, will let you read about, book, and pay for your shore excursions with a credit card on its Web site. If you take the time to do this right after you book your cruise, you will be guaranteed to get the excursions you want without having to wait in line on the ship at all. It is, quite simply, your best bet.

If you haven't booked your excursions in advance online, take your brand-new ship charge account and head straight to your ship's excursion desk the minute after you step aboard. There is no time to waste. Remember that you are one among thousands of people, and that the most popular excursions fill up first. Make a point of having your favorites at the top of a written list so you can book them in the order of your family's preference.

After you've taken care of your shore excursions, make a bee-line for the ship's spa and fitness center. Appointments for massages, facials, manicures, pedicures, and all the other pleasant offerings in your ship's spa will be snapped up just as fast as seats on those shore excursions. Before you can have your tension rubbed out of your shoulders later in the week, you'll have to exert a little energy to ensure that you get that massage appointment today.

Specialty Restaurant Reservations

You've gone through security in the cruise-ship terminal, deposited your luggage, gotten ship identification cards for your family, opened your shipboard charge account, booked your excursions, and made appointments at the spa. At this point, you're probably starting to get hungry—which should remind you that it's time to make reservations at the specialty restaurants of your choice.

Specialty restaurants are small eateries, often with themes such as Asian or Italian cuisine, where you can dine a few nights during your vacation to break up the monotony of eating in the main dining room. (You'll read more about that in Chapter 16.) These restaurants usually don't seat more than a hundred or so people, and as you might imagine, those seats are taken quickly. You will want to reserve yours right away, just as you did with shore excursions and spa appointments.

🧳 TRAVEL TIP

Before you get aboard your cruise ship, decide in what order of importance these extras fall: shore excursions, spa appointments, and specialty restaurant reservations. All three tend to book up fast, so make it a priority to reserve your spot first at the one that matters to you most.

You should have information about your ship's specialty restaurants in your cruise brochure. Some companies, such as Crystal Cruises, even provide sample menus for you to consider before your trip.

Finding Your Cabin

By the time you finish getting yourself and your family organized and reserved for every activity you want, your luggage will probably have been delivered to your cabin. Now you have to go find that cabin, which can be more challenging than you might expect.

Cruise ships are kind of like casinos—full of lights and sounds and smells that are exciting and distracting and, thus, can keep you a bit disoriented until you find your way around. If you are cruising aboard a luxury line, a personal steward will likely escort you to your cabin. If you are aboard a regular cruise ship (the majority of ships), you will have to find your own way.

Do yourself a favor and familiarize yourself with your cruise ship's layout before you even step aboard. Each cruise line has brochures and Web site pages that will show you deck plans for every level of your ship. From these you should be able to determine the correct deck, whether it is forward or aft (toward the back), and whether it is to port (the left side of the ship) or to starboard (the right side of the ship). Just knowing these slivers of information will help you find your way to your cabin after you step aboard—you can look for signs to the forward bank of elevators, for instance, if you know your cabin is in the front of the ship.

You usually will be handed a miniature ship map upon boarding, but if you have a large-scale one in your cruise-ship brochure, bring it with you. Tear the pages right out if you don't want to carry the whole brochure along. This deck plan will be larger with bigger print that is easier to see, and you will already be acclimated to the way it looks because you can study it before embarking. This will make it easier to follow as you wind your way around the ship and your new surroundings.

Unpacking *Everything!*

Unless you want to spend half your vacation time ironing, you should unpack everything immediately. Hang shirts and pants two or three to a hanger if you have to (you can always request more hangers later). Just get everything out of your bag before it has a chance to crease.

Pay special attention to the way you unpack and stow your toiletries. If they are not in a waterproof shaving kit or sealed zip-close bag, make sure that you place them in your bathroom vanity and drawers in a way that will keep them stable while the ship is under way. The last thing you want to do is perch a glass bottle of perfume on the edge of a shelf, only to see it tumble over in a seaway, crash down upon the floor, and stink up your entire cabin. Remember, ships *move*. Your things will, too.

If your cabin has a personal safe, place all your jewelry—as well as your passport—inside of it. Your expensive camera gear, portable DVD player, personal CD player, and wallet should go into the safe, as well. Cruise ships are secure places with professional cabin crews, but you don't want to tempt anyone unnecessarily by leaving your valuables out in plain sight.

Lifeboat Drill

Soon after you unpack, or maybe before you've finished, you will have to join all of the other ship's passengers at your assigned muster station for a lifeboat drill. This is the place where you should go if there is a serious problem aboard, and you will learn what sounds to listen for to alert you to emergency situations. The idea behind assigned muster stations is that everyone will get a lifeboat seat. If your children are wearing ship-required identification bracelets as part of anorganized activities program, the information on the bracelets will include the location of your muster station so that you can meet your children there after crew members deliver them.

During the lifeboat drill, you will be asked to put on a life preserver and to demonstrate that you know how to buckle it properly. This can be uncomfortable, especially in the heat of the tropics, but try to keep in mind that everyone else is feeling just as squirmy as you are. Tough it out, and know that you will need the information in the very off chance that your ship experiences a major problem.

≡FAST FACT

Cruise ships carry Type I life jackets, the big orange kind that are designed to turn an unconscious person face up in the water. Ships also carry Type IV flotation devices, such as the throwable white doughnuts you see mounted on various decks.

Ship Tours and Orientations

Usually, right after you step aboard your ship, you can ask about orientation tours. Sometimes these tours have designated times, and sometimes they are catch as catch can. Holland America, for instance, suggests that you go to the reception desk on embarkation day and hang around until a few other couples and families come over looking for orientation tours, as well. Once a group has formed, a crew member is summoned to lead the way. And usually, the wait is short.

Orientation tours usually include all the public spaces on a ship, and they are a good idea if you plan to let your children have the run of the ship for the duration of your cruise. That way, the kids will be less likely to get lost—and you'll have a good idea of where you might find them if they lose track of time before dinner.

Receptions

Most cruise ships offer at least one reception during your vacation. These can range from a welcome parade to a bon voyage pool party to the traditional captain's welcome reception, which is sometimes called the captain's dinner.

The captain's dinner is usually a formal event full of fancy hors d'oeuvres, free drinks, and sometimes a live band. There is usually a receiving line where you can meet the ship's officers and pose for a photograph with the captain. There will be a ship's photographer there, but you are welcome to use your own camera, too.

You might wonder whether you can score a seat at the captain's table for this formal reception. Obviously, a handful of people are chosen during each cruise, but how? The truth is that it varies from ship to ship, and from cruise line to cruise line. If you've cruised a lot with the same company, you might make the list; or you might be asked if you are celebrating a fiftieth wedding anniversary or other milestone event, such as a ninetieth birthday. If sitting at the captain's table is important to you, ask about it when you book your cruise. Your travel agent just might be able to pull a few strings on your behalf. No matter where you sit at the captain's welcome reception, you'll have a chance to meet some of your cruise ship's key officers. You'll feel a little more comfortable about this if you understand what each one does aboard.

Meeting the Officers

There's no need to be bashful about meeting your ship's officers. They are people just like you. Their jobs simply happen to be in the service and entertainment industry, with a very nice perk of getting to travel the world while working.

It takes hundreds of crew members to run a modern cruise ship, but a handful of people at the top are responsible for overseeing pretty much every general aspect of your vacation. The most important people whose hands you might want to shake include the captain, the cruise director, the hotel manager, and the food-and-beverage director.

The Captain

The captain is often lionized as an untouchable figure of almost mythic proportions, but he is essentially a very talented jack-of-all-trades. He must be a skilled and highly experienced seaman who can navigate the ship, oversee any engineering problems, and deal with protocol in ports of multiple nations worldwide. He also must be a leader who has the respect of hundreds of crew members, not to mention a charming host who can carry a conversation with VIP passengers throughout a lengthy five-course formal dinner.

You will see the captain at his welcome reception, and possibly during tours of the bridge, but don't expect him to be wandering around the ship at your disposal. If you spot the four gold bars on his uniform's epaulet in the middle of the day, consider yourself lucky.

The Cruise Director

Your cruise director is the person in charge of coordinating all of your ship's passenger activities. She will be highly visible and always smiling, acting as much like a cheerleader as the scheduling master that she is. The cruise-director job started out several decades ago as a sort of emceeing gig, with its primary responsibilities being to host live theater shows and socialize with the passengers. It has evolved into a top management position that dominates pretty much every activity you will have an opportunity to enjoy during your cruise. The best cruise directors also consider it their job to keep your mood, and everyone else's, as joyous as possible at all times.

≡ FAST FACT

Many cruise directors started out as theater performers, comedians, and the like, and worked their way up through the cruise-ship ranks. You may be surprised to learn that the woman coordinating your limbo contest is also a professional juggler!

The Hotel Manager

Aboard some ships, the hotel manager is still called the purser, but the job has evolved from days of old when all the purser did was stand at the front desk and answer questions about when cabins would be cleaned. Today's cruise-ship hotel manager, sometimes also called a hotel director, is responsible for your living accommodations—everything from how the room stewards treat you to where the plumbers need to go when you have a leaky faucet.

If you have any questions or compliments about your room or the service you receive there, you should seek out the hotel manager. He will always be happy to hear from you, since he certainly can't see what's happening in every cabin during every cruise.

The Food-and-Beverage Manager

The food-and-beverage manager is responsible for everything from provisioning the ship to overseeing the cooking and wait staffs. The provisioning alone is a huge job that requires keeping track of thousands of orders for hundreds of different kinds of foods and drinks. Think about it: The last thing you want to hear when you sit down for your first dinner aboard is that *somebody* forgot to order the lobster tails this week.

If you have a waiter or a maitre d' who offers you superb service, be sure to write a complimentary note and pass it along to the food-and-beverage manager. Anyone working in the ship's reception area can make sure it is delivered for you.

The Excursion Director

Your ship's excursion director is the person to see for information about which off-the-ship trips are the best for you and your family. This person has likely experienced all or most of the excursions your ship offers, and she can tell you from her own experience whether a given day trip is good or bad based on your children's ages, your budget, or even the weather.

If you would like to chat with the excursion director, don't wait until twenty minutes before your ship pulls into port. She'll be swamped with people asking questions. Instead, seek her out right after you board, or during a full day at sea. Those are the times when she's likely to be the least busy and thus have the most time for you.

CHAPTER 16

The Food!

SURE, IT'S NICE TO see pretty shorelines and smell fresh salt air and hear your kids laughing with delight as a dolphin brushes up against them in a wading pool, but your taste buds are really the luckiest of all five senses when it comes to cruising. The variety of restaurants, cafés, and buffet presentations aboard ships today is practically a vacation unto itself! Aboard the biggest ships, you can sometimes eat in a different setting every night. Even better, no matter what boat you choose, you can always have seconds . . . and thirds . . . and fourths . . . .

Dining Options

Celebrity Cruises puts out an interesting fact sheet about food aboard its Century-class ships. The 866-foot long *Galaxy*, for instance, carries 1,870 passengers who dine in a main restaurant along with several cafés. During a typical seven-night cruise, to feed that many people in those dining areas, the *Galaxy* brings along the following supplies in its galley:

- 25,250 pounds of fresh vegetables
- 21,900 pounds of fresh fruit
- 21,600 pounds of beef
- 11,760 pounds of fish

- 4,200 pounds each of chicken and turkey
- 3,250 pounds of lobster
- 2,500 pounds of potatoes
- 1,600 pounds of cookies
- 600 pounds of jelly

And that's not even half the supplies on board! You've got to wonder what thirty pounds of fresh herbs and spices looks like. Or 712 dozen eggs. Or nearly 10,000 tea bags.

If you can broaden your mind to consider all the food served aboard an entire fleet of ships during a week, try to imagine the twenty Carnival Fun Ships and the fact that they dish out about 17,000 gallons of fruit juices, more than 700,000 slices of bacon, and nearly a half-million shrimp *every seven days*. Just the thought of it might make you feel like you need to loosen the top button on your pants!

The sea-going smorgasbord that's available for breakfast, lunch, and dinner alike has always been a big selling point for cruise vacations, and things are no different today. All that's changed is the variety of restaurants aboard, with newer ships having small bistros, cafés, and specialty restaurants in addition to their main dining rooms. Whatever you want to eat, and whenever you want to it eat, it's out there waiting for you on a cruise vacation.

Main Dining Room

The main dining room is usually where you'll enjoy all your meals, unless you make arrangements to eat in a reservations-only restaurant aboard or pick up something at a poolside bistro. Breakfast and lunch tend to be at the same time every day, while dinner is traditionally offered as either an early (main) or late seating. On some cruise lines, you can choose the one you want—but you may have to stick with the same seating for the duration of the cruise. Aboard other cruise lines, you will be assigned a dining time either when you check in and register, or when you arrive in your cabin to unpack. If you don't like your assigned schedule, you should ask for a change. If you don't get the change you want, you should try tipping the maitre d'. Twenty dollars seems to be the going rate.

You will eat at the same table with the same people every night as long as you stay in the main dining room and forgo other meal-time options (which you'll learn about later in this chapter). If you are traveling with a large group, say on a family reunion, you can reserve a cluster of tables in the main dining room and switch seats however you choose during the length of your cruise. If there are just three or four in your family, though, you may end up sharing a table with the same other passengers every evening. That first evening's impression will go a long way toward making the duration of your cruise as enjoyable as it can be. Do your best to make friends fast—and that includes the wait staff. They'll be with you for the rest of your trip, as well.

 TRAVEL TIP

Want to make friends fast at your group dinner table? Memorize a few good jokes before sitting down. Make sure they're G-rated, and have a couple of new ones at the ready for every night of your cruise.

Early and Late Dinner Seatings

Should you choose the early or late dinner seating? It really depends on several factors. For starters, where is your ship sailing? If you are on a cruise to nowhere and the ship itself is your destination, you might try the early seating so that you can leave plenty of after-dinner time for the theater, casino, and other activities. If, on the other hand, you are cruising in a place where you plan to spend every minute you can exploring ashore—and returning to the boat late in the day—you probably will be happier with the late dinner seating. It will allow you time to get back aboard the ship, shower at a leisurely pace, and maybe even take a nap or look through your digital photos from the day's sights before you have to get down to the dining room.

If neither early nor late appeals to you, look for a ship that will let you split the difference. Holland America's Signature of Excellence Initiative, which will be completed aboard all its ships by 2006, includes the creation of four dinner seating times for added flexibility: 5:45 P.M., 6:15 P.M., 8:00 P.M., and 8:30 P.M.

Earlier seating, as you might imagine, does tend to be the preferred choice of seniors and families with small children. The kids usually get hungry earlier in the day, and retirees may want to head to bed around 9:00 P.M., when the late dinner seating is often hitting its stride. On the other hand, if your family is composed of adults and teenagers, you might be happier with the late seating, which enables you to linger and catch up over conversation for as long as you'd like after the meal is complete. (With no second seating following yours, there's no rush to get you up from your table.)

If you want to see the theater show at night, you will have to dine early aboard some ships, while others offer the theater show at two separate times to accommodate both dinner seatings. Check with your travel agent or cruise line about the options on your particular ship.

≡FAST FACT

Disney Cruise Line uses a rotation dining concept in which you have the same dinnertime and tablemates for each meal, but eat at three different restaurants during your cruise. The idea is to add new experiences as your vacation progresses, with everything from an elegant French dining hall to an animation-themed restaurant.

Open Dinner Seatings

If you don't want to be pinned down to a specific dinner schedule for your entire cruise, consider booking your vacation with one of the handful of cruise lines that have begun to offer open dinner seating policies. These enable you to choose your table and your dinner time in the main dining room, so if you like your group, you can stick with it—or you can enjoy a change of pace throughout the cruise to meet new people and accommodate the timing of different shore-side activities each day.

Norwegian Cruise Line, for instance, introduced what it calls Freestyle Cruising in 2000 and now offers it aboard all of its ships. It is meant to provide a more relaxed, resort-style vacation, including a less regimented style of dining. You can choose to eat in any of the main restaurants aboard an NCL ship anytime between 5:30 P.M. and midnight, and you can change the time that you eat each night throughout your cruise. You also may choose your dinner companions at tables that seat from two to ten people, and you may change companions every night. Within two scheduled time periods each night, you can even request meals cooked to order instead of having ones that are prepared banquet style.

Princess Cruises calls its open-seating program "Personal Choice Dining" and offers it from 5:30 until 10:00 P.M.—in addition to traditional dinner seatings at 6:30 and 8:30 P.M. if you prefer being assigned to a table for the duration of your cruise. As with the NCL program, Princess's program lets you choose your dinner companions and dining times on a daily basis in the main restaurant for more flexibility.

The luxury cruise line Silversea also offers open-seating dining that requires no reservations, except for special evenings in its smaller cafés. Tables are unassigned, so you can dine alone with your family or with a group of newfound friends.

Specialty Restaurants

Sometimes, you will want to leave the main dining room for a change of scenery, a change of company, or a romantic dinner for two. This is the time for you to try one of your ship's specialty restaurants.

If you think you might want to dine at a specialty restaurant during your cruise, your safest bet is to make reservations immediately upon boarding the ship. Some of these eateries are small, serving just thirty or so couples at a time, and the reservation books fill up fast. Don't wait until an hour before dinnertime and expect to get a table. You'll end up right back in the main dining room with the other thousand or so passengers.

Most specialty restaurants will require you to pay a surcharge in the neighborhood of $5 to $20 per person that can be added to your shipboard charge card and settled at the end of your vacation. If you want the change of pace or the intimacy, the surcharge is worth it—it's still far less than you would pay to dine ashore at a romantic restaurant.

Different cruise lines offer different kinds of specialty restaurants. Here's a look at some of the options that are available.

Crystal

Each of Crystal Cruises' three ships has at least two specialty restaurants in addition to its main dining room. The Crystal *Harmony* offers Kyoto and Prego, the Crystal *Symphony* offers Jade Garden and Prego; and the Crystal *Serenity* offers Prego, Silk Road, and The Sushi Bar. Each of these specialty restaurants is aptly named.

Kyoto is a Japanese eatery that serves sushi, sake, and dishes such as Salmonshio-Yaki (pan-roasted Alaskan salmon on traditional ponzo sauce with steamed fresh vegetables), Chicken Shouga-Yaki (broiled, skinless chicken breast in light ginger lemon sauce with satoimo, grilled zucchini, and eggplant); and Beef Teppanyaki (filet of steak on a bed of sauteed onions with teppanyaki sauce, steamed snow peas, green asparagus, and shiitake mushrooms). For dessert, you might try Kyoto green-tea ice cream.

Prego serves classic Italian fare from a seasonally changing menu called "Valentino at Prego." The dishes are based on offerings at Piero Selvaggio's Los Angeles and Las Vegas Valentino restaurants. Some of the menu's courses may include Scaloppine di Vitello Servite con Capelli d'Angelo (sautéed veal scaloppini in light lemon or mushroom sauce with angel hair pasta and seasonal vegetables); Linguine con Aragosta e Zucchini (linguine with lobster and grilled zucchini in a light tomato sauce flavored with Italian parsley); and Gamberoni Marinati alla Griglia (grilled marinated prawns with capellini tossed in eggplant, zucchini, and lemon-flavored tomato sauce).

Jade Garden's menu is Asian and includes Far East specialties along with dishes from Wolfgang Puck's restaurant Chinois on Main. Selections include wok-seared sea bass fillet in white truffle-flavored black bean sauce served on steamed Chinese baby greens and mushrooms; Thai lobster with wok-fried shiitake mushrooms flavored with Thai crushed herbs and hot sesame oil; orange-flavored chicken, lightly breaded, stir fried, and tossed in fresh orange peel sauce, and served with baby greens; and grilled Mongolian lamb chops with cilantro mint vinaigrette sauce, served with stir-fried green and yellow beans. The signature dessert at Jade Garden is a sampler of ginger crème brulee, chocolate spice cake, green-tea ice cream, lychee, and jackfruit.

≡FAST FACT

Jackfruit is actually a vegetable. It's a cousin of the breadfruit that can grow as big as three feet long and weigh as much as 100 pounds. It's reportedly the largest treeborne fruit in the world, growing from a tropical trunk that originated in western India.

Silk Road and The Sushi Bar serve dishes prepared by Nobu-trained chefs. The Sushi Bar offers Nobu's sushi and sashimi, while Silk Road serves more than two dozen of Nobu's signature appetizers, soups, salads, entrees, and desserts. Samples include Nobu-Style Lobster with Truffle-Yuzu Sauce (stir-fried lobster with garlic, asparagus, shiitake, snap peas, and truffle-yuzu sauce); Black Cod with Miso (Nobu-style saikyo miso-marinated and broiled black cod with lemon and hajikami); and Grilled Wagyu Beef Rib-Eye (steak grilled to taste with a choice of anticuccho or Nobu-style wasabi pepper sauce). For dessert, you can try a bento box filled with chocolate soufflé cake with shiso syrup and sesame ice cream.

Holland America

The Pinnacle Grill was added to Holland America's five-star ships as part of the company's Signature of Excellence program. It serves Pacific Northwest fare on Bvlgari china (with dinner plates alone worth about $300 each) and regional wines in Riedel stemware. The menu offers steaks and seafood, with dishes including:

- Cedar-planked lobster with roasted garlic scampi butter and herb crumbs
- Chicken marsala with Washington cherries
- Cedar-planked halibut with Alaskan king crab
- Two different cuts of filet mignon
- Smoked salmon tartare with grilled asparagus wasabi sabayon

If you can't choose just one meal from the list, a tasting menu with accompanying wines is also available.

Princess

Princess Cruise Lines promotes two specialty restaurants aboard its ships. The Sterling Steakhouse is a refined version of the steakhouse at your local shopping mall, serving everything from New York cuts to porterhouse steaks and prime rib at a carving station.

Sabatini's Trattoria is an Italian eatery that's open for both lunch and dinner. Everything is served in traditional Italian style, right down to the tiramisu on the dessert menu.

Radisson Seven Seas

The *Seven Seas Mariner* and *Seven Seas Voyager* each have four restaurants for passengers to try: La Veranda, an informal but elegant Mediterranean bistro; Compass Rose, an expansive dining hall; Signatures, which features chefs trained at Le Cordon Bleu; and Latitudes, an Asian-themed eatery. Aboard the *Seven Seas*

Navigator, you can try the Portofino Grill for Italian fare. And on the *Radisson Diamond*, you can dine while being serenaded by the waiters at Don Vito's.

Silversea

In addition to its main restaurant, your Silversea ship may have eateries including the Terrace Cafe, which serves Italian, French, and Asian cuisine; or a gourmet restaurant called either Saletta or Le Champagne that serves a menu created by German-born, Michelin two-star chef Joachim Koerper.

Buffets and Casual Dining Options

Still not tempted? That's okay—you can eat to your heart's content aboard most cruise ships without ever setting foot in the main dining room or specialty restaurants.

Carnival, for instance, has a program called Total Choice Dining that includes twenty-four-hour pizzerias, sushi bars, and a midnight buffet that includes hot and cold items alike. Celebrity Cruises calls its optional eating area the Casual Dining Boulevard, which includes a sushi Cafe, a pizza and pasta bar, light spa cuisine, themed lunches (Asian, Italian, and barbecue), soups, salads, sandwiches, and tortilla chips with salsa served during the sunset happy hour.

TRAVEL TIP

Bored with the regular fast-food offerings on your ship? Check out inspiring creations such as the three-fry braid and the pop 'n taco online at ✎*www.fastfoodfever.com*. You'll be combining your burgers with your nuggets in no time.

Holland America calls its casual eating program "Relaxed Lido Dining." It includes a buffet on the Lido deck for breakfast and lunch. For breakfast, the buffet includes cereal, yogurt, muffins, cholesterol-free egg substitutes, an omelet station, and fresh fruit. At lunchtime, the buffet offerings include a salad bar, freshly carved meat, seafood, a deli, pizza, pasta, tacos, nachos, fajitas, stir fry, hamburgers, and gourmet sausages. Disney Cruise Line also has breakfast and lunch buffets, as well as spots such as Pluto's Dog House for burgers and hot dogs, and Pinocchio's Pizzeria. Princess Cruises' buffet restaurant is open twenty-four hours a day, or you can eat at its tropical Café Caribe, late-night bistro (open till 4 A.M.), pizzeria, or burger and hot dog grill. Crystal Cruises has themed buffet luncheons that include American Classic and Nuevo Latino.

Room Service

Luckily, the cruise ships that offer twenty-four-hour room service usually don't charge you any extra money to enjoy it. Princess, Silversea, and Radisson Seven Seas are among these. Some lines, like MSC, offer twenty-four-hour room service that is free only for breakfast, with a limited menu during the rest of the day.

If you book a suite, the room-service options available to you are sometimes more substantial. Celebrity, for instance, offers twenty-four-hour complimentary room service to all cabins for orders of hot and cold sandwiches, gourmet boxed pizza (cheese, pepperoni, or vegetable), salads, and desserts. If you book a suite, you are automatically bumped up to butler service, which can include complete breakfasts and dinners, as well as afternoon tea and hors d'oeuvres.

Remember that regular and inside cabins are usually smaller than the average land-based hotel room, and that dining in them is not likely to leave you with a feeling of gourmet satisfaction. Unless you're fried from the sun or feeling seasick, you probably will enjoy the food more if you throw on a T-shirt and wander up to a poolside grill.

Poolside Grills

Poolside grills run the gamut from indoor-outdoor eateries with savory entrees to bars where you can grab a burger on the go. If you've had a big lunch or are waiting for a big dinner, they can be a terrific alternative to the main dining room.

Crystal's Trident Bar and Grill, for example, serves a late-risers' breakfast from 10 A.M. until 11:30 A.M. along with all-day-long hot dogs, hamburgers, veggie and chicken burgers, tuna melts, wrap sandwiches, and gourmet pizzas. By night, on select evenings, it becomes a casual restaurant where you can order light meals such as a grilled shrimp Caesar salad, a caprese salad with shrimp cocktail, or tandoori beef.

Aboard most cruise ships, you will at least have access to a poolside grill that serves hamburgers, hot dogs, and soda. If your children aren't big eaters, you might consider feeding them here and then dropping them off for an activity or with a babysitter while you enjoy a several-course evening in the main dining room.

Kids' Meals

There is no special trick to getting a kid's meal aboard a cruise ship—simply ask your server for one. Some ships even have separate menus for children in the main dining rooms, to make your options more readily apparent.

 RAINY DAY FUN

A cruise ship is a great place to expose your children to new foods. If you have to stay aboard because of weather, spend some extra time in the dining room—where you're allowed to order as many different dishes as you'd like. You can create your own sampler and indulge in an afternoon of interesting tastes.

Dress Codes

Most cruise vacations include at least one formal night. Royal Caribbean's ships, for instance, have one formal night aboard three- to four-night cruises, two formal nights aboard seven-night cruises, and three formal nights aboard ten- to fifteen-night cruises. Other nights, dining room attire can be casual or smart casual (meaning slacks and a jacket for men, and a nice pantsuit for women). During the day, casual clothes—including shorts and T-shirts—are fine in the main dining room.

Some people love formal nights and treat them like the prom. You'll see full-length ball gowns, pearl necklaces, and tuxedos with white jackets and silk bowties. Other people enjoy looking nice but aren't into penguin suits and girdles, so they wear a dark suit with white shirt and tie or a cocktail dress instead. You should wear whatever makes you feel comfortable within the boundaries of appropriateness. If you don't own a tuxedo, don't fret; you can usually rent one for a hundred bucks or so, including cummerbund and cuff links. It will be delivered to your cabin.

If you don't want to dress up at all, that's all right too. Most cruise ships offer casual dinner options in addition to whatever is happening in the main dining room, and some ships have gotten rid of forced formal nights altogether. Norwegian Cruise Line, for instance, asks that you dress in smart casual clothes for all dining room dinners and offers an optional formal night in other parts of the ship.

Most cruise ships do enforce the formal dress code for formal dinners, so don't try to get into the main dining room if you are dressed down. If you find yourself without a diamond barrette or black leather shoes, stroll to a more casual eatery aboard or try one of the increasingly popular specialty restaurants on today's cruise ships.

📋 TRAVEL TIP

Formal nights aboard cruise ships are just that—highly formal. You'll see men in white tuxedos with tails, as well as women in ball gowns and (on occasion) tiaras. Don't be shy about putting on the Ritz. This is the time to break out that fabulous outfit you've been saving for a special occasion.

Snacks

Fear not: You will not go hungry between mealtimes aboard your cruise ship. Snacks are available around the clock, in healthy and decadent varieties alike.

Some ships, like Disney's *Magic*, have poolside grills that specialize only in summertime treats like ice cream. Disney calls its ice creamery Scoops, while Crystal's moniker is the Trident Ice Cream Bar. At the Crystal station, you'll find lots to satisfy your cravings, including waffle cones, fudge brownies, cookies, sundaes, sherbets, sugar-free ice cream, low-carb ice cream, and nonfat frozen yogurt. You can top any of the above with fresh berries if you're feeling guilty.

Princess also has an ice cream bar, along with a patisserie that serves pastries, gourmet coffees, cappuccinos, and lattes. Carnival's Fun Ships also have patisseries for when your tummy grumbles.

Aboard ships that do not serve a midnight buffet, you will often be offered late-night snacks served on trays by wandering waiters. Disney offers late-night hors d'oeuvres served on trays, as does Celebrity, which calls its program "Gourmet Bites." It occurs during three nights of every seven-night cruise. White-gloved waiters tour the ship from midnight until 1 A.M. serving nibbles such as vegetable and fish tempura, chimichangas, salmon and vegetable wraps, roasted vegetable pizza, California vegetable rolls, carved Midwestern spiced turkey breast, and roasted garlic-lemon chicken. For dessert, you can have a taste of strawberry cheesecake, brownie, or apple pie.

Afternoon Tea

The tradition of afternoon tea began in the mid-1800s, when the Duchess of Bedford insisted on having a tray of tea with bread and butter to satisfy her appetite between noontime lunch and an 8 or 9:00 P.M. dinner. It became something of a social event as she invited friends over to join her, and today, the tradition has found its way aboard cruise ships in a variety of styles.

Disney, for instance, calls its afternoon service "Tea with Wendy Darling." Instead of the hot stuff, Peter Pan's pal joins you for a round of iced tea with cookies. She's very forgiving if you forget to raise your pinky with your cup.

Celebrity goes the more traditional route and serves an Elegant Tea each afternoon. You can take your choice of flavorful, steaming teacups served from rolling trolleys with light sandwiches and freshly baked pastries.

Special Dietary Requests

Just reading about all of the food options aboard cruise ships can leave you feeling bloated if you're trying to stay on a diet or are determined not to pack on the pounds during your vacation. Luckily, as Americans' dietary preferences have begun to shift toward more healthy options, cruise-ship food offerings have changed along with them. In addition to newer preferences such as low fat and low carb, some cruise ships also let you order everything from kosher to low-sodium meals.

Holland America, for instance, includes a "Light and Healthy" section on its lunch and dinner menus in its ships' main dining rooms, as well as on the posted Lido buffet menu. Each of these menu items is low in cholesterol and sodium. Sugar-free and low-fat desserts are also available, as are kosher entrees and entrees prepared with low sodium, low cholesterol, low fat, and in keeping with the vegetarian lifestyle.

 TRAVEL TIP

If you will require a special meal—kosher, low-sodium, low-cholesterol, sugar-free, or the like—make your requests known in advance through your travel agent or cruise-line contact. Your safest bet is to reserve these meals at the time you book your trip, so they will become part of your passenger record from day one.

Crystal Cruises also offers a light menu with entrees that are low in salt, fat, sugar, and cholesterol. The cruise line introduced a low-carb menu in 2004 inside both the main dining room and several specialty restaurants aboard its ships. You can order three-course, low-carb meals for lunch and dinner alike. Kosher meals are also available with Crystal, but you must request them at least ninety days before your ship sets sail.

Celebrity will also make you vegetarian, diabetic, low-sodium, low-fat, low-cholesterol, or lactose-frees meals as long as you request them no later than fifteen days before your cruise begins. (Kosher dinners are also available upon request, but not breakfasts and lunches.) Radisson Seven Seas Cruises asks that you make any special dietary requests four to six weeks before your embarkation date.

CHAPTER **17**

Onboard Facilities and Services

THE BEAUTY OF TODAY'S cruise ships is that they have enough things for you to do aboard that you never have to step ashore to be entertained. Not once. If it pours rain and you can't bear the thought of donning a slicker and wading down the gangway, you can do anything from sitting quietly under a poolside umbrella to taking in a lecture about a port's history to buying investment-quality artwork at an auction. Whether you want to lose a few pounds, finally see that major motion picture you missed back home, or learn how to dance an Irish jig, you can.

From the Fun to the Functional

It's actually quite startling to think about just how many different kinds of facilities are packed aboard today's biggest, most luxurious cruise ships. Think about it—a full-scale planetarium? Didn't they use to have those only in America's biggest cities? And how about ice-skating rinks? Who would even think to bring skates when packing for the tropics? Dance clubs and live-performance theaters, well, they've been a staple aboard cruise ships for years. But how about dedicated cigar and wine bars? They're the logical place to relax, you see, after an afternoon spent practicing your drive in the golf simulator.

These kinds of on-board facilities really put into perspective the size of some of today's fleet flagships. They really are floating cities, not just figuratively, with populations that dwarf some of the smaller communities and towns in the rural United States. As with any place that wants to attract a large number of people, today's cruise ships offer a little bit of something to suit nearly every person's interests.

Casinos

Casinos have been aboard cruise ships for many years, and they remain a popular spot for hard-core gamblers and nickel-slot lovers alike. Aboard ships that cater to children and families, casinos are sometimes one of the only places reserved for adults only. This can add to their popularity during daytime hours, though they usually are not open for business until at least mid-afternoon.

You'll find slot machines, roulette tables, and blackjack tables inside most onboard casinos, no matter which cruise line you choose. Some companies add to the standards, such as Crystal Cruises, which has Caesars Palace at Sea casinos aboard all three of its ships, the *Serenity*, the *Harmony*, and the *Symphony*. The world-famous gaming company operates craps and baccarat tables in addition to the old favorites.

Holland America's casinos also offer additional games, including Caribbean poker. The 780-foot *Amsterdam* ship alone has five blackjack tables, a roulette table, a craps table, a stud poker table, a three-card poker table, and eleven slot machines. That ship even runs what it calls a champagne slot tournament, in which the bubbly flows just as fast as the coins.

 JUST FOR PARENTS

Princess Cruise Lines' *Grand Princess, Star Princess,* and *Golden Princess* ships have casinos designed by architects of Caesars Palace, with domed ceilings that change from dawn to dusk every twenty minutes. You can watch the show overhead between turns at the blackjack, poker, roulette, and craps tables.

Norwegian Cruise Line's *Norwegian Dawn* has all the standard gaming options plus mini-baccarat, Let It Ride slot machines, and a VIP card room. That ship (and several others in the NCL fleet) also offers free gaming classes, triple-play chip promotions, and slot and blackjack tournaments.

Cinemas

You might not think of going to the movies when you think of being aboard cruise ships, but watching a major motion picture can make for great fun on rainy days or on days when you simply need a break from the sun, the salt air, and the crowds. There's something about having the lights go down and the sound come up all around you that provides another level of escape during your cruise-ship vacation.

Crystal Cruises has one of the most heavily promoted cinema experiences on the water. All three of its ships have areas called the Hollywood Theatre that show recently released and classic movies at least twice a day. All of the cinemas feature Dolby sound and multilingual translation systems. They also are equipped with StarSound infrared hearing technology that is designed to enable hearing-impaired passengers to sit anywhere in the room while watching the film. That's a great benefit if your family group includes older grandparents.

RAINY DAY FUN

If your ship's cinema is packed with people and you can't get inside, hold a little family contest to see who can name the highest number of nautical movie scenes. Get the ball rolling with Rodney Dangerfield's anchor-dropping yacht in *Caddyshack*, Bill Murray's "I'm sailing!" speech in *What About Bob*, and, well, anything from *Titanic*.

Ships in the Silversea fleet promote a cinema experience of a different kind. They show movies under the moonlight in the open air on the pool deck—a lovely place to snuggle up for a nightcap after a hectic day of excursions ashore.

Clubs and Discos

Not too many years ago, nightlife facilities were a main focus aboard cruise ships. As disco dancing gave way to the Age of Madonna back in the United States, cruise ships plying the world's waters worked hard to inject dance-club environments into their passengers' experience—and to market them heavily.

Today, the techno beats are still pumping amid laser-light shows aboard most of the cruise ships that cater to North American passengers, but the discos are not as widely promoted. Instead, cruise companies are focusing on highlighting their "new millennium" amenities, trying to lure you with advertisements for herbal spas and lecture series.

Still, if you want to boogie oogie oogie till you just can't boogie no more (with apologies to the band Taste of Honey), you will be able to aboard most ships. The European-based Costa Cruises, for one, still takes nightlife as seriously as a morning hangover aboard several of its ships. The Crystal Club Disco aboard the Costa *Allegra*, for instance, has panoramic 360-degree views. It does double-duty by serving as an observatory by day and hosting sound and light shows by night. The Costa *Fortuna* calls its dance club the Vulcania Disco. It features a sixteen-foot-high moving statue of the god Volcano alight with fiber optics. The second deck of the two-story Vulcania Disco is surrounded by the ship's casino, creating a fully appropriate adults-only feel.

Princess Cruises also combines some of its dance clubs with other adult pursuits. The *Diamond Princess*, for instance, features the high-tech Club Fusion. It not only offers nightclub dancing and cabaret, but also boasts forty-two high-definition video screens and adult-only gaming areas.

Exercise Facilities

Truth be told, you could get plenty of exercise aboard any cruise ship without ever stepping into the gym. Snorkeling, scuba diving, swimming, hiking, and simply walking around your various ports of call will often be more exercise on their own than you are used to getting back home.

Of course, if you want the real gym experience instead, you will find it aboard virtually every cruise ship out there. Celebrity Cruises, for instance, has the fitness areas that you would expect, with treadmills, stair machines, NordicTrack cross-country ski machines, and Aero-Step machines (just to name a few), as well as personal training sessions for beginners and work-out mavens alike. Celebrity's "Metabolism Booster" class is an aerobic and strength-training program specifically tailored to target your personal problem areas. The "Mind, Body and Soul" program combines strength training and stretching with meditation and aromatherapy, while the "Help! I Don't Belong to a Gym!" program is run by an instructor who will show you how to train with weights in a way that will be easy for you to continue after you disembark and head back home.

If you prefer to get your exercise outside, some of Celebrity's ships also have full-size basketball courts, compact football fields, paddle tennis areas, volleyball courts, golf simulators, and shuffleboard spaces.

JUST FOR PARENTS

Celebrity Cruises offers a special fitness program aboard its ships titled "Oh, My Aching Back!" It combines stretching with strengthening exercises during a thirty-minute session, with particular emphasis on your lower back area.

Costa Cruise Lines has fitness centers aboard its ships with Technogym equipment, free weights, life cycles, fitness walk classes, aerobics classes, strength training programs, and stretching and relaxation sessions. There's also a jogging track atop some ships, overlooking the pool deck. The Costa *Mediterranea* has a small-size tennis court that can be converted for groups wanting to play basketball or volleyball.

Crystal Cruises is proud not only of its gym equipment—including LifeFitness treadmills with individual flat-screen televisions—but of the place in which they stand: state-of-the-art gyms with panoramic ocean views. In the same fitness area, you can take part in yoga classes, Pilates sessions, body sculpting exercises, low-impact water workouts, tai chi sessions, and Cardio Ki-Bo circuit training (a combination of boxercise, kickboxing, and aerobics).

 TRAVEL TIP

If you want to get off the treadmill and break up your fitness routine, consider booking shore excursions that involve swimming, snorkeling, and scuba diving. If you weigh 150 pounds and scuba dive for just one hour, you can burn more than 800 calories.

Royal Caribbean's ships have jogging tracks and exercise rooms like other cruise lines, but this company's boats make a point of offering unique exercise options outdoors. For instance, every one of its ships has a three-story-high rock-climbing wall with paths designed to challenge you whether you're a novice or a veteran of Mount Everest. Royal Caribbean also has curvy in-line skating tracks aboard each of its Voyager-class ships, as well as the only ice-skating rinks at sea. Starting in July of 2005, the *Enchantment of the Seas* was scheduled to offer brand-new bungee trampolines.

Libraries

Libraries are often overlooked on cruise ships, taking a back seat to "sexier" spaces like nightclubs and gourmet dining rooms.

If you want to learn as much about your ports of call as possible, though, the library is the place for you.

Cruise ships that focus on excursions, such as Swan Hellenic's *Minerva II*, often have fantastic libraries to help you in your quest for knowledge. The *Minerva II* holds more than 4,000 books, including signed copies of some titles and books about every port of call you will visit.

Other cruise ships usually have a smaller number of volumes aboard, but their libraries often stock puzzles and games as well. If you or your family need a bit of quiet time, you usually can find it in your ship's library.

Lounges and Bars

Just as they have on land, lounges and bars have come a long way at sea. Gone are the days of one-design-fits-all sitting rooms. Today's socializing hotspots are often devoted to recreational pursuits beyond just finding other friendly faces.

The Carnival *Conquest,* for instance, has a piano bar and a separate wine bar in addition to its more traditional jazz club. Costa Cruise Line's *Tropicale* also has a piano bar that offers cocktails and light music, while its *Mediterranea* ship has a separate lounge for playing cards and board games. Disney Cruise Line has turned its Diversions bar into a traditional sports pub full of flat-screen plasma televisions for football, baseball, and basketball fans to stand around and cheer when they're not competing at trivia contests and karaoke.

At the other end of the ambience spectrum, NCL's *Norwegian Dawn* has a lounge called the Wine Cellar that seats just sixteen people for tastings, sometimes at romantic tables for two. The *Norwegian Dawn* also has a space called Gatsby's Champagne Bar, which is done up in art deco style to complement the piano player's tunes and the servings of martinis, pate de foie gras, and, of course, champagne. The ship's Java Cafe is a separate bar that serves frozen coffee, espresso, cappuccino, tea, Viennese pastries, and cookies. The *Norwegian Dawn* also has a few outside bars (in addition to its Pearly King's Pub). You can, for example, enjoy the Topsiders Bar, a Key West–style pool facility, or you can look out over the pool from high above while listening to the piano player in the Star Bar. There's also a Bimini Bar & Grill, done in a Bahamian-style beach atmosphere.

FAST FACT

Cruise-ship bars and lounges have come a long way in recent years. There are now specialty lounges for everything from cigar-lovers to wine tasters to sports fans. If you cruise aboard NCL's *Norwegian Dawn*, you can even enjoy an entire bar devoted just to ice cream, called Sprinkles.

Silversea has fewer offerings, but its bars and lounges are of a more refined nature. You can enjoy a wine tasting at Le Champagne or sip your cognac at The Humidor, a gentleman's club-style lounge with wood-paneled walls, comfortable leather chairs, and—most important—a dedicated ventilation system.

Smoking Rooms

Smoking rooms used to have a terrible connotation, with the mere mention of one conjuring visions of a smoke-filled closet where nicotine addicts got shoved out of sight of the rest of the passengers. Today, smoking rooms have grown up into full-scale lounges that offer far more than the standard old drag. They're downright luxurious in some cases.

Crystal Cruises has Connoisseur Clubs aboard each of its three ships, the *Serenity*, the *Harmony*, and the *Symphony*. The clubs are cigar lounges open for after-dinner drinks and conversation. The Radisson Seven Seas cruise ship *Voyager* also calls its smoking room the Connoisseur Club, and has it outfitted complete with English club chairs and hand-rolled cigars that are stored in climate-controlled humidors. NCL's *Norwegian Dawn* calls its smoking room the

Havana Club and also offers hand-rolled premium cigars, but for just twelve people at a time. If you're one of them, you can also order a glass of port, cognac, or malt whiskey.

Spas

What discotheques have lost in popularity in recent years, spas have gained—and then some. Like land-based resorts, spas have become a major selling point aboard cruise ships at all price levels. You are likely to be able to get a massage no matter what kind of cruise line you choose, but aboard the higher-end ships, you will often find treatments and services that rival the finest health spas in Paris and New York.

Celebrity Cruises, for example, boasts an AquaSpa aboard each of its ships. The services are run by Elemis, a leading manufacturer of premium spa products. Aboard Celebrity's Millennium-class ships, AquaSpa facilities measure fully 25,000 square feet and offer more than 40 treatments and therapies that range from ninety minutes to five hours long. Some examples include the Asian Ceremony of Stones (which lasts for five hours and includes aroma stone therapy and a frangipani hair and scalp ritual), the Tahitian Ceremony of Flowers (which also lasts for five hours and includes an exotic jasmine flower bath and Hawaiian four-hands therapy), and the Etruscan Chamber Rasul (in which you will find yourself covered in organic mud within a gentle steam bath that's specially designed for couples, followed by a tropical rainfall shower to rinse away the mud).

≡FAST FACT

The AquaSpa by Elemis aboard Celebrity's ships offers treatments that incorporate cultures you might find at various ports of call. Some examples include the Hawaiian lomi lomi massage, Chinese Tui Na sessions, the Balinese massage, Indian Ayurvedic treatments, the Swedish massage, and Japanese shiatsu.

The Radisson Seven Seas Cruises ship *Voyager* also paired with a big-name spa brand from exclusive health centers worldwide: Carita Paris. Costa Cruise Lines has not done the same, but it does have two-level Ischia Spa and Olympia Gym centers aboard its *Mediterranea* and *Atlantica* ships. You can enjoy a massage, hydrotherapy, or a Thalassic therapy treatment before you work out on the exercise machines and in the aerobics space. The Costa *Victoria* has a Pompei Spa with an indoor pool, a Turkish bath, saunas, and a 500-meter jogging track that connects to the ship's gymnasium. All of Costa's spas have floor-to-ceiling glass windows that look out over the sea.

Crystal Cruises' boats have spas that offer all the standards plus yoga and Pilates, as well as health-focused lectures and workshops. You'll also find Zen rock gardens, water fountains, rain and mist, aroma stone therapy, a private sundeck for relaxing before and after your treatments, and a sensory bed that you can enjoy alone or with your significant other.

Norwegian Cruise Line's ships all have treatments provided by Mandara Spa, a leading operator of resort spas throughout the world. While you can get in-stateroom treatments if you prefer your privacy, the spa offers hydrotherapy, Asian treatments, on-deck and poolside massages, and massages on secluded beaches in the Caribbean and South Pacific. The therapies you will find in Mandara Spas are meant to capitalize on the cultures of your ports of call. Cruises through the Hawaiian Islands, for example, include a coconut body polish done with freshly grated coconuts; a Balinese coffee scrub offered with freshly ground Kona coffee that is mixed with Balinese coffee and volcanic pumice; and traditional Hawaiian lomi lomi–style massages that include a technique of long, soothing strokes.

Not to be outdone, Royal Caribbean's Radiance-class ships all have traditional spa services plus unique thermal suites that include heated tile lounges, steam rooms, saunas, aromatherapy rooms, and tropical and fog showers.

≡FAST FACT

Aboard Norwegian Cruise Line's ships, the spas are called Mandara—
a word derived from a Sanskrit legend about the gods' quest for the
elixir of immortality and eternal youth.

Swimming Pools

You will find at least one swimming pool aboard almost every
major cruise ship in the world, even if it ends up running itineraries
for a few years in Alaska, where it's often too cold to take a dip.

Newer and bigger cruise ships tend to have more than one pool,
with different areas designed to appeal to different kinds of people.
Some pools are more kid-friendly, while others are sophisticated
and located near adults-only bars.

The Carnival *Conquest,* for instance, has an amidships outdoor
pool with a 214-foot spiral water slide in addition to a large pool with
a retractable dome on its aft deck. You can guess where the kids
will be aboard that ship!

Crystal Cruises has lap pools aboard its ships, plus indoor/
outdoor pools with retractable roofs to help keep the sun at bay.
Silversea also has lap pools aboard its ships, and in its case, they
are heated.

Theater

If you are a lover of song and dance, your ship's theater may
just well be the highlight of your cruise. Many of the productions
you will have a chance to see are of such high quality, they would
be right at home on the Las Vegas strip or even New York's famous
Great White Way.

Don't expect to be crammed into a tiny little room, either; many
cruise ships have massive multi-level facilities devoted exclusively
to creating award-winning musical productions. Costa's *Europa,*
for instance, has a two-deck-tall theater that holds a whopping 747

people. If that's not big enough for you, try Costa's *Mediterranea*, which has the three-deck-high Osiris Theater done up in an Egyptian theme.

As you might expect, the Disney Cruise Line boasts a theater designed specifically for its cartoon-character-inspired shows, much as you would find on land at Walt Disney World. The Walt Disney Theater is a 977-seater complete with a red carpet, fawning paparazzi, and a roving reporter, all of which makes the experience come alive before you even take your seat. The show designed just for this theater is called *The Golden Mickeys* (one you won't find at the company's theme parks), promoted as the most technologically advanced stage show at sea. Animated backdrops take you from outside to inside; three-dimensional illusions are created by films that race across stage-size screens; and there are surround-sound effects for all the scenes, including ones that take productions like *The Lion King* and weave them into the broader *Golden Mickeys* plot with new scenes.

If you prefer a more adult theme to cartoon characters in your theater experience, check out Holland America's productions. They have included everything from *Paparazzi*—created just for the company's ships by Tony Award–winner Tommy Tune—to a show called *Copacabana* that has been playing to capacity crowds since 1998, when singer Barry Manilow's production company created it for Holland America.

Auctions

Art auctions are becoming hugely popular as passengers realize that excellent bargains can be found on fine works of art. Often, your ship will give you a small print as a thank you for attending an auction, as well as chances to enter raffles for seriolithographs and other high-quality prints that you can take home and have framed. Actually, you don't even have to take them home if you don't want to; your cruise ship will often have them shipped for you, rolled in a special container to avoid wrinkles and tears.

■ TRAVEL TIP

You can find everything from Picassos to modern masters to animated-movie cells at onboard art auctions. Check with your particular cruise company to find out details about which artworks are expected to be available on your itinerary.

Aboard all cruise lines that offer art auctions, you should be able to see the appraised value of the artwork being offered. You might be tempted to think the valuations are some kind of scam, because you will be told that the price you will pay is far lower than what the artwork is actually worth. Don't worry—some passengers who purchase artwork and then go home to do independent research on its value find that they have made at least a few hundred dollars between the time they bought the print and the time they checked its worth after disembarking the ship. In fact, a few years ago, you might have read stories about expert art-buyers flocking to cruise ships for just this reason.

Medical Facilities

All cruise ships have medical personnel aboard to tend to their crew members. In most cases, however, these doctors, nurses, and physician's assistants are independent contractors—not employees of the cruise line. As such, they charge separate fees for their services. If you require medical assistance while onboard, the ship's medical staff may tend to you, or at the very least make an assessment that you require medical services ashore, but you are likely to be charged what most cruise companies call a "reasonable rate" in their brochures' fine print. Plus, the ship assumes no liability for the result of any instructions or diagnoses made by the independent contractor. Even though you are aboard a cruise company's ship, it is you and the doctor making your medical decisions and negotiating fees, period.

Do not expect a full-scale hospital aboard your ship, or even so much as a portable defibrillator like the ones now available in some land-based shopping malls. In most cases, your ship will offer basic treatment, a pharmacy stocked with common prescriptions, and basic emergency services. Some cruise lines, but not all, will have independent medical contractors who are also trained in cardiac life support. Be sure to ask about your particular ship's staffing in advance if you have major health considerations.

Your travel insurance policy (or your worldwide health insurance policy, if you are a frequent traveler) may afford you better care on shore—depending on where in the world your ship is. And whether you have insurance or not, if you become very sick, then the ship's personnel are authorized to demand that you disembark at the port of *their* choice. Of course, they cannot force you to go to a doctor on shore, but they can refuse to let you reboard the ship if they believe your medical condition is putting other passengers at risk of infection or disease.

The upshot is that cruise companies are vacation providers, not medical service providers. If you think you might have a problem aboard, prepare through insurance to handle it yourself.

Ship Services

There's a reason why your ship has an officer whose title is hotel manager: Each ship is essentially a large, floating hotel. As such, you will usually be able to find the same kinds of services you would in any Marriott or Sheraton, from Internet access to housekeeping to fax machines. Alas, though, as with most hotels ashore, you'll often be expected to pay an additional fee to use these services.

Internet/Computer Stations

So, you're one of those people who can't leave your work at home? Or perhaps you just like to remain connected with the world outside of your cruise-ship cabin?

You're in luck: More and more cruise lines are adding Internet cafés and even wireless access to their ships. In many cases, the services are pay-as-you-go in addition to your regular cruise fare, but they are available if you want them—often twenty-four hours a day.

Celebrity calls its twenty-four-hour Internet cafés Online@Celebrity Cruises. Depending on the ship you choose, you will find six to eighteen workstations that you can use for a fee of fifty cents per minute. You can bill your computer time on your signature card, so you won't have to carry cash. You will be subject to a program called CyberPatrol that is designed to limit offensive content and pornography. At each workstation, you will find a Logitech Quickcam camera that will let you take a picture of yourself and set it digitally against various backgrounds, to send to friends as an electronic postcard. The price for that service is $6.95 per postcard.

Celebrity also has a program called Connect@Sea aboard its Millennium-class ships (the *Millennium, Infinity, Summitt,* and *Constellation*) that provides you with twenty-four-hour Internet access from your cabin. The first fifty minutes are free, after which you will be charged $25 per day. You must bring your own laptop computer that runs on a Windows operating system in order to use this service.

≡FAST FACT

Royal Caribbean's newest ships have a feature called Cybercabin, which lets you use your laptop computer to connect to the Internet from your stateroom. You will be charged a flat rate of $100 for the service during a seven-night cruise, in addition to your regular cruise-ship fare.

Norwegian Cruise Line offers wireless Internet service that you can tap into with your own laptop computer or by renting one of the laptops aboard the ship. As long as your wireless card supports the 802.11B wireless protocol, you will be in business. There may be a separate charge depending on how you use the service, and it is only available in certain parts of NCL's ships. Often, you will have to leave your cabin in order to use it, in public spaces such as cafés, atriums, libraries, and, of course, Internet cafés—which are often open twenty-four hours a day and usually have plenty of workstations. The *Norwegian Dawn* alone has seventeen computer terminals.

Laundry Service

You will find multiple kinds of laundry services aboard different cruise lines, including everything from dry cleaning to self-service machines. As a general rule, you should not count on dry cleaning services being available unless you check with your specific cruise line, and you should expect to pay at least a nominal fee for laundry unless you have booked a high-end suite or penthouse.

≡FAST FACT

On higher-end cruise lines, such as Cunard, you can expect a full complement of services, including dry cleaning, valet laundry, and self-service washing machines.

Carnival Cruise Lines, for instance, does not offer dry cleaning but does have everything from valet laundry services handled by a room steward to self-service washing machines and dryers. If you choose to have the ship's crew handle your washing, you'll pay as much as $2 per T-shirt, $7.50 per dress, and $5 per skirt and blouse depending on the material from which they are made. Royal Caribbean, on the other hand, offers no self-service laundry but does provide dry cleaning and valet laundry services. Aboard Royal

Caribbean ships, you'll pay as much as $5 to have a dress washed and as much as $3.50 for a pair of slacks.

Maid Service

One thing you won't be doing at sea is making your own bed. Your cruise fare will include once-a-day maid service in your cabin or suite. Aboard some of the higher-end ships, you can expect twice-a-day maid service, including a bed turndown at night. Silversea, for instance, offers this level of service as part of your standard cruise fare.

Telephone/Fax Services

Many ships have telephones in each stateroom, but beware—the rates are substantially higher than on your cell phone, sometimes in the $10-per-minute range. Your friends who call the ship to reach you will be charged a similar per-minute rate on their credit card.

TRAVEL TIP

Depending on where you cruise, you may be forced to use the shipboard system instead of your cell phone because you may not have coverage, particularly when cruising overseas. A few companies are beginning to discuss mini-cellular towers aboard to enhance passengers' private cell phone signals, so you can ask your travel agent if your ship has that new kind of service—but don't count on it.

You will sometimes be able to send and receive faxes while you are aboard, but you may have to give your friends and family back home a special number or ship code. Again, check with your travel agent or cruise company about your particular ship.

Classes and Lectures

Facilities aren't the only thing that cruise ships offer nowadays. Aboard some cruise lines, half the fun is taking advantage of special classes, guest lectures, and activities like art auctions. You just might be surprised at how creative some of the cruise lines are becoming in this area, trying to outdo one another with celebrities and hobby-themed offerings like golf clinics and cooking schools.

Crystal Cruises, for instance, has PGA golf professionals at your disposal aboard all three of its ships. Morning lessons are included in the price of your cruise, while afternoon clinics are available at an additional charge. You will be able to work on your chipping and tee shots with onboard driving ranges, putting greens, and practice cages. Crystal even has a partnership with the TaylorMade company that enables it to provide clubs for men and women alike, in right-handed and left-handed models. Sometimes, during Crystal's golf-themed itineraries, you will even get a chance to share your ship with well-known PGA stars like Billy Casper.

If golf is not your game, Crystal's ships also have bridge lessons, including games supervised by accredited instructors from the American Contract Bridge League. Unlike the PGA stars, the bridge instructors are aboard for you on every cruise.

Holland America also offers bridge instruction, but only during itineraries that are at least ten days long. On the other hand, Holland America's ships have a few unique programs of their own, including instructional workshops where you can learn how to make marzipan and Dutch cheese fondue. By the end of 2006, every ship in the Holland America line will also have its own culinary arts theater where you can participate in guest-chef presentations, demonstrations, and small cooking classes. Each theater is intended to look like it belongs on the set of television's Food Network, with show kitchens like the one that famous chef Emeril Lagasse uses. The lessons and demonstrations are broadcast on televisions for the theater's audience, and you can even watch the shows from your personal stateroom.

Like Crystal and Holland America ships, the *Voyager* ship in the Radisson Seven Seas fleet also has a bridge instructor aboard, and Silversea Cruises promotes golf lessons through its Silver Links program aboard the *Silver Shadow* and *Silver Whisper.* The Silver Links program, in addition to including an onboard golf pro, provides pre-arranged tee times at whatever ports of call your ship is visiting.

Computer Instruction

As technology speeds ahead, so have the offerings that involve it aboard cruise ships. You can find classes for beginners and experts alike in basic word-processing programs and advanced digital photography techniques. These kinds of computer instruction classes are not as abundant aboard cruise ships as, say, casinos, but a few companies promote computer classes aboard at least some of their ships.

Radisson Seven Seas Cruises, for instance, has at least fourteen computers in the Club.com room aboard its *Voyager* ship. Free classes include "Introduction to E-Mail," "Advanced Word Processing," and "Digital Photography."

Crystal Cruises has an extensive twenty-course curriculum in computer instruction, all complimentary with the price of your cruise. Dell laptops and PCs are the teaching tools, and you can even get private instruction if you are willing to pay an extra fee. The beginner, intermediate, and advanced classes aboard Crystal's ships include "Introduction to Handheld Organizers," "Digital Photo Finishing," "Introduction to the Windows Operating System," "Web Site Design," and more. There is even a course available that will teach you how to research investments online and then prepare financial spreadsheets using the information you discover.

Dance Classes

From ballroom waltzes to steamy sambas, most cruise ships offer at least a few dance classes a week. They are, of course, a lot of fun for couples, but don't feel left out if you are cruising alone or your spouse bolts at the mention of dancing. Many cruise lines will provide a partner for you; ask about details from your ship's activities coordinator.

Guest Lectures

If you are the type of person who would rather listen to experts than try to become one, you'll be glad to know that many cruise ships have begun to offer lecture series. The topics cover a broad swath of human knowledge, sometimes directly related to your ship's ports of call and sometimes not related at all.

From Explorers to Chefs

The Radisson Seven Seas Cruises ship *Voyager*, for instance, offers Le Cordon Bleu workshops on select sailings. During these lectures, chefs trained in the classic French Le Cordon Bleu style give you an exclusive lesson in how to prepare some of their favorite dishes. This course is not usually included in your cruise fare, however; you should expect to pay at least $395 to attend.

Silversea Cruises has an entire enrichment series of lectures that it calls "The Spirit of Exploration." The company brings internationally acclaimed adventurers aboard select sailings to offer you presentations about their personal quests for discovery. In some cases, the expert even goes on shore excursions with you. Some recent lecturers have included Dr. Don Walsh, a retired Navy captain and oceanographer who gained worldwide fame during his fifty-five expeditions to the polar regions (he even has an Antarctic mountain range named for him, the Walsh Spur); Brian Jones, who with a partner completed the first circumnavigation of the Earth in a hot-air balloon; Dr. Joe MacInnis, a marine conservationist and one of the first people to dive on the wreck of the *Titanic*; and Belinda Sawyer, a senior expedition leader for Deep Ocean Expeditions, which offers submersible-vehicle expeditions as far as 20,000 feet below the ocean's surface to explore wrecks like the battleship *Bismarck* and areas of scientific interest like the Mid-Atlantic Ridge.

≡FAST FACT

Silversea also has offers a wine and culinary series on select itineraries. The series includes lectures, tastings, and guided excursions to wineries by top experts and winemakers. The lectures and culinary demonstrations are often followed by gourmet dinners with Relais & Chateaux-Relais Gourmands guest chefs.

Not to be outdone, Cunard brings in its enrichment speakers through a partnership with the prestigious Oxford University. Authors often host book-signings before leading discussions about their topics of expertise, which might include anything from cooking and wine to photography and British comedy.

Current Events and History

While adventurers have something to do with your cruise-ship experience—hey, you are, after all, on an adventure of your own—some cruise lines bring in speakers to lecture on specialty topics that have nothing to do with the ocean or cruising, but that are of interest to a large group of people.

Crystal Cruises calls its specialty-topic series the Crystal Visions Enrichment Program and brings in everyone from high-level ambassadors and foreign diplomats to guest chefs and wine connoisseurs, historians, humorists, authors, television journalists, movie celebrities, and financial leaders. Past guest lecturers have included Marlin Fitzwater, who served as U.S. press secretary under presidents Ronald Reagan and George H.W. Bush; and Dr. Harm de Blij, who spent seven years as the geography editor for ABC television's *Good Morning America* before beginning his current PBS series, *The Power of Place.*

Crystal also brings in lecturers on topics geared toward its theme cruises, including photography, golf, comedy, gardening, jazz, Big Band music, film festivals, Smithsonian voyages, and food and wine.

Local Culture

Perhaps some of the best lectures on board cruise ships are the ones given about the places you will be visiting. Nothing brings a port of call to life better than learning a bit about its history and culture before stepping foot ashore, and if your cruise ship offers such lectures, you should sign up immediately.

Holland America, for instance, brings a naturalist aboard every ship whose itinerary includes Alaska. The naturalists lecture and give slide presentations about the area's natural history and wildlife—everything from how glaciers and icebergs are formed to why salmon spawn in such droves every summer.

Radisson Seven Seas Cruises also brings guest lecturers aboard its *Voyager* ship to discuss your ports of call. Some of its speakers include leading university or museum experts, and the presentations often include slide shows. Imagine how much more you will enjoy a South American cruise, for example, if you learn about the Peruvian Incas along the way. Other lectures might include a discussion of Florence during the Renaissance during an itinerary of cruising around Italy.

CHAPTER 18

Programs for Children

THE NUMBER OF PARENTS choosing to cruise with children has grown exponentially in recent years. By Royal Caribbean's estimate, based just on its own ship bookings, there has been more than a 50-percent increase since 2000 alone. It's a trend that a lot of the cruise-ship companies recognized quickly, and many have created programs and partnerships specifically targeted to cruising families. Whether you have an infant, a toddler, a curious eight-year-old, or a teenager, nearly a dozen cruise lines have specific shipboard areas and activities that will help everyone in your family get the most out of your vacation.

Age Requirements

In general, cruise ships have kids' clubs broken down into age groups that make sense for kids and counselors alike. The teenagers are kept separate from the eight-year-olds, who are kept separate from the three-year-olds, and so on.

If you have one older child and one new member in your family, keep in mind that not all cruise lines offer services for children of all ages. Disney, for one, promotes a nursery for infants in addition to supervised activities for older siblings (beginning at age three); and Royal Caribbean announced a partnership with Fisher-Price in 2004 to create programs for children as young as six months (in addition to existing programs for kids age three and older). On the whole, though, babies will usually be your full-time responsibility. Unless otherwise specifically noted in your cruise-ship literature, you should *not* expect services on board for infants and newborns.

Carnival offers supervised activities for kids starting at age two, while Crystal, Costa, and Princess all offer supervised activities starting at age three. If your child is three years old but not fully toilet trained, he may not be allowed to participate in some of the programs. Be sure to check with your travel agent or your cruise-ship company for specifics; in some cases, the fine print says the use of pull-up diapers does not count when determining whether a child is toilet trained and eligible for the activities.

Holland America and Radisson Seven Seas Cruises begin offering supervised activities for children at the age of five (though Holland America is working on lowering that to age three). If you have a child younger than five and hope to cruise aboard one of these lines, you likely will have to supervise the child yourself or bring a babysitter or nanny at your own expense. Babysitting services are sometimes available on a first-come, first-served basis after your ship gets under way, but you should not count on them (see page 316 for more details).

 TRAVEL TIP

If you have an older child and an infant (and a budget that allows it), consider bringing your own babysitter aboard and booking an adjacent kids' cabin that has a third bed. Many ships offer plenty of activities for your older child, but babysitting for the child younger than age two might be iffy. Having the adjacent cabin and sitter will give you peace of mind.

Supervised activities occur all over the cruise ships (excluding the bars and casinos, of course), and some cruise ships have specially designed areas that are supervised for children's activities all day long. Different cruise lines have different amounts of supervised areas and programs available, and most companies limit the availability of supervised activities to when the ship is at sea—not in port. They assume you'll want to take the kids ashore with you to explore, so you should not expect to leave your kids on the boat under someone else's watch while you hit the town.

You should also note that some cruise companies work hard to appeal to childless customers and therefore do not have or promote children's facilities. Swan Hellenic, for instance, does not encourage passengers younger than age sixteen, while Oceana also discourages travel with children and—in a few cases of extreme rowdiness—has come close to asking parents and their children to leave before the completion of a cruise. Seabourn and Silversea also say their cruise programs are tailored for adult interests and prefer that you leave your younger kids at home when cruising on their ships. (Silversea does not allow children younger than one year old, and it reserves the right to limit the number of children aboard who are younger than three.)

Companies that *do* want your kids as passengers have named and packaged their children's activities into kids' clubs. Each of these cruise lines has different programs, some more educational than others.

Cruise Line Specifics

Of the companies that encourage cruising with children, each promotes different kinds of activities for different age groups. The easiest way to determine which company's offerings might be best for your family is to read about each program separately and then decide which one will be the best fit for your children's personalities. It's hard to compare these programs side by side because they are all coordinated differently company by company—and each company's individual ships have different spaces dedicated for kids' use—but you can learn about each cruise line's programming and make notes about the names of the activities that sound right for your child. The next step is to check your specific boat's brochure to find out what kinds of playrooms and arcades are aboard.

Remember that quality is often better than quantity when thinking about cruising programs for your kids. If you have a studious child, she might be happier aboard a cruise ship that offers a handful of great educational activities than aboard a cruise ship with dozens of video-game competitions. Conversely, if your son likes a lot of exercise outdoors, he may not be satisfied aboard a ship with super-duper indoor playrooms but no waterslide or mini-golf on the sun-drenched decks.

Carnival

Carnival promotes itself as being the creator of the "fun ships" and has tons of programs to support the claim. It is a top choice for many parents who want to cruise with kids, and, as such, you should expect activities areas to be packed with little people. Camp Carnival, as the youth program is known, was expected to support a half-million cruising kids between two and fifteen years old during 2005 alone. Your kids certainly won't lack for new friends—or new influences—aboard a Carnival ship.

Camp Carnival is divided into four age brackets, plus a fifth segment called "family activities" that includes things like sundae making, pool time, and a talent show. Programs are scheduled to run aboard the ship from 9:00 A.M. until 10:00 P.M.

≡FAST FACT

All Camp Carnival counselors are said to be college-educated, have professional child-care experience, or both. They supervise activities ship-wide in addition to providing babysitting services for you on an individual basis.

The youngest Camp Carnival group is toddlers, ages two through five. Activities for this group include finger painting, storytelling, face painting, Play-Doh time, sand art, Sony PlayStation 2 activities, and general arts and crafts.

Next come the juniors, ages six through eight. They can enjoy sand art and Sony PlayStation 2 activities, as well, but they also are given a chance to participate in a pirate hunt, an ice-cream eating contest, and an Olympics competition.

The intermediate level of Camp Carnival is for children ages nine through eleven. It includes nighttime swimming, karaoke, jewelry making, scavenger hunts, ping-pong tournaments, and board games.

Last is the teen bracket, for ages twelve through fifteen. These kids can play in video-game tournaments and enjoy disco parties in addition to some of the other activities previously mentioned.

RAINY DAY FUN

Carnival recently announced several new Camp Carnival activities, including youth spa treatments and H2Ocean, a science program that enables kids to make their own ice cream and mini-hovercrafts.

Activities that several of the age brackets can enjoy include an art program in which kids create works in papier-mache, oil paint, and watercolors. Camp Carnival also offers an EduCruise program that includes interactive projects tied to the cultures, landmarks, history, and geography of your particular ship's ports of call.

Celebrity Cruises

Celebrity's name for kid-friendly activities is the Family Cruising Program. It is available aboard cruises that take place during the summer months and during seasonal sailing dates (such as weeks when schools tend to be out of session for holidays).

Each Celebrity ship has a dedicated staff of eight to twelve youth counselors aboard, including one supervisor and one lifeguard. The company says each counselor is trained in child psychology, child development, education, or recreation studies in addition to having previous experience working with children aboard Celebrity or other cruise lines. Most counselors are from the United States or Canada.

≡FAST FACT

If your child is between ages three and ten and is participating in Celebrity's Family Cruising Program activities, he will be required to wear a wristband during the duration of the cruise for identification purposes. You also will have to sign your child in and out of the counselors' care and present your Celebrity Signature Card to verify your identity.

The Family Cruising Program is divided into four age groups: Ship Mates (ages three to six); Celebrity Cadets (ages seven through nine); Ensigns (ages ten to twelve) and Admiral T's (ages thirteen through fifteen, and sixteen through seventeen).

Activities for Ship Mates take place in a separate part of the ship from the other children's activities. There is a Fun Factory aboard the *Century, Constellation, Galaxy, Infinity, Mercury, Summit,* and *Millennium* ships, and there is a children's playroom aboard the *Horizon* and *Zenith* ships. In these spaces, your kids can enjoy clown parties, treasure hunts, Lego playtime, finger painting, dancing games, Sony PlayStations, ice cream sundae making, and more.

Cadet-level activities include pool Olympics, scavenger hunts, charades, T-shirt painting, movies, board games, ship tours, and more.

Ensigns begin activities later in the mornings and evenings than Ship Mates and Cadets, since Ensigns are a little bit older. Their programming includes karaoke, pizza parties, relay races, and more.

Admiral T's, like Ensigns, also get a later start on activities in the mornings and evenings because of their ages. Their activities include basketball tournaments, video games, a separate teen club aboard some ships (check your brochure), and team trivia contests.

Activities that bridge various age groups include the Young Mariners Club, in which your kids get to interact with different onboard departments and learn how the ship works. There is also a Junior Olympics tournament that's held poolside so you can cheer on your favorite contestant, as well as a clown party with face painting and a treasure hunt with "Celebrity pirates" lurking on your ship's decks. The Masquerade Parade will see your children making masks before parading about the ship, and magic lessons are available for kids of all ages. Your child can even have some one-on-one time with the professional magician.

RAINY DAY FUN

Celebrity offers a Summer Stock Theater program for children between the ages of three and twelve. The younger kids star in the show, which the older children direct. The older kids can also star in "commercials" between scenes if they want to have a few minutes in the spotlight.

Celebrity's Family Cruising Program hours are from 9:00 A.M. until noon; 2:00 P.M. until 5:30 P.M.; and 7:30 P.M. until 10:00 P.M. The hours remain the same whether your ship is in port or at sea. There are also two evenings dedicated to Parents' Night Out, in which counselors supervise a pizza party for your children while you dine elsewhere on the ship.

Costa Cruises

Costa Cruise Lines calls its youth program the Costa Kids Club and offers different levels of service for different age brackets depending on whether you are cruising in the Caribbean or the Mediterranean. In both destinations, the programs operate from 9:00 A.M. till noon, from 3:00 P.M. till 6:00 P.M., and from 9:00 P.M. until 11:30 P.M. All are closed for lunch and dinner and are usually also closed when ships are in port—except between 8:00 P.M. and 10:00 P.M. If you have a lot of kids on your ship or are traveling with a large group of children, you can request special activities outside of the scheduled programming times.

In the Caribbean, the Costa Kids Club is held at your ship's youth center, with groups divided into ages three to six, seven to twelve, and thirteen to seventeen. Activities for all ages include video-game competitions, arts and crafts, disco dancing, scavenger hunts, Italian language lessons, bingo, board games, face painting, and karaoke.

≡ FAST FACT

Costa Cruise Lines provides four full-time youth counselors for each Caribbean cruise. During Thanksgiving, Christmas, New Year's, and other traditional North American school holidays, additional counselors are brought aboard.

Also in the Caribbean, Costa offers its own program called Parents Night Out. On two different evenings, you can dine alone and enjoy adult ship activities while your kids eat at a supervised buffet or pizza party and do activities with other children aboard. Parents Night Out lasts from 6:00 P.M. until 11:30 P.M. and is included in the price of your cruise.

Costa promotes the children's programs for its European cruises differently. While the age brackets are the same, the programming is not. Juniors, who are the middle age group, can take part in jogging and aerobics, puppet theaters, and team treasure hunts, while the older teenagers can get guitar lessons, produce video shows, and enjoy sports and fitness programs. Costa does not offer the Parents Night Out program during its European cruising itineraries.

Crystal Cruises

Crystal Cruises offers a junior activities program aboard all three of its ships: the Crystal *Harmony*, Crystal *Symphony*, and Crystal *Serenity*. However, the ships are designed to cater to what the company calls "mature travelers," with luxuries and refinements as opposed to super-size indoor playgrounds. Far fewer parents bring their kids on these vacations than aboard some other cruise lines, and that is exactly how Crystal Cruises wants things to remain. The kinds of activities offered aboard each ship depend on how many children of each age are booked for each week's itinerary, so you should not expect full-time programming. Your three-year-old just may be the only one aboard, and other adults may not look as kindly toward rambunctious behavior as they would on the ships that cater to vacationing families.

The Junior Activities Program, as Crystal calls it, operates from 10:00 A.M. till noon, 2:00 P.M. till 5:00 P.M., and 7:00 P.M. till 9:00 P.M. It has two divisions: ages three to twelve, and ages thirteen to seventeen. Sometimes, teen programs are also offered from 10 P.M. till midnight. The company literature warns that you should not use activities programs as a babysitting service.

═FAST FACT

Crystal Cruises offers no programs for children six months old or younger. The company also reserves the right to restrict the number of children three years old or younger aboard each of its ships.

If you decide to bring your kids aboard a Crystal cruise, the Junior Activities Program includes a tour of the ship's galley with a chance for your children to decorate their own pastries; a backstage tour in the entertainment area, where your kids can see the dressing rooms and performers' costumes; and a tour of the bridge, as long as the captain grants permission based on weather conditions and the like. Each of Crystal's ships has a playroom with arts and crafts areas, Sony PlayStation video games, a large television, and board games. Two of the ships, the Crystal *Symphony* and Crystal *Serenity*, also have video arcades designed for teenagers, and all three ships have libraries with children's books and DVDs that can be enjoyed back in your cabin.

While there is a Junior Cruiser's menu, there are no segregated eating areas or supervised pizza parties for children aboard Crystal's ships. On the other hand, the ships sometimes award prizes for game tournaments if there is a demand based on the number of children aboard.

Arts and crafts that all ages can enjoy include puppet making, face painting, and macaroni art. The three- to twelve-year-olds can take part in scavenger hunts, movie nights, hula-hoop contests, and puzzle competitions, while the teenagers can play Trivial Pursuit, create their own pizzas, disco dance, and play poker.

Disney Cruise Line

It's hard not to think about kids when you hear the word Disney. For generations, Mickey Mouse, Donald Duck, and the entire Walt Disney family have been entertaining children of all ages at amusement parks on both coasts of the United States. Disney Cruise Line is no different, promising an experience just as magical as a trip to Cinderella's castle. And you can be sure this is the only cruise ship where your family will get to set sail with a bathing suit–clad Goofy.

≡FAST FACT

During a Disney Cruise Line vacation, your three- and four-year-old children can participate in Mousketeer Training—complete with a full-blown inspection by Mickey Mouse himself.

Disney divides its children's programs into five age groups, not including the aforementioned infant and toddler nursery, which it calls Flounder's Reef. The nursery has bubble murals done in a Little Mermaid theme and, more important, a staff of child specialists on duty to tend to your baby's needs.

The youngest age group in Disney's kids club is tailored for kids who are three and four. Activities are inspired by Disney characters that your kids may know from watching movies, with programming monikers such as "Do Si Do with Snow White" and "Nemo's Coral Reef Adventure." Older kids, those in the five- to seven-year-old category, can learn how to draw Disney characters or make up their own at a program called "Animation Antics." They also can make pirate flags that will be inspected by none other than Captain Hook himself.

Ages eight and nine are encouraged to use their heads as much as their hands, with programs such as "Hercules' Feats of Strength," in which your kids will learn to use basic physics to remove a tablecloth without breaking the dishes atop it. Your children in this age range also can become part of Goofy's Gum Shoe Investigators and learn how to identify people by using forensics clues. If your kids are ten to twelve years old, they can create their own animation cell and watch scientific demonstrations, including a vinegar-and-baking-soda "volcanic" eruption.

TRAVEL TIP

If you want to have the option of leaving your children at supervised programming but still have them be able to reach you at a moment's notice, consider a cruise with Disney. It offers pagers for you to take with you after dropping off your kids for activities.

Everyone thirteen or older is lumped into the teen category on Disney cruises, with activities including a dance party. If you want to give your teenagers something to do that isn't an officially coordinated program, tell them about the "Hidden Mickeys" all over the ship. Just as in Walt Disney World, the Disney cruise ships have Mickeys that designers slipped into the wallpaper, carpeting, and other parts of the ship as inside jokes. In fact, there's a whole Web site devoted to the public's search for them at ✑*www.hiddenmickeys.org*.

Holland America

The Holland America children's program is called Club HAL. It is organized in three age groups: five through eight, nine through twelve, and thirteen through seventeen—though the company is working on integrating programs for children as young as three aboard all its ships. On days when your ship is in port, the Club HAL activities start at 2:00 P.M. At sea, programs run from 9:00 A.M. until noon; from 2:00 P.M. until 4:30 P.M.; and from 7:00 P.M. till 10:00 P.M. Teen programs start at 11:00 A.M. and sometimes continue as late as 1:00 A.M. Holland America also offers programs you can enjoy with your children, such as family Olympics.

Club HAL has at least one staff member for every thirty children aboard your ship, plus one full-time director. The company says that half its directors have college degrees in education, while the others have experience in education, childhood development, or a related field.

≡FAST FACT

Holland America's Club HAL offers kids-only shore excursions that your children can take in Alaska and the Caribbean. Depending on your location, a guide leads your kids on treasure hunts, a tram ride and hike, and a visit to a totem pole center.

Typical activities for your five to eight year olds include storytelling, arts and crafts, ice cream parties, T-shirt painting, sing-alongs, and movie showings. As a security measure, you will need to follow a procedure of signing in and out for children this age, including providing a password when you want to retrieve your children at the end of activity time.

Your nine- to twelve-year-old kids in the Club HAL program can enjoy golf putting, disco parties, ping-pong matches, karaoke, and video games, while teenagers thirteen and older can take part in trivia contests, pizza parties, sports tournaments, and Monte Carlo Night activities.

In the Caribbean, Club HAL extends beyond the boat to Half Moon Cay, the private island Holland America owns. Shore excursions include supervised sandcastle building, beach volleyball, water-gun battles, and beach parties. In Alaska, your kids can participate in Club HAL's Junior Ranger program, in which they will be allowed to do activities with Glacier Bay National Park Rangers.

MSC Cruises

MSC calls its children's programming the Mini Club and offers it aboard all its ships, though the programs tend to be more detailed in the Caribbean (where the majority of young MSC passengers cruise). Scheduled activities are provided for children ages three to ten, though additional programming can be added upon request for older children. No children younger than three can participate.

Hours for the children's programming vary from ship to ship, and from itinerary to itinerary. Activities include arts and crafts, scavenger hunts, and pizza parties. (MSC is, after all, an Italian cruise line.)

Norwegian Cruise Line

NCL's programs are called Kid's Crew and Teen's Crew. The Kid's Crew, for ages two through twelve, is divided into two segments: Junior Sailors (ages two through five); and First Mates and Navigators (ages six through twelve). The Teen's Crew is for ages thirteen through seventeen. There are no supervised activities for children younger than age two. If your child is older than two but not toilet trained, you will be issued a beeper and asked to stay aboard the ship so that you can be called to change your child's diaper when necessary.

For all age levels, youth counselors supervise the programs. NCL says each counselor is chosen from universities and other organizations and undergoes training courses in safety, communication skills, and confidence building. Children younger than twelve are not allowed to leave their activities until a parent arrives to pick them up.

═FAST FACT

If you are aboard an NCL cruise ship and your child takes part in Kid's Crew activities, she will be required to wear an ID bracelet that includes her name, stateroom number, allergies, medications, and lifeboat station number.

Activities for Junior Sailors include painting, pizza making, and a treasure search. First Mates and Navigators can take part in scavenger hunts, video games, and storytelling, while teens are offered a disco on select ships, board games, card games, and sports.

A one-time Mom and Dad's Night Out is a complimentary service of the Kid's Crew Program; and you can purchase upgrades, including a $40 Kid's Crew backpack that includes unlimited soda and souvenir cup, baseball cap, and T-shirt. There is also a $34.50 Teen Passport upgrade that includes nonalcoholic drink tickets, an afternoon pizza and dance party, and a farewell party on the last night of your cruise.

The Kid's Crew program operates from 7:00 P.M. until 10 P.M. on all days. In addition, when you are at sea, there are activities from 9:00 A.M. until noon, and again from 2:00 P.M. until 5:00 P.M.

Princess

Princess Cruises has three different kids clubs divided by age group—and different services for those kids aboard its various ships.

When choosing to cruise with your family aboard a Princess ship, you would be wise to pay close attention not just to the company-wide programs but to exactly what facilities are offered aboard your specific ship.

The Princess Pelicans are ages three through seven, the Princess Privateers are ages eight through twelve, and the Off Limits group is ages thirteen through seventeen. Each of Princess's cruise ships— except for the *Royal Princess, Tahitian Princess*, and *Pacific Princess*— has a dedicated youth center with arts and crafts areas, game tables, movies, and more for each of the three age groups. Youth programs are offered aboard the *Royal Princess, Tahitian Princess*, and *Pacific Princess* when twenty or more children between ages three and seventeen are booked for a particular cruise, but if you are planning to be aboard one of these three ships, you should not count on children's services being available.

On the other hand, if you have a toddler and are traveling aboard the *Sun Princess, Dawn Princess, Grand Princess, Golden Princess, Coral Princess, Island Princess, Diamond Princess,* or *Star Princess*, you will have access to complete youth services plus a toddler play area. Keep in mind that toddlers sometimes require parental supervision, though, and don't expect to use the play areas as babysitting drop-off services.

 ## JUST FOR PARENTS

Princess is one of the few cruise lines that offers full-day children's activities aboard the boat on days when you are docked at a port. From 8:00 A.M. until 5:00 P.M., your kids can take part in supervised programming on your ship while you explore on shore.

On days when you are at sea, Princess operates youth programming from 9 A.M. until noon, 2:00 P.M. until 5:00 P.M., 7:00 P.M. until 10:00 P.M., and—for teens—10:00 P.M. until 1:00 A.M. On days when your ship is in port, activities run from 8:00 A.M. until 5:00 P.M., 7:00 P.M. until 10:00 P.M., and—again for teens—10:00 P.M. until 1:00 A.M.

Children ages three to twelve can take part in activities that include scavenger hunts, ice cream parties, disco dancing, karaoke, pajama parties, and "edu-tainment." Look for more details about your specific ship's offerings under the "Fun Zone" heading in your Princess brochure.

Radisson Seven Seas

Radisson calls its kids programming Club Mariner and focuses on children in three age groups: five through nine, ten through thirteen, and fourteen through seventeen. Most of its counselors are former teachers or adults who have worked with children in some other teaching capacity.

Activities for younger Club Mariner participants include coloring, cookie decorating, storytelling, doing puzzles, making totem poles, and completing word searches. Children ages eleven and older can participate in activities that include a singing contest modeled after the popular television show *American Idol,* karaoke, "Coke-tail" parties, and pizza-making. Teens are often allowed to choose their activities for the day, instead of having to sign up in advance for organized sessions, and the children's club services include a Parents' Night Out in which counselors watch your children from dinnertime into the early evening while you enjoy some of your ship's adult entertainment options.

Club Mariner hours of operation vary depending on your ship and itinerary.

Royal Caribbean

Royal Caribbean's Adventure Ocean program has five age groups: the Aquanauts (ages three to five), the Explorers (ages six through eight), the Voyagers (ages nine through eleven), the Navigators (ages twelve through fourteen), and the Guests (ages fifteen through seventeen). Aquanauts, Explorers, and Voyagers are offered activities from 9:00 A.M. till noon, 2:00 P.M. till 5:00 P.M., and 7:00 P.M. till 10:00 P.M. on days when your ship is at sea, and from thirty minutes before the first shore excursion through 5:00 P.M., plus again from 7:00 P.M. until 10:00 P.M., on days when your ship is in port. Navigators and Guests have daytime activities that vary according to the ship's schedule, but programs are always available from 9:00 P.M. until well after midnight.

≡ FAST FACT

Royal Caribbean's Adventure Ocean program includes Adventure Family activities that you can enjoy with your kids, such as shipbuilding regattas, talent shows, and ship-wide scavenger hunts.

Aquanauts do things like finger painting, Play-Doh sculptures, and building-block games; Explorers have sports tournaments and autograph hunts; Voyagers do karaoke; Navigators have pool parties and disco dancing events; and Guests enjoy DJ training and talent shows. The Adventure Ocean program also includes supervised on-shore activities for several age groups, including beach parties, hermit crab hunts, sand-castle building, and seashell collecting.

Also available is programming that Royal Caribbean calls "Edu-tainment" for children of all ages, including arts and crafts pegged to the cultures of the regions on your itinerary, and hands-on science experiments including "Mystery of the Motion of the Ocean."

If you plan to cruise with children younger than five, you can take advantage of Royal Caribbean's new partnership with the preschool toy-maker Fisher-Price. The two companies announced a joint venture beginning on all Royal Caribbean ships in early 2005 to develop programs for children as young as six months old. Aqua Babies is for children six to eighteen months old, while Aqua Tots is for children eighteen months to three years old.

Some of the programs include forty-five-minute playgroups in which you can learn how to incorporate skill-building into playtime through storytelling, creative arts, music, and—you guessed it—the use of Fisher-Price learning toys and games. For instance, the "Get

Up and Go" program teaches motor skills by having your children use Fisher-Price's Stride-to-Ride Walker, and the "Fun on the Farm" activities will find you using the toy-maker's Little People characters and Animal Sounds Farm as props.

 **RAINY DAY FUN**

Royal Caribbean's partnership with Fisher-Price led to the creation of television programming that you can watch in your cabin. It includes shows you might recognize from home, including the *Baby Development* and *Little People* series, as well as tips for traveling with children.

If you participate in either Aqua Babies or Aqua Tots, you will get a newsletter each day describing each session's objective and offering you tips for continuing to strengthen your child's skills after you leave the ship at the end of your vacation.

Babysitting Services

Different cruise lines offer different kinds of babysitting services, from group sitting that's available virtually on request, to private, in-cabin sitting that you must register for as much as twenty-four hours in advance after you get aboard your ship. The babysitting services almost always are provided for an additional fee, and in some cases you will be expected to pay cash instead of simply adding the total to your general cruise-ship checkout bill.

As with supervised children's activities, there are age restrictions that differ from cruise company to cruise company with regard to babysitting. Rates and times are subject to change, so you should verify all details with your travel agent or cruise company before booking your trip on any cruise line.

Carnival

Carnival offers group babysitting every day of your itinerary from 10:00 P.M. until 3:00 A.M. On days when your ship is in port, your children ages two and younger will also have babysitters available from 8:00 A.M. until noon.

The charge is $6 per hour for one child, plus an additional $4 per hour for every extra child from the same family.

Celebrity Cruises

Celebrity offers both private and group babysitting aboard its ships. Group babysitting for children between the ages of three and twelve is available from 10:00 P.M. until 1:00 A.M. The cost is $3 per hour for one child, and $5 per hour for two or more children from the same family.

If you require babysitting outside those evening hours, you must request private, in-cabin babysitting through your ship's Guest Relations or Stateroom Services departments. The service is available on a limited basis, so you should not count on it. You will be charged $8 per hour per family for a maximum of two children.

Costa Cruises

Group babysitting is available aboard Costa Cruises for children ages three and older who are out of diapers. The daily babysitting service operates on request from 6:30 P.M. until 11:00 P.M. every day. On days when your ship is in port, additional babysitting is available from 8:30 A.M. until 12:30 P.M., then again from 2:30 P.M. until 6:30 P.M.

You must check for pricing information when you request the sitting services onboard.

Crystal Cruises

Crystal does not promote group babysitting services. Instead, you may book in-your-cabin babysitters through your ship's concierge at least twenty-four hours in advance.

The price is $7.50 per hour for one child, $10 per hour for two children, and $12.50 per hour for three children. You cannot leave more than three children with a sitter at any time.

Disney

The Disney Cruise Line offers group babysitting for children from twelve weeks to three years old in its Flounder's Reef Nursery. You must sign up for this service on embarkation day. Space is limited, and rates and times vary depending on the ship's itinerary.

The fee is $6 per hour for one child, plus $5 per hour for additional children. You will be required to pay a two-hour minimum fee even if you do not leave your children at the nursery for that long.

Holland America

Babysitting services aboard Holland America's ships are not guaranteed. They are promoted as being available on request at each ship's front office, but the sitters are staff members who must be available and volunteer for the extra work.

Prices are $8 per hour for one child, plus $5 per hour for each additional child from the same family.

MSC Cruises

MSC offers in-cabin babysitting aboard all its ships, but no group babysitting services. Prices and hours of availability vary; check with your travel agent or the cruise company about your particular ship and itinerary.

TRAVEL TIP

Cash is best when tipping your children's onboard babysitter. Some people think it's nice to bring the sitter a souvenir from shore as a thank you, but keep in mind that sitters (like all cruise-ship employees) live in cramped quarters. They usually don't have space for even the smallest of knickknacks.

Norwegian Cruise Line

NCL offers group babysitting services as part of its Kid's Crew program. The cost is $5 per child per hour, plus $3 per child per hour for children in the same family. On days when your ship is at sea, group babysitting will be available from 10:00 P.M. until 1:00 A.M. as long as you sign up before noon each day. When your ship is in port, group babysitting will be available from 9:00 A.M. until 5:00 P.M. (you must sign up before 5:00 P.M. on the previous day), and again from 10:00 P.M. until 1:00 A.M. as long as you sign up before noon on that same day.

If your child is not toilet trained, you will be required to carry a beeper and remain aboard the ship after dropping off your kids with the babysitting service. You will be beeped when your child needs to be changed.

Princess

Group babysitting for children ages three to twelve is available from 10:00 P.M. until 1:00 A.M. at a price of $5 per hour, per child.

You can book the service aboard any of the following Princess ships: *Grand Princess, Golden Princess, Star Princess, Crown Princess, Regal Princess, Sun Princess, Dawn Princess, Sea Princess, Ocean Princess, Coral Princess, Island Princess,* and *Diamond Princess.*

Radisson Seven Seas

You shouldn't count on babysitting services being available aboard a Radisson cruise. Private, in-cabin babysitting may be available if a female member of the crew is willing to volunteer for the job in addition to her usual duties, but there are no regularly scheduled group babysitting services.

The price for in-cabin babysitting is $25 per hour, billed in full for the first hour no matter what, and then in half-hour increments after that. You will be expected to pay the babysitter at the time services are rendered.

Royal Caribbean

Royal Caribbean offers group and private in-cabin babysitting services as long as your children are at least three years old and fully toilet trained. The cruise line specifies that your children will not be eligible for the babysitting service if they use any kind of diapers or pull-up pants. Group babysitting takes place from 10:00 P.M. until 1:00 A.M. in each ship's Adventure Ocean Center, where you will be charged $5 per hour per child.

If you would rather have a private babysitter in your cabin, you must book one through the Guest Relations desk at least twenty-four hours in advance. This service is only available if your children are at least six months old, and you will be expected to pay in cash. The price is $8 per hour for as many as two children from the same family, and $10 per hour for as many as three children from the same family. You will be charged for two hours as a minimum rate.

Nannies

Your best bet for having child care when you need it and exactly how you want it is to bring your own nanny aboard. Of course, this will increase the total cost of your vacation. You will have to pay the nanny not only for her services but also for her trip expenses, including excursions you want her to take with your kids.

If your children do not already have a full-time nanny at home, a cruise ship is not the best place to introduce them to the concept. They will be in a foreign environment and will already feel separated from your daily routines and family structure. Adding a new full-time caretaker in this situation is difficult, at best. The kids may be worried, you may be worried, and you may not feel that you spent your vacation dollars very wisely.

However, adding a part-time nanny during your children's first cruise is a reasonable idea that might help to put your mind at ease. For instance, if you have a favorite babysitter at home, you might offer to treat her to a free cruise if she would be willing to watch your children during afternoons and evenings. That way, you will have the option of going ashore and enjoying evening adult activities but will still have family time every morning while your part-time nanny takes a break.

TRAVEL TIP

If you bring a favorite babysitter along on your cruise to act as a part-time nanny, remember that she will need a break from your kids for at least a few hours every day. Be sure to take advantage of the ship's existing supervised children's activities to give your sitter some breathing room.

Even better, if you already know and trust the babysitter from her work in your home, you might feel comfortable booking a single cabin with an extra (third) bed adjacent to your cabin, and letting the sitter stay in the same room as your kids. It will feel like a giant field trip for them, and you will always know where they are and who they are with.

Playrooms

Playrooms and activity centers come in all different shapes and sizes depending on your cruise line and, in addition to that, your specific cruise ship. Carnival, for example, has at least one ship with a teen club and video arcade, plus a separate children's playroom with outdoor play area, and an additional area with a 214-foot spiral water slide. At least one of Royal Caribbean's ships has an Adventure Ocean Youth Area in addition to a teen disco, while another of its ships has a separate children's pool area but no teen disco.

By the same token, you will find that some cruise ships' indoor play areas have multiple computers for educational activities in addition to fun and games, while others are simply spaces set aside to keep kids out of the adults' way.

Your best bet is to request a detailed layout of your ship from the cruise company you choose—including, if possible, the square footage of children's spaces and the number of children each room has the capacity to hold. Also request a detailed activities list, and be sure to ask whether the majority of the space is devoted to playtime or educational activities. Some playrooms will have a dozen Sony PlayStations but only two computers, while others may have the opposite ratio.

In some cases, you can even get a color brochure with photographs of the rooms in which your kids will be spending the bulk of their time during activities programming. That's your best option for really scoping out a facility.

CHAPTER 19

Excursions and Shopping at Sea

YOUR SHIP OFFERS PLENTY of things for you to do that are included in the price of your cruise, but you can do a whole lot more if you are willing to spend a little money when you head ashore. Okay, in some cases it's a lot of money, but you can make your choices according to your budget. You can take a guided tour or explore on your own, window-shop or clean out the racks at the local boutiques, or enjoy a traditionally prepared meal. Heck, it's vacation. Why not do it all?

Guided Tours

Traveling to foreign countries can be exciting and challenging all at once. It's a thrill to walk into a place that looks nothing like your neighborhood at home or, even better, nothing like anything you've ever seen before. But the more you look around—especially if you don't travel often—the more you might feel out of place and a tad nervous. Perhaps the local language is something other than English. If it's Spanish or Italian, you might pick up a few words here and there, but if you're in Greece, well, it will all be Greek to you. The roads might be old and winding like alleyways, laid out in a way that makes it hard for you to follow the twists and turns on your guide-book map. And when you look up at the street signs, you might not be able to read them. Especially if they are written in, say, Arabic.

These are the times when you may be happier if you choose a guided tour. If you're a novice traveler or are visiting a country that is dramatically different from your own, guided tours can make the difference between truly understanding and enjoying your surroundings versus wandering around, getting lost, and anxiously making your way back to your ship. You will have traveled very far and spent a good amount of your savings in an effort to see a new part of the world. Why not do everything you can to make that experience a pleasure?

Every cruise ship offers several guided tours at each port of call, and in most cases, they are organized to appeal to different people's interests. Take, for instance, a few of the guided shore excursions that Princess Cruises offers in Rome, Italy. They are similar to what other cruise lines offer in this popular world city, and each is tailored with a different theme:

- **The Eternal City:** This is a tour by car, van, or bus that includes a visit to St. Peter's Basilica and the Sistine Chapel in Vatican City, plus the Colosseum.
- **Imperial Rome:** This group vehicle tour also includes St. Peter's Basilica and the Colosseum, but skips the Sistine Chapel and instead adds the Roman Forum and the Church of St. Peter's in Chains.
- **Treasures of Rome:** This is a walking tour on which you will see the Trevi Fountain, the Spanish Steps, the Pantheon, Piazza Navona, and St. Peter's Basilica.
- **Tarquinia's Etruscan Tombs and Museum:** This is a tour for passengers who have already seen the major sites in Rome and want to explore the city's archaeological history, including the Etruscan National Museum and tombs that stretch across the countryside for three miles.

As you can see, the way a guided shore excursion is organized will have a hefty impact on what you learn about a place and the memories you will take home. In the Colosseum alone, you can walk around by yourself and marvel at the architecture, or you can follow a guide who is part archaeologist, part historian. With the guide, you'll do more than have your photo taken under one of the many impressive archways. You'll learn that you are standing in a stadium built as a monument to the people in defiance of a selfish emperor who hogged most of the city's best land for his private use. (That's not all you'll learn, of course, but what an impressive nugget of knowledge to take home!)

Guided shore excursions are usually offered in large groups or, for an extra fee, in private cars where you can be alone with your family. If your cruise line doesn't offer the private tours and you would prefer one to the group setting, you can usually book a private tour guide through your travel agent or through your own research on the Internet.

 **TRAVEL TIP**

Booking a guided shore excursion through a local company instead of your cruise ship can definitely get you away from the crowds. However, make sure that you will be returned to your ship in time for its departure. Local companies are not always as familiar with your cruise schedule as the ship's tour guides are.

The other thing to consider when deciding whether to take a group tour is safety. As the adage goes, there is safety in numbers. If you are traveling with small children and want to focus on the sites instead of on looking over your shoulder when coming around every corner, perhaps you should stick with the group tour instead of venturing off on your own.

Exploring on Your Own

The downside to taking a guided tour is that, well, you will be part of a guided tour. You will be one among at least a dozen other people craning your necks to see and cupping your ears to hear as you move from photo op to photo op, sometimes with precious little time for reflection and contemplation. Or perhaps you will get stuck in a group with an incessant complainer, or with people who want to walk faster than you do, or with people who want to walk slower than you do, or with people who constantly talk when the guide is trying to speak, or with people who are . . . well . . . *other people.*

If you are willing to give up "seeing it all" in exchange for the opportunity to spend real quality time at one or two sites that truly interest you, perhaps you would be better off exploring on your own. In major European cities, for instance, this is usually no problem. Rome, Paris, London, and Barcelona all have tourist-friendly maps, police officers, and at least a handful of signs in English that will help you find your way. Even Eastern European cities such as Athens, Greece, make getting around fairly easy for you. They expect to see tourists and want you to come ashore, feel comfortable, and spend some money in their stores. You most certainly won't be the only person doing so.

In the Caribbean, too, you are likely to feel at ease wandering around islands without a group tour. Most islanders in the Caribbean speak English, though with a thick accent in some cases. If you've got a strong Texas drawl and are trying to communicate with some-one from the Jamaican countryside, for instance, you might think you're speaking two different languages. Simply slow down your speech, smile often, and use gestures. Your point will get across, and you likely will get the help that you need.

■ TRAVEL TIP

If you decide to go exploring on your own instead of as part of a guided tour, remember to keep your valuables secure and your money out of sight. Even in the safest ports of call, lone travelers will attract the attention of thieves much more often than groups do.

Australia and New Zealand, too, are excellent places to go exploring on your own. Again, the accents may throw you off, but English is the native tongue and all the signage should be easy for you to understand. Even in parts of the world where Spanish is the predominant language, such as South America, you often will be able to find bilingual people to help you make your way around your port of call.

Exploring on your own gets tricky when you're in a place where tourism is a newer concept, or where the predominant language is so different from your native English that you'll have trouble puzzling out even the most basic of words. The Far East, for instance, can be tricky to navigate because signs are often written in characters that are nonsensical to English-speaking people. And your odds of finding bilingual shop owners in Beijing who speak, say, Mandarin Chinese and English are a lot worse than they would be of finding bilingual shop owners in Mexico who speak Spanish and English.

If you want to explore on your own in more exotic ports of call, make sure you've done your homework first. Have a guidebook with maps, basic phrase translations, and local behavior customs (such as when to ask for your check in a restaurant) that you can carry with you in case you get lost or need help. Memorize key phrases before you head off on your mini-adventure so that you will be seen as a respectful tourist and get the assistance you need. If you learn just a dozen or so words, you should be able to make your way around without too much trouble:

- Hello
- Excuse me
- Please
- Thank you
- Right, left
- Cruise ship port
- Restaurant
- How much is this?
- I need help!

Also, talk with your cruise-ship excursions director about the area where your ship will dock, what the nearby neighborhoods are like, their record of public safety, and any cute little places he has learned about during his previous visits there. Sometimes, you can stay very close to your ship and still have an incredibly authentic experience as all the other passengers bolt past you on their way to tours on the outskirts of town. After all, it's usually the ship's crewmembers who know the "real" areas in any port the best.

What to Take Ashore

The most important thing to remember when you head ashore at any port of call is that you must bring your ship identification card with you. *You will not be allowed back on your cruise ship without it.* Also carry another form of identification with you, such as a driver's license with photograph, in case there are any questions or problems.

Of course, you'll need money. Some cruise destinations, such as the Bahamas and the Galapagos Islands, have currencies that are linked to the U.S. dollar. You don't need anything in your pockets that you wouldn't normally have, and you will be able to do anything you want.

═══FAST FACT

Curious about how the U.S. dollar compares to other currencies around the world? There's a Web site that will tell you with the click of a mouse. You can compare Uncle Sam's greenbacks to the euro, British pound, Japanese yen, and nearly a hundred other currencies at *www.xe.com*.

In most other countries, though, you will need the local currency if you want to pay for things with cash. Your best bet is to exchange your U.S. dollars for the currencies of the countries you will be visiting before you board your plane in the United States. Major international airports all have currency exchange booths, and if you do all your transactions at once, you will only be charged a single fee. This will save you time and money compared with trying to exchange currency at every new port of call, especially if you are visiting different countries that each use different currencies.

Credit cards and traveler's checks, too, are usually accepted at major tourist sites. Visa and MasterCard are the most widely used, but Discover is a decent backup in many locations, too. If you're sticking with group tours and don't plan to venture into quaint little areas on your own, you probably can get by without any cash. You'll be doing most of your shopping at the major tourist stores that take credit cards. In addition to money and your ship identification card, you'll want to have a few other things with you when you head ashore:

- A guidebook of the area, including a map that shows your ship's port
- Sunscreen
- A sun hat
- Your camera
- A large bottle of water from your ship, or your own thermos filled with the ship's water
- Snacks like granola bars and apples in places where the local food is questionable
- A number you can call to reach your ship if you get lost or need help

Frequent travelers often toss all of these items into a backpack, since it has thick straps that distribute weight evenly and prevent theft when used properly—and offers plenty of extra room to add souvenirs along the way. And of course, if you're traveling with small children, you'll want to have any additional items they need with you, as well.

If you're planning to carry a backpack in a destination where pickpockets are common, consider using your tiny luggage locks to keep your backpack pockets closed. If possible, use a separate, smaller "fanny pack" for your wallet, cellular telephone, shipboard identification card, and any other valuables. You can often hide this type of pack under your clothing, close to your body.

Shopping

Shopping in ports of call is one of the best parts of any cruise-ship vacation. Certainly, you'll want to find keepsake mementos that will help you remember your cruise for years to come. The trick is to know when to browse and when to buy.

If you've never been on a cruise before, you might be tempted to start plunking down money at the first row of shops you see. Don't do it! In a lot of ports of call, you will find the same T-shirts, ashtrays, and statuettes on block after block—and eventually, you'll find them in a store where the owner is willing to haggle over the price. Patience pays off in most ports of call when it comes to shopping. Browse the entire shopping district first, then walk back toward your ship and make your purchases right before you board. The shop owners will know they only have a few minutes left to offer you a reasonable bargain, and you can buy with the confidence that you have gotten the best possible deal.

Keep in mind that you're going to have to pack everything you buy before you leave your ship to head home. If you're purchasing large or bulky items and the store offers you the option of shipping them directly home, you should do it. It's a little bit of money that will save you a whole lot of hassle in the airports—and if you pay with your credit card, you may be entitled to shipping insurance at no extra charge. Check your policy before you leave home, or call your credit card company for information.

Dining

Some cruise-ship passengers shy away from eating ashore simply because of the added cost. Yes, it's true that all your meals are included in your cruise price, but one of the best ways to really get the feel for the culture at any port of call is to enjoy a leisurely meal there. What could be better than sipping Italian red wine at a *trattoria* in the shadow of the Leaning Tower of Pisa? Or ordering a table full of Spanish *tapas* to sample as the locals in Buenos Aires whiz by? Or seeing how the fried rice in Hong Kong differs from the greasy stuff they serve at your local Chinese restaurant? Or trying a taste of curried goat made by a woman known only as "Ma" down in the Caribbean?

In highly trafficked tourist areas, you will find menus written in English as well as the native language. This will simplify things for you, of course, but you may not feel that you are getting the entirely local experience. (After all, you'll be surrounded by other tourists.) For a bit more authenticity, you might have to venture off the well-eaten path and poke your head inside smaller eateries where the locals outnumber the tourists. If you plan to do this, make sure you know a few key words in the local language, such as "water," "beef," "chicken," and the like. Or, at the very least, be prepared to point at other diners' meals and smile.

≡FAST FACT

The majority of illnesses that cruise-ship passengers acquire in ports of call come from undercooked food and untreated water. Consider ordering your meals well done, and bring bottled water with you from the ship.

Shipboard Stores

If you're on a transatlantic cruise or a cruise to nowhere—or if you simply prefer to do your shopping on your ship—you'll have plenty of ways to spend your money. The biggest, newest ships out on the ocean today have entire areas devoted to boutiques. It's like a small shopping mall right there aboard your ship.

You'll find jewelry, fragrances, cosmetics, clothing, souvenirs, sundries, artwork, antiques, and more. And sometimes, you'll find them at up to 30 percent off retail prices in the United States, since they are for sale duty-free along with liquor, cigarettes, and chocolates.

If you spot an item you simply must have, you should buy it right away—quantities, after all, are limited to whatever can fit in the boutique's stowage area during your cruise. On the other hand, if you're on the fence about a purchase, you might wait until the end of your vacation to buy. Some cruise lines hold sales on select items toward the end of each itinerary.

And no matter what or when you decide to buy, remember to save some money for the products that will be for sale in your ship's spa. You can pick up some great soaps and lotions when you get a nice neck rub after you're done trying on all your new clothes and carrying them back to your cabin.

Clothing

Today's cruise ships are like high-end outlet stores. You'll find designer names such as Gucci, Armani, Burberry, DKNY, Nautica, Tommy Bahama, Tommy Hilfiger, Calvin Klein, Ralph Lauren, and Fossil. If you're a shopper, you might consider leaving some extra space in your suitcase and purchasing a few outfits after you embark. You won't be disappointed aboard cruise lines such as Cunard, Crystal, and Princess, which promote shopping as a favorite onboard activity and devote a lot of space to their boutiques. You may even stumble across Mont Blanc pens and pricey Rolex wristwatches in between the souvenir coffee mugs and picture frames.

Of course, you'll also find standard-size shops aboard even the oldest of ships in any fleet, with shelves full of logo-emblazoned T-shirts, hats, and the like. These can be great souvenirs for your kids, especially when they're sold as two-for-one deals.

Sundries

If you've unpacked everything and realize you've forgotten a few basic toiletries, you should be able to find them in the ship's sundry store. Most cruise ships offer a selection of shampoos, razors, toothbrushes, toothpaste, deodorant, hairspray, Q-Tips, sanitary products, and the like.

The prices are usually reasonable, and the shop is far more convenient than anything you'll find wandering around a port of call.

Going Home and Going Again

IF YOU ENJOY YOUR cruise-ship vacation, the odds are good you'll want to book another one in the future. It may be in the near future, or it may be in the far future, but it is likely to be within the next couple of years if you're anything like the typical passenger. The cruise companies know this, so they make it as easy as possible for you to stick with their fleets instead of going home, checking out the competition, and, well, jumping ship. It's time to pack up, assess your experience, and start thinking about your next trip.

Packing

Oh, the dreaded moment when you realize your suitcase won't close. Those hand-carved bongos you found on St. Vincent and the super-size T-shirts you nabbed on Antigua sure seemed like good ideas at the time, but now, faced with airline luggage weight restrictions and stunningly inflexible suitcase zippers, you're probably not so sure. And as you look around your cabin, you realize you might be missing a few things that you know you had when you came aboard. Uh oh.

Relax. Take a deep, cleansing breath and realize that you are simply one among hundreds of people experiencing the same exact moment aboard your cruise ship. Packing up to go home is sad to begin with. (Vacation should last forever, right?) Add a week or two spent collecting souvenirs and tossing your belongings around your cabin, and packing can also be a headache—your first reminder of the "real life" waiting for you at the bottom of your ship's gangway.

You can start sucking the stress out of this situation by referring to the inventory you made before your trip of all the belongings in your suitcase. (You did make one, didn't you?) As you pack your things, place a check mark next to every item on the list. If you have nothing else to pack and there are still a few unchecked items on your inventory, you know you've left something behind. Check deep in the back of drawers and down in closet corners. If you still can't find your missing windbreaker or flip-flops, contact the ship's lost-and-found department.

If you've got everything you're supposed to—and then some—and can't get your luggage closed, you have a couple of options. For starters, you can use the spare, empty suitcase that you packed as a pre-emptive solution to this very problem. If you didn't bring a spare, perhaps you can reshuffle a few things in your family members' suitcases to make extra room. You can also use souvenir bags as carry-ons to hold extra stuff, whether you bought the bags in your ports of call during the week or a few minutes ago from your cruise ship's boutiques. Most airlines will allow you one carry-on plus one personal item, so you can add a souvenir bag to the burden on your shoulders just long enough to get everything home.

≡FAST FACT

On the night it began operations—April 17, 1973—Federal Express delivered 186 packages to twenty-five U.S. cities. Today, the corporation serves more than 220 countries and territories worldwide.

When you come to the realization that you're just not going to be able to get everything home on your own, shipping becomes your best bet. Some of the things you've purchased during your cruise—large sculptures from shore-side shops, framed prints from your ship's art auctions—will already be headed to your home in shipping containers. Talk to your ship's purser about whether your cruise line offers shipping of your personal belongings. If it doesn't, ask if you can find the service at the airport. Some major international airport hubs do have this service available.

If you're aboard a luxury line such as Silversea, you can arrange before your trip to have your luggage shipped through Federal Express from your home to your ship, and then back again at the end of your cruise. That way, you won't have to worry about this problem at all.

Cruise Surveys: Rating Your Experience

As you prepare to disembark, cruise-line personnel may come around asking you and other members of your group to complete a survey about your experience. You may also receive a customer satisfaction survey in the mail when you return to your home. Fill it out! The only way cruise lines in general, and your company in particular, will continue to improve is through honest, specific feedback from passengers like you.

Be as detailed as you can, even naming crew members who made your trip especially enjoyable. Mention particular meals that left you satisfied or unhappy. Discuss children's programming both in terms of its content and the times when it is offered. Explain which features in your cabin you liked the best, and what you would like to see done differently on new ships the company is planning to build. This is, quite frankly, your best chance to make your voice heard.

You also may choose to post your personal review on any one of the general-information Web sites that focus on cruise-ship vacations. (See Appendix A for a list.) For a few years now, a community of cruise-ship passengers has come together on the Internet to share unbiased, unfiltered information with one another about specific ships, itineraries, and excursions, as well as about cruise lines in general. Just as you may find someone else's review helpful in planning your next cruise, a novice will look to your posting when comparing notes and making a decision for her family's first seagoing vacation.

Discounts for Booking Aboard

Some cruise lines will give you an additional savings—beyond early-booking fares, senior-citizen discounts, and the like—if you book a future cruise before you even finish the one you're taking. It makes sense, if you think about it. You're having a good time already, so they might as well get you to commit to your next vacation before you have time to go home and think about doing something different. Most cruise ships have a purser or future-cruise consultant aboard to help you sort through your options.

Aboard some cruise ships, you will be asked to provide a deposit of as little as $100 toward your next cruise. Other times, you will be allowed to wait until you get back home to confirm the future booking by making your deposit then. The policies vary from cruise line to cruise line, so you need to check with the company of your choice.

 TRAVEL TIP

If you decide to book your next cruise while still aboard your first, make sure you join that particular cruise line's frequent traveler program. You'll immediately start earning loyalty points that will get you perks later.

Companies that offer these onboard booking discounts include Celebrity Cruises, Crystal Cruises, Cunard, Holland America, Norwegian Cruise Line, Princess Cruises, Radisson Seven Seas Cruises, Royal Caribbean, and Seabourn. The majority of them allow you to combine any discounts you receive with other special fares that are available on their ships, but a few companies restrict your savings to just the onboard booking rate. Norwegian Cruise Line has historically offered only the onboard booking discount, but with so many of its competitors allowing you to combine that discount with others, look for NCL to change its policies and get more in line with the industry standard.

The discounts you receive will also vary from cruise line to cruise line, from a $50-per-stateroom credit all the way up to a 5-percent discount on the total price of your next cruise. Again, check with your travel agent or the specialist aboard your cruise line of choice for specific details.

Frequent Travelers' Clubs

If you plan to cruise even just one more time in the future, a cruise club is guaranteed to help you save at least a few bucks. If you intend to cruise year after year all over the world, you'll be throwing away hundreds or perhaps thousands of dollars if you don't join. The clubs just plain make sense.

Almost every major cruise line has a frequent travelers' club, sometimes called a loyalty program, with the goal of getting you not only to book again, but to book again aboard the same fleet of ships. They want to offer you as many perks as it takes to keep you coming back to *their* ships instead of giving your hard-earned vacation dollars to a competing company.

Royal Caribbean, for instance, calls its loyalty program the Crown and Anchor Society. It has several levels of membership, ranging from Gold (you're eligible after your first cruise) to Diamond Plus (you're eligible after you have completed twenty-four cruises, or twelve cruises with a suite booking). You get added benefits during your cruise, such as complimentary wine tastings, private departure lounges, priority wait listing for sold-out shore excursions and spa appointments, and preferred dining-room seating. You also get benefits in between cruises, such as savings certificates within the

Crown and Anchor magazine, members-only contests, and special offers on rates for balcony and suite staterooms.

Princess Cruises has a similar program, called the Princess Captain's Circle. It has three levels ranging from gold (you're eligible after your first cruise) to elite (you're eligible after your fifteenth cruise). As a member of the Captain's Circle, you automatically become part of the Referral Rewards Program, which lets you refer your friends to Princess via the company's Web site. If your friends book their first Princess cruise, they get a discount. After they complete their trip, you get the same discount offered to you. Other Captain's Circle benefits include upgraded cabin assignments aboard and priority room assignments ashore, free upgrades to higher levels of travel insurance, complimentary dry cleaning and laundry services, and discounts at the ships' boutiques.

Sometimes, a cruise company's loyalty program will not help you financially on every future cruise, but will help you substantially with select itineraries. The Silversea Venetian Society is a good example of this concept. If you become a member, you can in some cases get as much as a 10-percent discount in addition to early-booking savings and advance payment bonuses. However, the discounts only apply to certain cruises. Check with the company before joining the loyalty program to see if the next cruise you have in mind might qualify for the added discount. In some cases, you might find a better deal with another cruise-line company.

 TRAVEL TIP

If you cruised with a certain company once before and are planning to go back for another cruise, ask if you are still eligible for the company's customer loyalty program. Even if it's been a few years, you might still be entitled to substantial repeat-client savings and perks.

Carnival Corporation, the parent company of Carnival Cruise Lines, takes the customer loyalty idea a step further with its Vacation Interchange Privileges program. If you cruise aboard a Carnival Corporation ship, you will be entitled to the "past guest" savings offered aboard every other cruise ship company under the same corporate umbrella. The cruise lines that participate, in addition to Carnival Cruise Lines, include Costa, Cunard, Holland America, Princess, Seabourn, and Windstar.

If your cruise company of choice wasn't mentioned in the preceding paragraphs, don't worry—odds are good that it has a loyalty program similar to one of the others described here. Ask your travel agent for details, or check the fine print in the back of your brochure.

Payment Options

As you might imagine, the vast majority of cruise-ship passengers pay for their trips with a major credit card—Visa, MasterCard, and American Express being the most popular. Some cruise companies also accept the Discover and Diner's Club cards.

It seems almost quaint nowadays to think about actual paper money, but many cruise lines do accept cash and checks. In some cases, you may need to get a certified check or a money order from your bank, but at least you won't have any worries about running up your credit card bills. In many cases, a personal check will suffice.

Technology makes direct deposit another possibility for paying your cruise-ship bill nowadays. Just as you might have your paycheck deposited directly into your bank account every two weeks, you can arrange to have direct deposits sent from your bank account to your cruise-ship company of choice. You can set up incremental or lump-sum deductions from your account, depending on how you prefer to pay and on what deadlines the cruise company has for your balance due.

If you prefer to pay onboard your ship, ask if your cruise line has an express checkout plan. Princess Cruises, for instance, offers a system much like the ones you find in mid-range to upscale hotels, whereby you provide a credit card when you check in (or at any other time during your cruise) and simply let the cruise ship charge your balance to it.

Gratuities

Different cruise lines have different policies on tipping. Some include gratuities in the price of your cruise, others leave tipping entirely up to you, and still others use a hybrid system in which you are automatically charged for some gratuities but encouraged to leave others in cash.

If you need to tip cruise-line personnel on your own, it is customary to tip bellboys as services are rendered but everyone else at the end of your cruise—including children's counselors, housekeeping, the restaurant's maitre d', and your restaurant waiters. Also remember that shore excursion leaders usually are not cruise-company employees, so if you want to tip them, you will have to do so at the end of each excursion.

Be sure to check the fine print in the back of your brochure for your particular cruise line's policy on gratuities. The following sections describe where most of the major companies stand.

Carnival

Carnival charges $10 per passenger, per day, as gratuities for dining and stateroom services. The amount is automatically added to your shipboard charge account, which you pay at the end of your trip. (On "Cruises to Nowhere," the $10 per guest, per day gratuities must be prepaid.) Carnival also adds 15 percent to your onboard beverage purchases as gratuities.

You have complete discretion to adjust these gratuities in any way you wish before you settle your account. You also are encouraged to tip your maitre d' and room service staff as they render services (if they provide exceptional service), although you may still choose to wait until the end of the voyage if you wish.

≡FAST FACT

Americans are typically generous tippers in the context of the world-wide market. Europeans, for instance, tend to tip about 5 percent for boat crew members, while Americans often top 20 percent in their offerings.

Celebrity

Tipping is at your discretion aboard Celebrity ships. The cruise line suggests that you wait until the last day of your cruise, then use the following per-day rate as the basis for your gratuities:

- Waiter: $3.50
- Assistant waiter: $2
- Butler (suites only): $3.50
- Assistant maitre d': $0.75
- Stateroom service: $3.50
- Stateroom service (Concierge Class): $4
- Assistant chief housekeeper: $.75

Costa

Gratuities are your responsibility, to be left at your discretion.

Crystal

As with Costa, gratuities are your responsibility, to be left at your discretion, except for the 15 percent that is charged to your tab for all bar drinks and wines. You may charge the rest of your tips to your shipboard charge account if you would like, including gratuities for the maitre d', headwaiter, assistant stewardess, and night room-service personnel. Crystal offers the following guidelines on a per person, per-day basis:

- Stewardess: $4
- Waiter: $4

- Assistant waiter: $2.50
- Butler (penthouse decks): $4
- Specialty restaurant wait staff: $6
- Spa and salon personnel: 15 percent of service charge

Disney

Gratuities are your responsibility, to be left at your discretion.

Holland America

Holland America adds a gratuity of $10 per guest, per day, to your shipboard charge account. You may adjust the amount up or down before settling your bill. The cruise line also adds a 15-percent tip to all your bar and wine purchases.

MSC

Gratuities are your responsibility, to be left at your discretion.

Norwegian Cruise Line

Norwegian Cruise Line adds a gratuity of $10 per guest, per day, to your shipboard charge account. For children between three and twelve years old, the gratuity charge is $5 per guest, per day. There is no charge for children younger than three, and you may adjust the total amount on your account up or down before settling your bill.

You are not required to tip further, but the cruise line encourages cash tips in addition to the daily service charge for crew members who enhance your experience outside the norm. NCL also suggests that you add a 15-percent gratuity to all bar and wine purchases.

═══FAST FACT

Don't like the sound of the word gratuity? Try these: tip, gravy, grease, palm oil, sweetener, token, or "little something."

Princess

Princess Cruises adds a $10 per day, per guest, gratuity to your bill for dining and stateroom personnel. You may adjust this amount at your discretion before settling your account. The cruise line also adds a 15-percent bar gratuity to every liquor or wine purchase you make.

Radisson Seven Seas

Gratuities are not expected onboard. They are included in your cruise fare.

Royal Caribbean

Royal Caribbean adds a 15-percent gratuity to all your bar and wine purchases but leaves the rest of the tipping at your discretion. You will find envelopes in your stateroom where you can leave cash gratuities on the last night of your cruise. You may also leave gratuities on your shipboard charge account, or you may prepay them at the time of your reservation.

The cruise line offers the following guidelines for tipping on a per person, per-day basis, for adult and children passengers alike:

- Suite attendant: $5.75
- Stateroom attendant: $3.50
- Dining room waiter: $3.50
- Assistant waiter: $2
- Headwaiter: $.75

Seabourn

Gratuities are not expected onboard. They are included in your cruise fare.

Silversea

As with Seabourn, gratuities are not expected onboard. They are included in your cruise fare.

Swan Hellenic

Tipping is included in your fare, and the cruise company tips excursion companies where appropriate.

Disembarkation Procedures

Australian writer Alan Walker rightfully refers to disembarkation day as D-Day—just as dreaded as it is inevitable. You will have to get up earlier than usual to get breakfast. You will feel anxious as your luggage is swept out of your control and taken off the ship, and you may become bored and frustrated during the hours you will be required to wait before stepping foot ashore.

If you understand the process going on all around you, you might find D-Day a bit easier to handle. The disembarkation process is intended to get you and the several other thousand passengers off quickly, load supplies for the next cruise, and check in the next trip's passengers before nightfall. Consider the level of coordination and hustle required to pull this off, and cut your ship's crew members some slack. Try to look like a seasoned pro instead of a curmudgeonly novice. Keep a positive attitude as you wonder about your luggage, and bring along a good book to read while you wait (and wait . . . and wait . . .) for your turn to climb down the gangway.

Luggage

You'll have to say goodbye to all of your checked luggage the night before disembarkation day. Your ship will give you written instructions or will broadcast instructions on your cabin television telling you exactly when you can begin to put your bags out in the hallway, and you can be certain that the ship's personnel will start collecting it immediately. After all, they need to get you and your stuff off quickly so they can clean your cabin before the next cruise passengers arrive in just a few short hours.

Your luggage will be taken to a central location on the ship where it can be offloaded easily by forklift. After you disembark, you will have to find your bags among the hundreds of others with which it was offloaded. Consider tying a ribbon to your suitcase handle, or wrapping a colorful bungee cord around your bag (which is great both for identifying it and keeping it closed in transit). It will make your personal search-and-recovery mission much easier.

 **TRAVEL TIP**

Remember to leave yourself a change of clothes to wear home on the last morning of your cruise. More than a few passengers have been known to pack all their outfits into their suitcases before having ship's personnel carry them away the night before disembarkation day, only to wake up without a pair of pants to wear to the airport.

Biding Your Time

Your brochure may say that your ship arrives back in port at 7 A.M. on the last day of your cruise, but that's not when you should expect to step onto shore. You will be assigned to a disembarkation group (by numeric or color-coded system, usually) that takes into account your flight or transfer time, your VIP status, and the needs of guests who require special assistance. If you have an early flight and booked a suite, you will probably be one of the first people allowed to leave the ship. If you were in one of the least expensive inside cabins and plan to drive a half-hour back to your home, expect to settle in for a few hours' worth of waiting.

Expect to wait in the ship's public areas until your disembarkation group is called over the loudspeaker or by crew members. Sometimes you can hang out in your cabin, but the housekeeping teams are usually out in full force by breakfast time, trying to get the ship ready for the passengers arriving later that day. You'll find a lot of people waiting by the gangway, or in the public areas closest to it, so if you don't like crowds you should get as far away from those spots as possible. (Just stay within earshot of the disembarkation announcements.)

You will need your passport and U.S. Customs Declaration Form if your ship cruised outside of U.S. waters. Clearing customs, of course, adds to the time needed to get the several hundred or several thousand passengers off your ship. Try to be patient.

If you plan in advance for this long morning of delays, your family will be much happier in the long run. Have books, a deck of cards, and other keep-busy items on hand. If you don't expect to make it out of bed in time for the early breakfast in the dining room, make sure you have some snacks in your carry-on bag. The few eateries still open on the ship during disembarkation will have long lines, and you'll save yourself a lot of hassle if you simply pack a granola bar to tide you over until you get to the airport.

Transfers to Airports and Trains

Once you have collected your luggage, if you live near your final port of call and have a car waiting for you, congratulations—you're done! If you're from out of town, you have one more leg of travel to endure. It's time to transfer to mass transportation such as airlines and trains.

If you booked your own transportation, you should see someone waiting outside the cruise-ship terminal with your name on a sign, just as limousine drivers wait in airport baggage handling areas with signs for their customers. If you booked your transfers through the cruise company, ship's personnel will instruct you on which signage to follow to meet your bus. There should be plenty of porters around to help you with your luggage, as well as assistants to help you if you feel lost or have questions.

Your bus will drop you and any other passengers who will be flying on your airline at the airport terminal. Once you are inside, you are officially on your own and headed back home. That is, until the departure date for your next cruise vacation comes along.

Bon voyage!

Useful Numbers and Web Sites

ALL OF THE MAJOR cruise-ship companies have their own Web sites, and some will let you do everything from research itineraries to take video ship tours to book port-of-call excursions months in advance. In addition to those sites, a healthy number of general-interest Web sites offer all kinds of great third-party information about cruising in general and specific cruise lines in particular. If you want an independent review of a particular ship or itinerary, check the general-interest sites before logging on to the cruise company's Web address.

Major Cruising Companies

These companies are the ones you are most likely to find on travel Web sites and to see in newspaper and magazine advertisements. Their Web sites usually include direct booking, ship details, itinerary and shore excursion information, general terms and conditions, and more.

Carnival.com

This is the official site of Carnival Cruise Lines, which is consistently ranked as providing good-value cruises for families.
✍ *www.carnival.com*

CelebrityCruises.com

This is the official site of Celebrity Cruises, which targets passengers who earn at least $75,000 per year.
✍ *www.celebritycruises.com*

CostaCruises.com

This is the official site of Costa Cruises, which is based in Italy and has ships that carry anywhere from 820 to 2,700 passengers.
✍ *www.costacruises.com*

CrystalCruises.com

This is the official site of Crystal Cruises, which operates three ships at a level meant to be comparable to Ritz-Carlton hotels on land.
✍ *www.crystalcruises.com*

Cunard.com

This is the official site of the Cunard cruise line, which runs the world's largest ocean liner, the *Queen Mary 2*.
✍ *www.cunard.com*

DisneyCruises.com

This is the official site of Disney Cruise Line. The site allows you to connect to the broader Walt Disney World Web site as well.
✎*www.disneycruises.com*

HollandAmerica.com

This is the official site of the Holland America cruise line. One of its features enables you to download printable PDFs of its glossy destination brochures.
✎*www.hollandamerica.com*

MSCCruises.com

This is the official site of MSC Cruises, a value-priced cruise line based in Italy.
✎*www.msccruises.com*

NCL.com

This is the official site of Norwegian Cruise Line, which operates fourteen ships with home ports in the United States and Canada.
✎*www.ncl.com*

Princess.com

This is the official site of Princess Cruises, which has fifteen ships that carry from 670 to 3,110 passengers apiece.
✎*www.princess.com*

RSSC.com

This is the official site of Radisson Seven Seas Cruises, whose biggest ships carry just 700 people each.
✎*www.rssc.com*

RoyalCaribbean.com

This is the official site of Royal Caribbean cruises, which is consistently rated among the best values for cruising families.
✎*www.royalcaribbean.com*

Seabourn.com

This is the official site of Seabourn Cruise Line, a luxury brand whose three identical ships carry just 208 passengers apiece.
✎*www.seabourn.com*

Silversea.com

This is the official site of Silversea Cruises, a luxury brand whose four ships carry between 296 and 382 passengers each.
✎*www.silversea.com*

SwanHellenic.com

This is the official site of Swan Hellenic Discovery Cruises, a company whose itineraries make destinations the focus of your cruise.
✎*www.swanhellenic.com*

Other Cruising Companies

The companies on this list certainly do not represent the rest of the entire cruising industry. There are countless operators that have one ship apiece operating in ports all over the world, so many that it would simply be impossible to list them all.

Having said that, if you want to look outside of the mainstream, heavily promoted cruise lines for your cruise vacation, a lot of smaller and uniquely organized companies out there want your business.

AmericanWestSteamboat.com

The American West Steamboat Company offers classic-style steamboat cruises in Alaska's Inside Passage and along the Columbia and Snake rivers in Oregon and Washington state.
✎ *www.americanweststeamboat.com*

CruiseWest.com

CruiseWest has a fleet of smaller ships—the largest is 295 feet long and holds 114 passengers—that cruise in Alaska, Costa Rica, Panama, Mexico's Sea of Cortez, Japan, the South Pacific, California Wine Country, the Columbia and Snake rivers in Oregon and Washington state, and Canada's British Columbia.
✎ *www.cruisewest.com*

Deilmann-Cruises.com

Peter Deilmann Cruises offers nine vessels that cruise along the rivers in the heart of Europe. Options include the Danube, Seine, Rhone, Elbe, Rhine, and more.
✎ *www.deilmann-cruises.com*

DeltaQueen.com

The Delta Queen Steamboat Company offers classic-style paddle-wheel cruises aboard three different ships along the Mississippi River from Minneapolis, Minnesota, all the way south to New Orleans, Louisiana; and along the Ohio River beginning as far east as Pittsburgh, Pennsylvania. Some trips include tributaries, as well.

✐*www.deltaqueen.com*

GreatLakesCruising.com

The Great Lakes Cruise Company operates five ships that cruise in places including the Thousand Islands, the Erie Canal, Quebec City, the St. Lawrence River, Chicago, Ottawa, and Nova Scotia.

✐*www.greatlakescruising.com*

HL-Cruises.com

Hapag-Lloyd Cruises is a German company whose four ships cruise everywhere from Antarctica to the U.S. Great Lakes. The ships carry 164 to 420 passengers apiece, and service is often on a par with what you will find aboard lines like Cunard, Celebrity, and Holland America.

✐*www.hl-cruises.com*

Expeditions.com

Lindblad Expeditions is one of the few cruising companies that has won awards not just from magazines like *Conde Nast Traveler,* but also from organizations such as the National Audubon Society and the United Nations Environment Programme. Ecotourism plays a large role in its itineraries.

✐*www.expeditions.com*

CoastalVoyage.com

This is the official site of Norwegian Coastal Voyage, which offers cruises on a dozen different ships to thirty-four ports of call along the western shore of Norway. You can cruise year-round, despite the cold winters.

✒*www.coastalvoyage.com*

OceanaCruises.com

This is the official site of Oceana Cruises, which operates two ships that take 684 passengers apiece. Itineraries include the Caribbean, Europe, Africa, and Asia.

✒*www.oceanacruises.com*

OrientLines.com

Orient Lines operates the *Marco Polo*, a 578-foot ship that carries 826 passengers on twelve decks. Destinations for 2006 are expected to include Antarctica, the Panama Canal, and Europe.

✒*www.orientlines.com*

POCruises.com

P&O Cruises is a British company that operates six ships carrying 914 to 2,388 passengers apiece. It is considered a mass-market brand in the worldwide industry, although its prices are in pounds—currency that has had more value than the dollar in recent years, and thus may not be a good bargain until the dollar rebounds.

✒*www.pocruises.com.*

SeaCloud.com

Sea Cloud Cruises has two sailing cruise ships and two river ships that operate in Europe and the Caribbean. The sailing ships are small, carrying fewer than 100 people per cruise.

✒*www.seacloud.com*

SeaDreamYachtClub.com

The Sea Dream Yacht Club operates two ships that are each 344 feet long and carry no more than 110 passengers per cruise. The ships are based in the Caribbean and Mediterranean, where captains have the authority to extend or shorten ports of call along the itinerary depending on what you and the other passengers want to do.

✐*www.seadreamyachtclub.com*

StarClippers.com

Star Clippers operates two tall sailing ships, one 360 feet long and the other 439 feet long. The ships carry 170 and 227 passengers, respectively, and cruise in the Caribbean, Mediterranean, and Far East.

✐*www.starclippers.com*

TravelDynamicsInternational.com

Travel Dynamics has three ships that take 34, 106, and 114 passengers apiece. The company promotes education-oriented cruising worldwide.

✐*www.traveldynamicsinternational.com*

Uniworld.com

Uniworld River Cruises offers itineraries aboard twenty-one ships on rivers in Europe, Russia, China, and South America.

✐*www.uniworld.com*

VikingRivers.com

Viking River Cruises is the world's largest river cruise line, operating twenty-five ships on rivers in China, Russia, and Europe. River itineraries include the Rhine, Main, Moselle, Danube, Elbe, Seine, and Rhone in Europe; the Volga in Russia; and the Yangtze in China.

✐*www.vikingrivers.com*

Windjammer.com

Windjammer Barefoot Cruises operates five ships (four tall sail-boats and one motor-ship) in the Caribbean, Bahamas, and Virgin Islands. The largest ship takes 119 passengers, and you can learn to sail along the way if you're interested.

✍*www.windjammer.com*

WindStarCruises.com

Wind Star Cruises operates three sailing ships, the largest of which is 535 feet long and carries 308 passengers. Itineraries are in the Caribbean and Mediterranean.

✍*www.windstarcruises.com.*

General Cruising Web Sites

It's always hard to say whether you can trust the independent information on third-party Web sites. You never know what writers took which free cruises in exchange for writing a rave review that will generate thousands of dollars in business for the cruise company.

Having said that, there are some good cruising sites on the Web that can enhance your general knowledge about what's out there, what you should expect aboard, and what experiences other people have had during similar cruises. Hey, it never hurts to do a little extra snooping around before you hand over your credit card number, right?

CruiseMates.com

This Web site includes cruise line and specific ship reviews by experts as well as by readers—including teenagers when reviewing topics of interest to younger passengers. There are also general-interest articles about everything from first-time cruising to gay and lesbian cruising to family and singles cruising. The site's editor is Anne Campbell, former editor and co-founder of Cruise Critic on America Online. The links are easy to follow and may lead you to related topics that will be helpful and that you might not have considered on your own.
www.cruisemates.com

CruiseCritic.com

This Web site also includes cruise line and specific ship reviews, as well as informative features about everything from teen cruising to senior cruising to destinations worldwide. You can search for cruises based on your personality—everything from "Romance" to "Soft Adventure," and find good deals in a special section called "Bargains."
www.cruisecritic.com

Cruise 411.com

Here is another Web site that includes cruise line and specific ship reviews, as well as other features including last-minute deals and discounts. A section called "Cruise Buzz" offers snippets of information about new programs from the major cruise lines. Other sections display weather and ground transportation information in popular ports of call.

✍ www.cruise411.com

CruisePage.com

This site claims to offer information about more than 11,000 itineraries and more than 300 cruise ships. What's nice about this site is that it divides the cruise lines into searchable categories such as premium, mass market, river cruises, and specialty cruises. If you're new to cruising and want to get a good overview of the industry, this site's home page is a great place to start.

✍ www.cruisepage.com

SeaLetter.com

This site calls itself an online cruising magazine and includes everything from cruise company to specific ship reviews. There are features written by experts and readers about topics as diverse as tipping, luggage tags, seasickness remedies, and maintaining your weight while on vacation. Humor columnists are on this site as well, along with the kinds of quizzes and surveys you might expect to find in traditional print magazines.

✍ www.sealetter.com

CruiseReport.com

This site has less story and review content than some others, but it has a nifty search feature that enables you to plug in a destination and a date and automatically see which cruises are offered by all the major companies at once. It can be a real time-saver if you know where and when you want to go but are trying to comparison shop among ships.

www.cruisereport.com

CruiseOpinion.com

This site is a database of more than 4,500 cruise reviews posted by anyone who cares to type a few words about their trip. It is run by a travel agency that encourages its customers to share their thoughts with other potential customers about specific ships, itineraries, and the like.

www.cruiseopinion.com

ICruise.com

This site has general-interest articles as well as a search feature that enables you to plug in a date and destination and find cruises being offered by multiple companies. It also promotes hot deals and lets you book your cruise directly through the site.

www.icruise.com

CruiseWeb.com

This is a travel agency site where you can book cruises aboard all the major cruise lines. It has informative write-ups about each of the big cruise companies as well as the most popular cruising destinations.

www.cruiseweb.com

WorldOfCruisingMagazine.com

This is the Web site for the print-version of *World of Cruising Magazine*. You can read sample articles from past issues, including ship and destination reviews. Of course, you can also use this site to subscribe to the magazine.

✍ *www.worldofcruisingmagazine.com*

CruiseDiva.com

The brainchild of freelance cruise travel writer Linda Coffman, this site includes everything from cruise company and ship reviews to general-interest articles and columns. One of the most useful pages it offers is called "Hot Tips for Cruisers," which includes tidbits that will help you with everything from packing dirty laundry to thwarting pickpockets during shore excursions.

✍ *www.cruisediva.com*

Cruise-Addicts.com

This site is a place where you can read reviews and book cruises, but its best feature seems to be its forums. You can post specific questions about anything from lost luggage to a particular itinerary, and other people who have taken cruises provide the responses. It's a nice cyber-community if you'd like to join the broader cruise-ship discussion.

✍ *www.cruise-addicts.com*

PassengerShipSociety.com

This site has passenger reviews of some ships, as well as links to major cruising companies.

✍ *www.passengershipsociety.com*

Helpful Travel Sites

General-purpose travel Web sites can help you do it all these days: Book just a cruise, or a cruise plus airfare, or a cruise plus airfare and hotel, or a cruise plus airfare and hotel and rental car—and then some:

- *www.cheaptickets.com*
- *www.expedia.com*
- *www.orbitz.com*
- *www.priceline.com*
- *www.travelocity.com*
- *www.travelzoo.com*

If you plan to book your cruise directly through the cruise company or through a travel agent, but want to research airfares on your own, try these two sites:

- *www.kayak.com*
- *www.sidestep.com*

These sites search many of the travel sites like Orbitz.com and Expedia.com at the same time as they search airlines' individual Web sites. If airfare is all you need, these two sites can save you plenty of time and money.

Additional Reading

THERE ARE DOZENS OF other cruise-ship books out there for you to purchase after you've finished reading this one––and that's not even counting guidebooks that focus on destinations alone. Some books are definitely better than others, and you may find that as you cruise more frequently, you will want to move from beginner's books about cruising in general to specific books about the places you will visit on your itineraries. With the wealth of information that's available, you'll never lack for something to read.

General Cruise Information

If you want to learn more about cruising in general or about individual ships and itineraries in particular, there are several titles you should consider buying. Some are written from the insider's perspective of cruise-ship employees, while others are written in review style by experts who have cruised all over the world.

Unofficial Guide to Cruises

The Unofficial Guide series of books are the closest thing you'll find to a *Consumer Reports* of travel guides. *The Unofficial Guide to Cruises*, written by Kay Showker and Bob Sehlinger, won the prestigious Lowell Thomas Award for Best New Guidebook on its first printing in December 2003. It is not family-focused, but does include family cruising information on cabins, itineraries, dining, service, entertainment, facilities, shore excursions, and—most important—getting the best value for your buck.

Cruise Chooser: Buyer's Guide to Cruises

This book, written by Mary Fallon Miller, is meant first and foremost to be a money-saving guide. It includes twenty-five different programs that reportedly will help you find better bargains and even offers a special "$500 Guarantee" that you will get a great deal when booking your vacation.

The Essential Little Cruise Book

An interesting twist with this book is that it is written by former cruise director Jim West, who has been aboard more than 500 cruises with tens of thousands of people. You'll get an insider's perspective on everything from finding the right travel agent to curing seasickness, and West even prints his personal phone number in case you have any questions after you're done reading.

100 Best Cruise Vacations of the World

Author Ted Scull limits the general-interest information in this book and instead focuses on 100 specific itineraries and ships that he rates as the best in the world. He discusses not only the areas where each cruise takes place, but also how being aboard different ships when you pull into different ports can really make a difference in your vacation.

Selling the Sea: An Inside Look at the Cruise Industry

If you want to dig a little deeper into what's really going on in the cruising world, get this book by Carnival Cruise Line president Bob Dickinson and travel expert Andy Vladimir. It will give you the insider's business-oriented take on how cruising has become such a mass-market phenomenon. Don't expect fun and light reading, though—this book is all about the almighty dollar.

Cruise Ship Blues: The Underside of the Cruise Industry

Ross A. Klein may depress you with his look at the things you won't find in any cruise brochure: ship-created pollution, widespread food poisoning, passenger safety concerns, workers' conditions, and the myth of the "all-inclusive" deal. This book is muckraking in its finest sense, though some reviewers have said it's too full of touchy-feely complaints about what is, after all, a worldwide multibillion-dollar business.

Destination Information

If you've picked out your ship or already know how to get the best deals on your favorite cruise line, you'll probably want guidebooks that talk less about cruising basics and more about the destinations on your itineraries. There are plenty of options here, as well, no matter where in the world you hope to cruise.

Berlitz

Berlitz Publishing makes everything from guidebooks and maps to books that help you learn the basics of the language wherever you plan to travel—including those helpful little pocket phrase books you can carry along with you on shore excursions. The company offers titles about more than 100 destinations, as well as *Ocean Going and Cruise Ships*, an industry guidebook that is updated regularly.

✎*www.berlitzpublishing.com*

Fodor's

Fodor's has a team of more than 700 people running around the world doing research and updating its guidebooks annually. Its catalog has somewhere in the neighborhood of 450 titles broken into series such as "Gold Guides" (complete travel planning), "Exploring Guides" (with in-depth cultural information), and "See It Guides" (heavily illustrated guidebooks). No matter where you plan to cruise, you will be able to find a Fodor's book that tells you everything about it from where to stay to how much to tip.

✎*www.fodors.com*

Frommer's

Beloved bargain-hunter Arthur Frommer started this company in 1957 when he published *Europe on $5 a Day*. The company still publishes a series of "$ A Day" guidebooks, as well as its complete travel guides and pocket-size guides to cities and countries all over the world. Some editions are updated annually, others every two years. If you travel frequently with children, check out the series of "Frommer's with Kids Guides."

www.frommers.com

Lonely Planet

Lonely Planet publishes more than 650 guidebooks in fourteen different languages. More than 150 authors from nearly two dozen countries do the writing, and the company makes a point of noting that its writers never accept kickbacks or freebies in exchange for favorable reviews. These books are terrific if you want to get an over-view of a place and its culture, with specific hotel prices and the like mixed in.

www.lonelyplanet.com

Neos

Neos Guides are put out by Michelin Travel Publications, which targets European travel as its core market. Neos is actually an acro-nym that stands for "New, Expert, Open (to all cultures), and Sensitive (to the atmosphere and heritage of a foreign land)." You'll find sec-tions about social etiquette and the home life of residents in addition to tourist information about more than forty European areas.

www.viamichelin.com

General Travel Information

General travel books range from places-to-see-before-you-die titles to bargain-hunter specials on everything from hotels to rental cars. If you want to be your own travel agent, these books will give you more vacation ideas than you could experience in a dozen cruises.

The Travel Book

Lonely Planet got its authors together to create this whopping 444-page book that offers short profiles of every country in the world—every single one! You won't find in-depth knowledge in these encapsulated reviews, of course, but you will find just enough information to leave you drooling for more. You'll also discover places you might never have imagined visiting, but suddenly can't seem to live without exploring.

The Encyclopedia of Cheap Travel

This book is updated annually with tips on getting the best rates on everything from hotel rooms and rental cars to mass-market cruises and private chateaux. There's even advice in this book about how to get great travel stuff for free.

Worst-Case Scenario Survival Handbook: Travel

You've no doubt seen at least one version of these tongue-in-cheek, pocket-size "survival guides" in your local shopping mall. The travel edition includes advice on everything from tarantula encounters to leaping across rooftops. It makes a great pre-vacation gift for friends and family who might be coming along with you on a cruise or taking one of their own.

Activity Schedule

WITH ALL THERE IS to see and do on a cruise, both on land and aboard ship, you might want to keep track of all the things you and your family will want to experience during your trip. The following pages can serve as a tool to help you plan a daily schedule and make the most of your vacation.

Day #:_____
Date:_____
Day of week:_____

Morning Activities

Time	Location	Activity Description

Afternoon Activities

Time	Location	Activity Description

Evening/Nighttime Activities

Time	Location	Activity Description

Index

Everything® Family Travel Guides from Adams Media

This accessible, informative series contains all the
information a family needs to plan a vacation
that every member will enjoy!

The Everything® Family Guide to Hawaii
1-59337-054-7, $14.95

The Everything® Family Guide to New York City, 2nd Ed.
1-59337-136-5, $14.95

The Everything® Family Guide to RV Travel & Campgrounds
1-59337-301-5, $14.95

The Everything® Family Guide to Las Vegas, Completely Updated!
1-59337-359-7, $14.95

The Everything® Family Guide to the Caribbean
1-59337-427-5, $14.95

The Everything® Family Guide to the Walt Disney World Resort®,
Universal Studios®, and Greater Orlando, 4th Ed.
1-59337-179-9, $14.95

The Everything® Family Guide to Washington D.C., 2nd Ed.
1-59337-137-3, $14.95

The Everything® Guide to New England
1-58062-589-4, $14.95

The Everything® Travel Guide to the Disneyland Resort®, California
Adventure®, Universal Studios®, and the Anaheim Area
1-58062-742-0, $14.95